Women As Asylum Seekers:
A Legal Handbook

Heaven Crawley

With a foreword by Helena Kennedy Q.C

Published by Immigration Law Practitioners' Association (ILPA)
and Refugee Action

Immigration Law Practitioners' Association (ILPA)
Lindsey House
40-42 Charterhouse Street
London EC1M 6JH
Tel: 0171 251 8383
Fax: 0171 251 8384
email: ilpa@mcr1.poptel.org.uk

ILPA is the UK's professional association of lawyers and academics practising in or concerned about immigration, asylum and nationality law. ILPA is a company limited by guarantee, registered in England and Wales, Reg. No. 2350422

Refugee Action
240a Clapham Road
Stockwell Road
London SW9 0PZ
Tel: 0171 735 5361
Fax: 0171 587 3676
email: refugee1act@gn.apc.org.uk

Refugee Action provides community development advice, training, publications and information for refugees and asylum seekers living throughout England and Wales. Operating from offices in London, Birmingham, Bristol, Leeds and Manchester, Refugee Action is funded by the Home Office, the London Borough Grants Scheme and by Charitable Trusts. Refugee Action is a company limited by guarantee, Reg. No. 1593454, and a registered charity, Reg. No. 283660.

A catalogue record for this book is available from the British Library

ISBN 1 901833 00 3

Printed and bound by Postprint, Taverner House, Harling Road, East Harling, Norwich

The **Refugee Women's Legal Group (RWLG)** was established by individuals and organisations concerned about the impact of changes in immigration law on refugee women in the UK. Central among its aims is the development of a feminist perspective on refugee law and policy. This book is part of a long-term strategy to advance standards of representation and decision-making, and to increase awareness of the gendered experiences of refugee women fleeing persecution. It is essential reading for all those representing women in the asylum process.

Heaven Crawley is a researcher based at the University of Oxford (Nuffield College) currently in the latter stages of a PhD on the experiences of refugee women seeking asylum in the UK. She has contributed to a number publications including *The Myth of Community; Gender Issues in Participatory Development* (1997) and *Engendering Forced Migration: Theory and Practice* (forthcoming).

The production of this Handbook would not have been possible without the contributions of the members of the RWLG and especially **Victoria Tennant (Refugee Legal Centre), Hildegard Dumper (Refugee Action), Jane Coker (ILPA), Minoo Jelali (Avon and Bristol Community Law Centre), Monireh Moftizadeh (Asylum Aid), Hannana Siddiqui (Southall Black Sisters), Alison Stanley (ILPA), and Brigitte Boldy (ILPA).**

We are grateful for the advice and support which we have received from a number of individuals and organisations and in particular Susan Rowlands (ILPA) and Rick Towle (UNHCR). Oxfam (with assistance from the National Lottery Charities Board), Barrow Cadbury Trust, Rathbones, ILPA and Refugee Action have shown very generous support providing substantial financial and other assistance for this publication.

Special thanks are due to the refugee women who gave us their powerful testimony.

We dedicate this book to all refugee women and hope it will make a difference to their lives.

Contents

List of Abbreviations

ADIMA	Australian Department of Immigration and Multi-Cultural Affairs
CA	Court of Appeal
CEDAW	Convention on the Elimination of All Forms of Discrimination Against Women
CIRB	Canadian Immigration and Refugee Board
CCR	Canadian Council for Refugees
CRDD	Canadian Refugee Determination Division
ECHR	European Convention on Human Rights
ECRE	European Council on Refugees and Exiles
E Ct HR	European Court of Human Rights
ELR	Exceptional Leave to Remain / Enter
EXCOM	Executive Committee of UNHCR
FGM	Female Genital Mutilation
FORWARD	Foundation for Women's Health Research and Development
IAT	Immigration Appeal Tribunal
IFA	Internal Flight Alternative
IGLHRC	International Gay and Lesbian Human Rights Commission
ILPA	Immigration Law Practitioners' Association
Imm AR	Immigration Appeal Reports ('Green Books')
IND	Immigration and Nationality Department (UK)
INS	Immigration and Naturalisation Service (US)
QBD	Queen's Bench Division
SBS	Southall Black Sisters
SCQ	Self-Completion Questionnaire
SSHD	Secretary of State for the Home Department
UDHR	Universal Declaration of Human Rights
UNHCR	United Nations High Commision(er) for Refugees
WAR	Women Against Rape

List of Annexes

Table of Cases

- This table refers *only* to case law (IAT and above) from the UK. International jurisprudence is referred to in the footnotes of the text.
- Reported cases can be found in the *Immigration Appeal Reports* (Imm AR) or 'Green Books'
- Unreported Immigration Appeal Tribunal (IAT) decisions cited here, and unreported adjudicator determinations found in the text can be obtained from Thanet House, 231 Strand, London WC2
  Tel: 0171 353 8060 Fax: 0171 583 1976

Foreword by Helena Kennedy Q.C

When women turned the spotlight upon legal institutions, their examination began to expose ways in which law had failed women. It became clear that legal rules or categories often discriminated against them. Law had developed from a male perspective, reflecting the circumstances and behaviour of men, and it could fail to acknowledge the reality of women's experiences. The trials of rape, sexual assault and domestic violence manifestly displayed the problems women have as the victims of crime, where the effects of trauma have not always been understood and where the woman's own behaviour has been measured for propriety. Cases of battered women who kill their abusers also showed ways in which black letter law and legal definitions denied women's experience or cumulative abuse.

These problems usually exist because of the historical processes which have produced law. There was no conscious conspiracy of men in long wigs. The law was developed with men in the driving seat, either as judges adding to the body of caselaw through their judgements, as legal commentators affecting laws development through scholarship, or as legislators in Parliament. Inevitably the law reflected their view of the world given the absence of women in those influential roles.

There has been a growing acceptance in the international legal community that behind law's apparent neutrality there can exist assumptions, stereotypes and narrow interpretations which discriminate against women. The courts in Britain have been slow in accepting that women can be disadvantaged by such processes although there has been some acknowledgement in the criminal courts and some other fields. Nonetheless there has been a failure to appreciate potential inequity in asylum. Although some countries do already recognise the specific needs of refugee women, as recently as 1996 the United Kingdom maintained to the United Nations High Commission for Refugees that Britain had not so far encountered any particular difficulties in the consideration of claims by female asylum seekers. However, immigration law advisers and legal practitioners are much less sanguine and believe that women applicants can be denied asylum because their experiences as women are not fully understood.

The stereotype of the political asylum seeker is of an activist who protests, organises, writes pamphlets, speaks at public meetings or offers physical resistance. Whilst some women have similar political backgrounds to men and experience asylum procedures in the same way, many women less often fit this bill because they are more likely to operate in the private rather than the public sphere. Their opposition to oppression takes different forms: providing support and refuge, passing messages, working with women's organisations. Women's political activity can be the refusal to subscribe to social mores or abide by discriminatory laws about what they can or cannot do. Gender is specifically an issue where women suffer for refusing to comply with society's expectations about female behaviour; for example pregnancy outside marriage can invoke stoning in some Islamic states whilst the refusal to conform to dress codes can have terrible consequences. These activities may not be in the full public glare but, even so, the response by oppressive regimes is just as persecutory.

One of the problems faced by some refugee women is securing recognition that what they undergo is indeed 'serious harm' and amounts to persecution. Too often the rape or sexual abuse of women is seen as the isolated aberrant behaviour of individual men wanting sex rather than as anything to do with governments. Indeed, it can be precisely because of women's gender and reproductive capacity that they are the focus of attacks as we saw so clearly with ethnic cleansing. The humiliation and sexual violation of women can be a means of socially controlling the political group or minority of which they are a part.

Adjudicators, tribunals and courts grapple with what constitutes 'serious harm'. The trauma of sexual violation, domestic violence or sexual abuse can set up varied and sometimes suprising responses in women which can serve to undermine their credibility as asylum applicants. They have great difficulty in giving voice to the detail of what they went through. They often distance themselves from events as a means of psychological survival and instead of being tearful, distraught witnesses give their history in a flat, unimpressive way, as though they are emotionally anaesthetised. Women are often filled with shame, even though they were the victims, and this feeling of self-disgust may be even greater where they hold strong religious beliefs. Those assessing the credibility of women asylum seekers can misread their demeanour in the absence of knowledge about the long-term effects of such abuse.

This handbook shows that legal processes can be unjust to women if the full context of their lives and their experiences are not understood. It also shows how good practice can be developed to avoid injustice. The United States, Australia and, particularly Canada, have been leading the way in attempts to combat gender bias in the law by introducing guidelines and legal reforms and pioneering judicial education on gender issues. The United Nations has also produced guidance on gender, specifically related to refugees, recommending that member states make the asylum process more accessible for women. It is essential that the same steps should be taken here in Britain. For some this handbook will be a source of revelation and for others an acknowledgement of what they have always known. For everyone, however, it will be a powerful tool in the cause of justice.

Helena Kennedy Q.C

Chapter 1 REFUGEE WOMEN AND THE ASYLUM
DETERMINATION PROCESS

1.1 The Aim of this Handbook

"That women and children constitute eighty percent of the refugee population is a widely used statistic, [but] its implications for programming and policy development have not been fully integrated into decision-making."[1]

There has typically been no gender attached to the term 'refugee' and limited attention has been focused on the protection needs of women as asylum seekers in the UK. This reflects in part an implicit assumption by some of those involved in the refugee determination process that gender does not make a difference to the experience of being a refugee. There is increasing evidence however, that refugee women may be unable to benefit equitably from protection and assistance efforts. Although some countries have begun to recognise the specific needs of refugee women and have taken appropriate measures to ensure their access to protection and material assistance, much more still needs to be done in the UK to respond to the ways in which gender shapes the experience of seeking asylum. These concerns, which are both procedural and substantive, have been the driving force behind this Handbook.

In recognising that women may experience persecution differently from men, this Handbook provides advice on how representatives can best approach claims where gender has had implications for the kind of persecution or harm suffered and the reasons for this treatment:

"Even where gender is not the central issue, giving conscious consideration to gender-related aspects of a case will assist representatives in understanding the totality of the environment from which an applicant claims fear of persecution or abuse of their human rights."[2]

It should be noted however, that it is not intended that this Handbook be regarded as a substitute for existing sources used by representatives.

---

[1] Forbes-Martin 1991, 5
[2] ADIMA *Guidelines on Gender Issues for Decision Makers* July 1996, paragraph 2.15 (Annex 6)

This Handbook aims to give representatives, and ultimately decision-makers, an additional level of understanding of the particular needs of women within existing policy frameworks for refugee and humanitarian applications. As such, it does not replace other relevant advice, but is intended to complement it.

Whilst every effort has been made to include relevant information from a wide range of sources and to provide an overview of existing case law on gender-related asylum claims in the UK, the situation is a constantly evolving one and representatives should ensure that they keep up-to-date with developments subsequent to publication.

1.2 Refugee Women and Protection

Refugee women suffer the same deprivation and hardship that is common to all refugees and they are frequently persecuted for reasons which are similar to their male counterparts. In addition female refugees and asylum seekers, by virtue of the fact that they are women, are victims of further hardship and have protection needs and concerns which reflect this. The material presented in this Handbook and elsewhere suggests that some women are denied refugee status for reasons that seem to have to do less with refugee law than with gender.[3] As Spijkerboer (1994) suggests, the authorities in these countries might justify this by claiming that women will less often qualify as refugees than men because they are less involved in political activities. However this kind of reaction leaves a number of questions unanswered. Do women participate in political activities less often than men? How exactly is political activity defined? Who is seen as 'deserving' of protection?

Women along with their dependants, are often the first victims of political, economic and social repression in significant part because of laws and social norms which dictate gender-related behaviour and treatment.

The experiences of refugee women in their country of origin often differ significantly from those of men. Many are targeted because they are political activists, community organisers, or persist in demanding that

---

[3] See for example Spijkerboer 1994. In most western countries, including the UK, about one third of asylum seekers are female yet statistics show that in some countries women get disproportionately fewer status. The lack of gender-disaggregated data regarding determinations makes it difficult to substantiate this statistically in the UK

their rights or those of their relatives are respected. Others are targeted because they are vulnerable - young women who can easily be sexually abused or mothers who will do anything to protect their children. In addition the authorities in some countries have exploited family relationships to intensify torture and ill-treatment.[4] Some women are subjected to human rights violations simply because they are the wives, mothers or daughters of people whom the authorities consider to be 'dangerous' or 'undesirable'. These women are threatened, held as substitutes for their relatives, tortured or even killed as governments attempt to exert their will over those closely connected to them. An attack on women may also represent an attack on their ethnic group; because they have a reproductive role, women may be viewed as the embodiment of a given ethnic identity's maintenance.

> **"In conflicts between different political or religious groups, sexual violence against women has been used as a means of aggression towards an entire section of the community or as a means of acquiring information about the activities and location of family members."[5]**

In many of these scenarios, *gender-specific forms of harm* are inflicted by the persecutor. Rape by government agents is a common method of torture inflicted on women, but sexual abuse takes many forms in addition to rape including sexual contact falling short of rape, verbal humiliation, threats of violent attack or forced acts intended to degrade. This kind of abuse constitutes a particularly humiliating assault and one which often carries traumatic social repercussions which range from shame and social stigma to reprisals by relatives. Rape victims may be ostracised by their communities and rejected by their families, and as a result refugee women who have been sexually abused often blame themselves for their tragedy. Such gender-specific forms of persecution are additional to non-gender-specific abuses and can have significant implications in the refugee determination process, both procedurally and substantively. As a result they form an important focus for this Handbook. However, a further issue related to the protection of women has emerged in the international arena more recently, and concerns the need to recognise as refugees those who suffer persecution in their own country because of their sexual status. In many parts of the world women

---

[4] See Amnesty International 1991
[5] Siemens 1988, 22

who do not live up to the moral or ethical standards imposed on them by their societies can suffer cruel or inhuman treatment.

Refusing arranged marriages, having sexual relations outside marriage, providing unsatisfactory dowries, or even wearing certain dress can result in physical persecution, if not death. Because of social and economic constraints, relatively few of these women manage to flee to other countries for protection yet, when they do, their experiences tend to be interpreted as discriminatory as opposed to persecutory.

Following years of inattention to the needs of refugee women, a new awareness and willingness to take gender into account in policy development and implementation has emerged and there have been many encouraging recent developments legitimising the factual basis for women's asylum claims. Human rights groups in particular have increasingly focused their attention on gender-specific human rights abuses and human rights abuses imposed on women because of their gender. Meanwhile the UNHCR has also begun to turn its attention to gender-related persecution and Canada, the United States and, most recently, Australia have extended their interpretation of the Convention to women making claims on this basis. The approaches and recommendations made in the existing guidelines on refugee women and protection have been substantially incorporated into this analysis.

At the time of writing however, the concerns of those working with refugees in the UK about the problems facing women seeking asylum have yet to be even acknowledged by the Home Office:

"Casework experience suggests that in practice few, if any, asylum applications made in the UK by women turn solely on the question of gender-based persecution...The UK has not so far encountered any particular difficulties in the consideration of claims by female asylum seekers."[6]

In this context and knowing what we do about the problems faced by refugee women seeking asylum in this country, this Handbook aims to alert representatives to some of the issues affecting their female clients and ultimately, through good practice, increase pressure on the Home

---

[6] UK response to a questionnaire to governments participating in the UNHCR *Symposium on Gender-Based Persecution* February 1996, Geneva (unpublished)

Office, adjudicators and judges to both monitor the situation and formulate a response which is in line with that of other refugee receiving countries.

Incorporating a gendered approach into the process of refugee determination will take time. It will also meet with either passive resistance, because it shakes the routine and the comfortable assumption of stereotypes, or active opposition, because it ultimately challenges traditional gender roles.

Many of the problems faced by refugee women in the UK are procedural. They are caused in significant part by a process of refugee determination which does not recognise that women's experiences differ from those of men. These differences can undermine both access to the determination process itself and the credibility of refugee women's testimony. These issues form the focus of Chapter 2. In addition there are substantive problems for refugee women which reflect the way in which the UN Convention Relating to the Status of Refugees is currently being interpreted.

1.3 The UN Convention Relating to the Status of Refugees

According to Article 1(A) of the 1951 Convention the term 'refugee' shall apply to any person who:

"Owing to a well-founded fear of being persecuted for reasons of race, religion, nationality, membership of a particular social group or political opinion, is outside [her] country of origin and is unable or, owing to such fear, is unwilling to avail [herself] of the protection of that country; or who, not having a nationality and being outside the country of [her] former habitual residence as a result of such events, is unable or, owing to such fear, is unwilling to return to it."[7]

The international community's response to refugees is based on the 1951 Convention and 1967 Protocol Relating to the Status of Refugees (the Convention) and the principle of *non-refoulement*. Protection is at the heart of the responsibility that the international community bears towards refugees. In order to be granted protection, individuals have to show that they have a well-founded fear of persecution on account of their race,

---

[7] UNHCR *Handbook* 1979, paragraph 34

religion, nationality, political opinion or membership of a particular social group. Acts of persecution or feared persecution must also have been committed by the government or by groups that the government either cannot or will not control. The basis for women's fear is therefore not always consistent with a typical asylum claim despite the fact that the nature and the degree of the violence perpetuated against refugee women constitutes serious, if not egregious, violation of their human rights.

It is assumed that international law is objective and that international law norms directed at individuals within states are universally applicable and gender-neutral. International refugee instruments are based upon the assumption that all refugees - irrespective of their sex - face the same problems and will be treated equally. Yet whilst there is nothing which explicitly precludes a woman being recognised as a refugee,[8] the interpretation of these instruments by states both reflects and reinforces gender biases:

"By portraying as universal that which is in fact a male paradigm, women refugees face rejection of their claims because their experiences of persecution go unrecognised."[9]

"Refugee law has developed within a male paradigm which reflects the factual circumstances of male applicants, but which does not respond to the particular protection needs of women."[10]

In many respects, the failure to incorporate the gender-related claims of refugee women seeking asylum is a product of the general failure of refugee and asylum law to recognise social and economic rights and its emphasis instead on individual targeting and specific deprivation of civil and political rights. This is despite the fact that social and economic rights may be violated for political reasons. However, it is also related to a larger criticism of human rights law and discourse - that it privileges male-dominated 'public' activities over the activities of women which take place largely in the 'private' sphere.

---

[8] Johnsson (1989) notes however that to the extent that gender is revealed in these legal texts, the masculine language used suggests that the male refugee was in the mind of the drafters.

[9] Greatbach 1989, 518

[10] Kelly 1993, 674

> "The key criteria for being a refugee are drawn primarily from the realm of public sphere activities dominated by men."[11]

> "Refugee law is dominated by a prototype of the 'refugee' that looks more or less as follows; the critical intellectual, active and with a high profile in illegal resistance, organised, ideologically well-versed."[12]

Women's political protest and activism may manifest itself in ways that differ from the familiar modes expressed by men. However whilst overt expression of a political opinion through traditional means such as involvement in political parties and organisations may be considered as a basis for political asylum, less traditional means of political resistance, such as refusal to abide by discriminatory laws or to follow prescribed rules of conduct, are often categorised as personal conduct. Women are also more likely to be involved in so-called 'low-level' political activities or in providing supporting roles, so that what appears to be a non-political activity by women may, on more careful inspection, turn out to be a form of political protest or activism. Many refugee women face similar problems with regard to establishing the failure of the state to provide protection when the harm to which they are subjected takes place within the home or community.

In the context of a largely male oriented body of law women's cases are often formulated in ways which reflect the advocate's understanding of the law rather than the reality of the applicant's experiences.

1.3.1 Content versus Interpretation

> "Gender-specific claims to refugee status are, in fact, no different than any other claims to refugee status. You don't need a new definition. You don't need to manipulate the current definition. Gender-specific claims to refugee status ought to be assessed on exactly the same grounds as every other claim to Convention refugee status."[13]

---

[11] Indra 1987, 5
[12] Steendijk 1992, 668
[13] Hathaway 1990, 1

7

Whilst the Convention does not specifically name gender as one of the bases upon which protection can be granted, the key issue is the failure of decision-makers to incorporate the gender-related claims of women into their interpretation of the existing enumerated grounds. In interpreting the Convention, decision-makers have largely failed to recognise the political nature of seemingly private acts of harm to women. For example, because rape is frequently viewed as a sexual act rather than as an act of violence, the rapist, even when a government official or a member of an anti-government force, is perceived as acting from personal motivation. The sexual nature of the harm may serve to personalise the event in the eyes of the adjudicator.

One of the central objectives of this Handbook is to demonstrate the need for a *reinterpretation* of the Convention definition on refugees to include victims of oppression and discrimination on the basis of their gender. It will be suggested that both actual (and imputed) political opinion and 'membership of a particular social group' within the meaning of Article 1(A) of the Convention can provide a legal basis for the recognition of women as Convention refugees.

Furthermore it will be argued that the interpretation of other terms in the Convention, most significantly 'persecution' itself, must take into account harm inflicted upon women which is both specific to their gender and/or takes place at the hands of non-state agents. The problem which is the focus of this Handbook, and which is particularly relevant for those representing refugee women, is the way in which the experiences of women and their claims for asylum have been *represented and analytically characterised.*

1.3.2 Framework for the Analysis

As is noted in the UNHCR *Handbook*, the phrase a 'well-founded fear of persecution' is central to the definition of a refugee and is said to exist if the applicant can establish, to a reasonable degree, that her continued stay in her country of origin has become intolerable.[14] This fear may be based on personal experience, or on the experiences of persons similarly situated.[15] However, the UNHCR *Handbook* also accepts that there is no universally accepted definition of 'persecution' and that various attempts to formulate one have met with little success. According to well-

---

[14] UNHCR *Handbook* 1979, paragraph 42
[15] ibid., paragraph 43

recognised commentators, this omission of a precise definition was deliberate so as to permit a case-by-case determination of whether any given conduct constitutes a persecutory act.[16] Yet the lack of any intrinsic meaning is also highly problematic in terms of objective assessment of individual refugee women's claims for asylum.

This Handbook argues that given the problems of interpretation associated with the refugee definition as it currently exists, and in particular surrounding the central concept of persecution, a gendered critique is needed of all of its aspects. Following Hathaway (1991) the definition will be divided into its six essential elements.

> - **Alienage**
> - **Genuine Risk**
> - **'Serious Harm'**
> - **Failure of State Protection**
> - **Grounds for the Persecution**
> - **Needs and Deserves Protection**

It should be noted however that whilst the concept of alienage has attracted comment elsewhere,[17] neither it nor the cessation and exclusion clauses contained within Article 1 C (1) to (6), D, E and F will be examined in detail here. Rather the analysis in this Handbook centres around two key aspects. The first of these is Hathaway's insistence that the concept of persecution contains two elements: firstly the issue of whether harm apprehended by the claimant amounts to persecution, and secondly whether the state can be held accountable, in some measure, for the infliction of the harm.

'Persecution' = 'Serious harm' + 'The Failure of State Protection'

These elements are critical to any assessment of whether 'persecution' can be said to have taken place, yet rarely are the two components

---

[16] See for example Grahl-Madsen 1966; Goodwin-Gill 1983; Hathaway 1991
[17] See for example Castel 1992; Goldberg 1993; Kelly 1993, 1994. Castel (1992) makes a general point about the concept of alienage from a gendered perspective. Noting that the majority of the world's refugee claimants are men, she suggests that for women facing persecution, travelling to potential countries of asylum to make a claim for refugee status is particularly difficult owing to their responsibility for the care of their children, their lack of financial resources, and cultural and other restrictions.

distinguished and analytically addressed. The persecution ground will also form a significant part of the substantive analysis in this Handbook because it represents that element of the definition which has provided the principal focus for concerns about the gender-related persecution claims of refugee women.

1.3.3 The Meaning of 'Serious Harm'
Women are frequently subjected to *forms* of persecution which are similar to those of their male counterparts, but they also face physical harm or abuse which is *specific to their gender* including sexual violence and rape, discriminatory social mores, female genital mutilation, bride burning, forced marriage, domestic violence, forced sterilisation and forced abortion. A key issue in these cases concerns the definition of 'serious harm': does the treatment to which the applicant was subjected in the past or which the applicant fears amount to persecution? Chapter 3 discusses a number of forms of gender-specific violence which women as asylum-seekers may have experienced in order to encourage active reflection and discussion among those who are acting as women's representatives. Although *it is by no means definitive or exhaustive,* this information is intended to raise awareness of the gender-specific forms of harm and assist representatives in arguing that there is a legal basis for the asylum claim.

1.3.4 The Failure of State Protection
A person seeking to establish eligibility for asylum must show more than that he or she has suffered or has a well-founded fear of suffering serious harm. In order to constitute persecution, such harm must be at the hands of the state or a force that the state cannot or will not control. The state may be said to have failed in its duty to protect when it is actively involved in the persecution (through legislature, police officials and the military), where it offers active assistance to, or condones, persecution through a non-official agent, or where it is unable to provide protection. In addition therefore, to identifying the human rights potentially at risk in the country of origin, a decision on whether or not an individual faces a risk of 'persecution' must also comprehend scrutiny of the state's ability and willingness effectively to respond to that risk. Insofar as it is established that meaningful state protection is available to the claimant, a fear of persecution cannot be said to exist. Evidence suggests however that establishing a failure of state protection may be particularly problematic for some women where persecution is based upon gender-

discriminatory legislation or where it has occurred at the hands of non-state agents. These issues form the focus of Chapter 4.

1.3.5 Establishing the Persecution Ground

> "Although gender is not specifically enumerated as one of the grounds for establishing Convention refugee status, the definition of *Convention refugee* may properly be interpreted as providing protection for women who demonstrate a well-founded fear of gender-related persecution by reason of any one, or a combination of, the enumerated grounds."[18]

> "It should be noted that these guidelines do not advocate gender as an additional ground in Refugee Convention definition. However, it should be accepted that gender can influence or dictate the type of persecution or harm suffered and the reasons for this treatment."[19]

This Handbook advocates an approach to persecution ground which is comparable to both the Canadian and Australian guidelines, and which suggests that 'political opinion' is a preferable line of reasoning in the cases of many, although not all, refugee women fleeing gender-related persecution.

> "Most of the gender-specific claims involving fear of persecution for transgressing religious or social norms may be determined on *grounds of religion or political opinion*. Such women may be seen by the governing authorities or private citizens as having made a religious or political statement in transgressing those norms of their society, even though UNHCR Conclusion No. 39...contemplates the use of 'particular social group' as an appropriate ground."[20]

It is critical to the asylum applications of refugee women that those who are acting as their representatives challenge the normative - and

---

[18] CIRB *Guidelines on Women Refugee Claimants Fearing Gender-Related Persecution: UPDATE* November 1996, A.I (emphasis in original) (Annex 5, 187)

[19] ADIMA *Guidelines on Gender Issues for Decision Makers* July 1996, paragraph 2.15 (Annex 6)

[20] CIRB *Guidelines on Women Refugee Claimants Fearing Gender-Related Persecution: UPDATE* November 1996, A.III (emphasis in original) (Annex 5, 190-191)

paradigmatically masculine - interpretation of the grounds enumerated within the Convention.[21]

1.4 The International Protection Framework

The evaluation of gender-related asylum claims must be viewed within the framework provided by existing international human rights instruments. There are a number of international instruments for the protection of women's human rights to which reference is made throughout this Handbook.

International Instruments for the Protection of Refugee Women[22]

- **Universal Declaration of Human Rights (UDHR) (1948)**
- **1949 Geneva Conventions on the Laws of War and the two Additional Protocols of 1977**
- **European Convention for the Protection of Human Rights (ECHR) (1950)[23]**
- **Convention on the Consent to Marriage, Minimum Age for Marriage and Registration of Marriages (1962)**
- **Convention on the Elimination of All Forms of Racial Discrimination (1965)**
- **International Covenant on Civil and Political Rights (ICCPR) (1966)**
- **International Covenant on Economic, Social and Cultural Rights (ICESCR) (1966)**
- **Convention on the Elimination of All Forms of Discrimination Against Women (CEDAW) (1979)[24]**
- **UN Convention Against Torture and Other Cruel, Inhuman or Degrading Treatment or Punishment (UNCAT) (1984)**
- **Convention on the Rights of the Child (CROC) (1989)**
- **UN Declaration on the Elimination of Violence Against Women (1993)[25]**
- **UN Platform for Action (1995)[26]**

---

[21] This will also require detailed information about the social, political and legal position of women in their country of origin. See this volume at 2.7

[22] Information on where copies of these instruments can be obtained is provided in Annex 1

[23] See Annex 2

[24] See Annex 3

[25] ibid.

[26] ibid.

In addition there have been a number of recent international initiatives which have increased awareness of human rights violations against refugee women and suggested approaches to gender-related asylum claims. It is important that representatives and others within the asylum determination process keep pace with, and where possible utilise, these developments.

1.4.1 UNHCR

In addition to the *Handbook on Procedures and Criteria for Determining Refugee Status* (1979), the Executive Committee (EXCOM) of the UNHCR has issued a number of notes and conclusions relating specifically to refugee women.[27] The UNHCR has also issued several publications of interest to those representing refugee women as asylum seekers. These include *Guidelines on the Protection of Refugee Women* (1991) and *Sexual Violence Against Refugees; Guidelines on Prevention and Response* (1995). Both sets of guidelines address gender-related persecution and recommend procedures to make the asylum determination process more accessible to women. The information they contain about the gendered experiences of women asylum applicants is of considerable use to representatives and reference is made to these publications throughout this Handbook. Although the UNHCR materials do not have the force of law or form part of the Convention and therefore cannot override express terms of the Immigration Act(s) or Rules, they can provide guidance and are aids to interpretation of the Convention and may be relevant to the exercise of a broad discretion.[28]

1.4.2 Canada

On March 9th 1993, the CIRB issued its ground-breaking *Guidelines on Women Refugee Claimants Fearing Gender-Related Persecution* which were developed after extensive consultation with interested governmental and non-governmental groups and individuals. The *Guidelines* attracted considerable interest internationally because they were the first national guidelines to formally recognise that women fleeing persecution because of their gender could be recognised as Convention refugees. Four years after their release, the Canadian guidelines remain a model for gender-sensitive asylum adjudication and the CIRB released an updated version in November 1996, necessitated by

---

[27] For details see Annex 4

[28] Macdonald and Blake *Macdonald's Immigration Law and Practice in the United Kingdom* 1995, 377 paragraph 12.12

the volume of jurisprudence that has emerged in the field of gender-related refugee claims since the original guidelines were issued.[29] The update also provides a framework for analysis which is useful for representatives. This Handbook draws heavily on the information provided by the CIRB not least because there is evidence from appeal hearing determinations that some adjudicators will consider their significance where they are relevant to the appellant's claim:

> "Whilst not themselves binding they are a tool to ensure that vital issues are objectively canvassed in weighing refugee claims where gender is a factor...we would commend the use of the Canadian Guidelines to adjudicators."[30]

1.4.3 The United States
In June 1995 the INS issued its *Considerations for Asylum Officers Adjudicating Asylum Claims from Women* which were designed to assist asylum officers in interviewing women refugees and in making asylum decisions in light of well-established international human rights and refugee law principles. In so doing, the United States became the second country to adopt formal guidelines recognising that the persecution of women based on their gender could be the grounds for political asylum. The guidelines promulgate specific instructions to decision-makers that recognise rape and other forms of sexual violence as persecution and also recognise that women who are beaten, tortured, or subject to other such treatment for refusing to renounce their beliefs about the equal rights of women may be considered for asylum protection. The INS guidelines also emphasise the importance of creating a 'customer-friendly' asylum interview environment that allows women claimants to discuss freely the elements and details of their claims.

1.4.4 Australia
Australia's refugee and humanitarian intake has two components: an 'off-shore' or overseas programme and an 'on-shore' programme. There is a special category in the off-shore programme that offers protection to 'women-at-risk' in addition to standard Convention obligations. Responding to concerns about gender bias in both the definition of a refugee and in procedures for processing applications, ADIMA issued *Guidelines on Gender Issues for Decision Makers* in July 1996 which are

---

[29] See Annex 5
[30] *Almaz Woldu Gimhedin v SSHD*, IAT 1st October 1996 (14019) (unreported)

perhaps the most comprehensive of all those which so far exist, and which are referred to throughout this Handbook:[31]

"The guidelines provide practical advice on procedural issues which can influence women applicants and which may affect their ability to present their claims, for example, in relation to receiving applications, managing interviews and ensuring confidentiality of information. They also offer assistance with the interpretation of the regulatory requirements of the various protection, refugee and humanitarian visa classes as they relate to claims put forward by applicants with gender-based claims, with the aim of ensuring that the assessment process is sensitive to gender issues."[32]

1.4.5 Europe

In 1984 the European Parliament adopted a resolution calling upon states to consider women who have been the victims of persecution as belonging to a 'particular social group' within the definition of the Convention and therefore qualifying for refugee status. Since that time however there appears to have been very little progress on this issue. The process of asylum determination varies significantly between states. This was reflected in the written responses of governments to the recent questionnaire issued by the UNHCR concerning gender-based persecution in general and the social group issue in particular, which provided the basis for discussion at the *Symposium on Gender-Based Persecution* held in Geneva in February 1996. In addition, moves towards harmonisation suggest that standards for protection are being reduced to the lowest common denominator.[33]

Perhaps the most significant aspect of the European system therefore is the fact that it has its own *European Convention for the Protection of Human Rights* (ECHR) which, by creating a European Commission as well as a European Court of Human Rights, sets up the only truly effective system for the protection of human rights at the international level.[34] The right of individual petition is also important for

---

[31] See Annex 6

[32] ADIMA *Guidelines on Gender Issues for Decision Makers* July 1996, paragraph 1.3 (Annex 6)

[33] See for example UNHCR *An Overview of Protection Issues in Western Europe: Legislative Trends and Positions Taken by UNHCR,* European Series No 3, 1995 and Elspeth Guild *The Developing Immigration and Asylum Policies of the European Union* 1996

[34] See ECRE *Asylum in Europe: An Introduction* 1993 for further details and Annex 2

asylum seekers and refugees. Although Article 3 is most often referred to, asylum seekers and refugees may also invoke a number of other Articles in support of their claim for protection from persecution, and representatives should ensure *at an early stage* that they are fully aware of the additional protection that may be available to some refugee women through the ECHR.[35]

---

[35] Contact the AIRE Centre for further information on how representatives can utilise the protection mechanisms available through the ECHR (Annex 9)

Chapter 2 PROCEDURAL ISSUES

"The Home Office do not understand what I have been through. I have felt like a criminal, going to interviews with officials, attending a court, living in hiding in case I was arrested. I have had to speak about very personal issues. I have left interviews crying and with severe headaches. I have been unable to sleep and I suffer nightmares. I have lived on my own without money. I have missed my family and I always worry about them, and especially my husband. The Home Office's procedures I have had to follow in this country have only added to my pain. I will never forget this experience."[1]

Procedures for refugee determination are critical for those seeking asylum in the UK. However whilst all applicants may experience serious difficulties, technical and psychological, in submitting their case,[2] there is increasing concern that these difficulties are exacerbated for female refugees because the procedures themselves are modelled on the assumption that asylum seekers are *politically active men* who have been persecuted by the authorities as a result of those activities. The result is that if asylum procedures allow for the experiences of women at all, they tend to regard them as dependent wives, daughters and mothers. This is reflected in the fact that information on the human rights situation of women in countries of origin is all too often lacking, despite the fact that such information is necessary for the evaluation of any claim to asylum.

The evidence presented in this chapter suggests that the asylum determination process itself can be more responsive to the experiences of refugee women if representatives and others are aware of the particular procedural difficulties that they face. Whilst there remain problems in the way adjudicators assess the credibility and demeanour of female applicants, careful consideration of a number of procedural issues can improve both access to, and representation within, the process of asylum determination in the UK.

---

[1] Testimony of a refugee woman from Zaire seeking asylum in the UK, extracted from a press release on 'How asylum procedures failed Mrs. X and how the Short Procedure (SP) will lead to a further deterioration of standards', Hackney Community Law Centre and Women Against Rape, 1996

[2] UNHCR *Handbook* 1979, paragraph 190

2.1 Derivative Status or Independent Claim?

EXCOM Conclusion No. 73 "calls upon states and UNHCR to ensure the equal access of women and men to refugee status determination."[3]

As is acknowledged by the UNHCR in its *Guidelines for the Protection of Refugee Women* (1991), women who arrive as part of a family unit are sometimes not interviewed or are cursorily interviewed about their experiences, even when it is possible that they, rather than their husbands, have been the targets of persecution. Their male relatives may not raise the relevant issues because they are unaware of the details or ashamed to report them.[4]

"Women coming into the country with their spouses are often assumed to be dependants. The majority opt for that because of natural deference to their husband, not being accustomed to being addressed as an individual, and fear. They are not invited to a separate interview. Some are interviewed with their male relatives, brother, father, cousin. Very often the last person a woman can bear to tell her story to is her husband."[5]

Yet as the UNHCR has also noted, a woman's claim to refugee status may in some cases be as strong or stronger than that of her husband.[6] If her experiences only emerge some time after the initial application or once the claim has been refused by the Home Office, she may be unable to make the case convincingly for being granted her own refugee status because the delay will undermine the credibility of her application.[7] There is also increasing concern that if only the husband's experiences

---

[3] EXCOM Conclusion No.73 (XLIV) 1993, paragraph c (Annex 4)
[4] UNHCR *Guidelines on the Protection of Refugee Women* 1991, paragraph 57
[5] Gill Hinshelwood 'Interviewing Female Asylum Seekers', paper presented at the UNHCR *Symposium on Gender-Based Persecution* February 1996, Geneva (unpublished)
[6] UNHCR *Guidelines on the Protection of Refugee Women,* 1991. The strength of a woman's claim relative to that of her husband can be seen in the recent case of *Abdollah Fathi and Mashid Ahmady v SSHD*, IAT 1st December 1996 (11544) (unreported), where the appeal of a woman from Iran was allowed whilst that of her husband was refused.
[7] See this volume at 2.6 and Rule 349 of HC395 (as amended in particular by CM 3365)

are considered during a family's request for asylum, this may have significant implications for her future. For example, there may be problems for a woman if she is entirely dependent on her husband for her status, especially if that status is ELR. Should the family break up, a woman who has accompanied or joined her husband may find herself without any protection from forced return. She also risks expulsion if the application of her family member is denied or if he unilaterally decides to renounce his claim even though she may have a valid claim for protection in her own right.

> **"It is important to identify the person included in an application who has the strongest claims. An application written by, or an interview with, a male head of household may place little or no emphasis on a female family unit member's experience of persecution or discrimination, even though her experiences may carry the most weight. A woman who is included in the application as a member of a family unit should be given the opportunity of a separate interview so that she is able, with appropriate assurances of confidentiality, to outline her experiences."[8]**

It is essential that women are given equal access to the refugee determination process from their initial application. Where a woman arrives as part of a family unit, regardless of whether she is the principal applicant, she should be interviewed by the representative. Consideration should be given as to whether it is appropriate to submit a separate claim and/or a statement at that time. Accuracy is essential because of the possibility of discrepancies leading to adverse inferences on credibility. Any discrepancies must be explained; different perceptions of the same event may appear inconsistent.[9]

> **"It should also be noted however that if gender-related claims are revealed separately from the rest of the family, *representatives must treat the information provided with great care*. This is particularly necessary if the woman has indicated that other members of the family are unaware of her experiences."[10]**

---

[8] ADIMA *Guidelines on Gender Issues for Decision Makers* July 1996, paragraph 3.10 (Annex 6)

[9] See ILPA *Best Practice Guide to Asylum Appeals* 1997

[10] ADIMA *Guidelines on Gender Issues for Decision Makers* July 1996, paragraph 3.28 (Annex 6). Representatives should be aware of professional duties of confidentiality and the potential for conflict of interests.

2.2 Finding Out About Women's Experiences

"Women face special problems in making their case to the authorities, particularly when they have had experiences which are difficult and painful to describe."[11]

Responding to these concerns, the guidelines recently issued by both the US and Australia make a number of procedural recommendations for the handling of gender-related claims[12]. The aim of these recommendations is to create a 'customer-friendly' asylum interview environment, in which women claimants may freely discuss the elements and details of their claims. Despite these international developments, representatives and advisors should be aware that, as yet, the Home Office has not acknowledged any particular problems which women may experience during the asylum process:

"The particular need for sensitivity in dealing with asylum applicants and the procedural and policy considerations involved in assessing the merits of asylum claims apply to both sexes. We have not yet identified a need to issue *separate* guidance on dealing with applications from female asylum seekers in the UK...Our current approach to asylum claims from women is generally compatible with that set out in the US Guidelines."[13]

2.2.1 The Interview
The experiences of women refugees indicate that there are a number of issues which need to be addressed during the interview process and which representatives should take into consideration during discussions with their female clients. The UNHCR has itself made a number of recommendations regarding the use of gender-sensitive techniques to

---

[11] UNHCR *Guidelines on the Protection of Refugee Women* 1991, paragraph 58

[12] See INS *Considerations for Asylum Officers Adjudicating Asylum Claims From Women* 1995 and ADIMA *Guidelines on Gender Issues for Decision Makers* July 1996 (Annex 6)

[13] UK response to a questionnaire to governments participating in the UNHCR *Symposium on Gender-Based Persecution* February 1996, Geneva (unpublished) (emphasis in original)

obtain information from women during the status determination process.[14]

> **"Female applicants who are survivors of torture and trauma, in particular, require a supportive environment where they can be reassured of the confidentiality of the gender-sensitive claims they are making."[15]**

For refugee women in particular, a *non-confrontational* interview is critical to allow for the full discussion of past experiences relating to their claim, yet the reality in many cases is an asylum interview which is harrowing for women, and in particular for those who have experienced sexual violence. There are a number of interrelated reasons why the interview process is particularly difficult for many women.

> **"Women refugee claimants who have suffered sexual violence may exhibit a pattern of symptoms referred to as Rape Trauma Syndrome, and may require extremely sensitive handling. Similarly, women who have been subjected to domestic violence may exhibit a pattern of symptoms referred to as Battered Wife Syndrome and may also be reluctant to testify."[16]**

For women who have been sexually abused there is the additional problem of conflicting interests. It is clear, and usually will be clear to the applicant, that it is important to tell the determining authorities about experiences of sexual violence. On the other hand, there are good reasons not to tell, which can range from the fact that it is very hard to do, to the fear that her experiences may become known to others and lead to her being ostracised from her family and/or community.[17] Women from societies where the preservation of virginity or marital dignity is the cultural norm may be very reluctant to disclose certain information relevant to their asylum claim or that of other members of their family.[18]

---

[14] See Annex 7

[15] ADIMA *Guidelines on Gender Issues for Decision Makers* July 1996 paragraph 3.12

[16] CIRB *Guidelines on Women Refugee Claimants Fearing Gender-Related Persecution: UPDATE* November 1996, D (Annex 5, 195)

[17] Spijkerboer 1994, 61

[18] See CIRB *Guidelines on Women Refugee Claimants Fearing Gender-Related Persecution: UPDATE* November 1996, D (Annex 5, 195) and also UNHCR *Guidelines on the Protection of Refugee Women* 1991, paragraph 60

"Rape sometimes appears to be used as a form of torture because those responsible realise that their victims may be constrained from revealing what has occurred after their release from custody. The shame associated with rape can be a strong inducement to silence."[19]

2.2.2 Presence of Family Members

"Female victims of violence, discrimination and abuse often do not volunteer information about their experiences and may be reluctant to do so in the presence of family members."[20]

Refugee women should be given the opportunity to be interviewed outside the hearing of other members of their family, especially male family members and children. Whilst the testimonial process is a highly stressful experience for anyone, woman applicants may communicate experiences of sexual abuse or other kinds of harm more freely when family members are not present. Sexual violence in particular may be viewed as a failure on the part of the woman to preserve her virginity or marital dignity. In this context discussing her experience in front of family members may become a further source of alienation.

2.2.3 Interviewers and Interpreters[21]

"In the vast majority of cases women who have suffered torture and/or trauma have suffered these abuses at the hands of men. Coupled with a fear and distrust of authorities, this fact is likely to seriously inhibit the capacity of a female applicant to divulge details of her experiences to a male interviewer."[22]

"The female victim of sexual torture obviously may be reluctant or find it very difficult to talk about it, particularly to a male interviewer."[23]

---

[19] Amnesty International 1991, 22

[20] ADIMA *Guidelines on Gender Issues for Decision Makers* July 1996 paragraph 3.12

[21] Interpreters should be reminded that their role is to interpret and not to advise, or make judgements about, the applicant and her experiences.

[22] ADIMA *Guidelines on Gender Issues for Decision Makers* July 1996 paragraph 3.13

[23] UNHCR *Guidelines on the Protection of Refugee Women* 1991, paragraph 60

It is also recognised in the guidelines from Canada, the US and Australia, that testimony on sensitive issues such as sexual abuse can be diluted when received through the filter of a interpreter. Some of these problems may be linguistic. For example, during the interview both the interviewer and the interpreter should be aware of the difficulties in interpreting particular words, such as 'rape' or 'assault', which may have different meanings or connotations in the applicant's language. In addition however, it is not difficult to imagine the reluctance of a female applicant to testify about her experiences through a male (or even female) interpreter who is a member of her community.

"In particular, during interviews where an interpreter is used, a woman applicant may be reluctant to divulge information for fear that the interpreter may be an informer for the authorities in the country of origin or that they will divulge their story to others in the community. The applicant should be assured of the confidential nature of the interview process."[24]

This problem, and its implications for the applicant's credibility, has yet to be recognised by the Home Office. In one recent case the representative pointed out to the IAT that the appellant, being a Pathan woman, would have been frightened to explain her fears regarding sexual violence at the asylum interview, because both the counsellor and interpreter were male Muslims.

"We reject that contention as it appears to us that the appellant is an educated and sophisticated woman. She was not a rural agricultural worker from a remote village and we do not believe that had she anything to say she would not have done so simply because there were male Muslims present. Accordingly, in our view, our finding must reflect adversely on the credibility of the appellant."[25]

As has been noted elsewhere, merely being female does not guarantee gender-sensitivity.[26] Nonetheless every effort should be made to ensure that female interpreters and interviewers are available where it appears

---

[24] ADIMA Guidelines on Gender Issues for Decision Makers July 1996, paragraph 3.13 (Annex 6)
[25] Salma Jamil v SSHD, IAT 25th June 1996 (13588) (unreported)
[26] See for example Oosterveld 1995

that the presence of a man may prevent the claimant from presenting her case.

"Before scheduling the interview, ensure that appropriate arrangements have been made for interpreters who are sensitive to any special requirements of the applicant regarding language, dialect or ethno-cultural sensitivities. If an applicant has made claims of a sensitive or traumatic nature every effort should be made to ensure an interpreter and interviewing officer of the same sex."[27]

"Where an officer suspects, as a result of researching the country information relating to the case, that gender-related claims may be raised or discussed, every effort should be made to engage an interpreter of the same sex, with regard to any cultural or religious sensitivities, wherever possible."[28]

2.2.4 Asking the Right Questions

The questions that are asked during the asylum interview are typically oriented at male asylum-seekers.[29] They tend to be about political activities narrowly defined rather than background activities in which women may be involved. They also tend to be specifically about 'torture', which female applicants may not equate with the types of harm that they fear, for example, sexual violence, female genital mutilation, and forced sterilisation or abortion. Female applicants are not routinely asked questions about gender-related persecution and even if it is mentioned by the applicant during interview, there may be no follow-up questions to ascertain details or the applicant's full experience.

For her claim to asylum to be successful, the asylum applicant must be allowed to clearly state what her fear of persecution consists of. There are a number of measures which can be adopted by representatives in response to some of the difficulties outlined above. It is important for example that prior to the interview, research is conducted to establish familiarity with women's status and roles in the country from which the applicant has fled,[30] but the information revealed during the course of the interview may also reflect the way in which questions are asked.

---

[27] ADIMA *Guidelines on Gender Issues for Decision Makers* July 1996, paragraph 3.16 (Annex 6)
[28] ibid. paragraph 3.17 (Annex 6)
[29] See Schilders 1988; Steendjik 1992; Spijkerboer, 1994
[30] See also this volume at 2.7

- **Specific questions concerning issues that are relevant to women can be incorporated into the existing interview structure**

- **Open and/or indirect questions can be asked in order to establish the applicant's reasons for fleeing and to obtain indications about whether gender-related harm has occurred**

The types of questions to be asked might include the following:

- **are women treated differently than men?**
- **were you, as a woman, treated badly?**

To answer the first question, the woman may give relevant information about how women in her country are treated without necessarily speaking about herself, and yet may indirectly refer to herself. When asking the second question, it is essential to use the word 'bad'. This is understood by most cultures and is not confrontational. The statement by the asylum applicant that she has been 'badly treated' may be a euphemism for sexual violence and/or rape. Moreover if the applicant is directly asked whether she has been raped her answer may be negative although she may have been subjected to other forms of sexual abuse.[31] If there are indications that the applicant has experiences which are in some way related to her gender, it is essential for the success of the claim that more direct questions are asked to ascertain specific aspects of the woman's experience:

- **What are the (possible) consequences of having experienced gender-specific harm, especially sexual violence including rape, for the refugee woman?**

- **Can it be said that the authorities and/or the community provided protection?**

- **What fear of persecution awaits a woman when she is forced to return to her country?**

---

[31] See this volume at 3.1

2.2.5 Culturally Sensitive Communication

"After the first interview we had a second interview at Gatwick. The man who did the interview was very rude. When I explained some things about my culture he just laughed. For example I was saying that my father and mother had only me and then he had another woman with whom he had a son. He had five children with her and my father had three wives altogether. He just started laughing. I asked him why. I explained that he should understand and shouldn't laugh. I was very frustrated and humiliated. I was not comfortable."[32]

The failure to appreciate cross-cultural differences can jeopardise the quality of the information revealed by a female applicant and the way in which that information is then responded to by both the interviewer and the decision-maker. In the UK the lack of culturally sensitive communication between the interviewing officer and the applicant is clearly a problem in some cases, despite protestations from the Home Office to the contrary:

"The particular need for sensitivity in dealing with asylum applicants is recognised and stressed in our training and guidance to staff involved in the asylum process. This focus ensures that all applications are handled sympathetically and that caseworkers appreciate cultural differences."[33]

Where possible, representatives should challenge interviewing officers who do not communicate with their clients in a manner which is sensitive to cultural differences. In addition, however, they should also be aware of cultural sensitivities during their own interviews with refugee women. As the Australian *Guidelines* indicate, this can most appropriately be demonstrated by attentive listening, including the following:

---

[32] Testimony of a Somali refugee woman during an interview with the author, September 1996

[33] UK response to questionnaire to governments participating in the UNHCR *Symposium on Gender-Based Persecution* [speaking note] February 1996, Geneva (unpublished)

- **reflective listening (i.e. paraphrasing what has been said by the applicant);**

- **not talking at the same time as the applicant;**

- **not making judgmental comments;**

- **maintaining composure if the applicant gets angry or upset;**

- **nodding affirmatively when appropriate;**

- **ensuring minimum interruptions and/or distractions;**

- **ensuring the interpreting is an accurate reflection of the applicant's testimony (eg. relative length of translation, reaction from the applicant).[34]**

Discretion and tact are especially critical when dealing with deeply rooted traditions such as female genital mutilation. In addition the UNHCR has emphasised that interviewers should be conscious of possible reactions to trauma and familiar with culturally different patterns of behaviour and language.[35]

"The level of emotional distress exhibited by a female applicant during the recounting of her experiences should not automatically add more credibility to her claims than that of another who may be very calm and quiet when describing a similar event. A lack of emotion displayed at interview does not necessarily mean that the applicant is not distressed or deeply affected by what has happened. Cultural differences and trauma often play an important role in determining demeanour."[36]

---

[34] ADIMA *Guidelines on Gender Issues for Decision Makers* July 1996, paragraphs 3.22 to 3.26 (Annex 6)

[35] UNHCR *Sexual Violence Against Refugees; Guidelines on Prevention and Response* 1995

[36] ADIMA *Guidelines on Gender Issues for Decision Makers* July 1996, paragraph 3.29 (Annex 6). Issues of demeanour and credibility are addressed in more detail in this volume at 2.6

2.3 A Note on Short Procedures[37]

> Ms D travelled to the UK with two other women and eight children. The women and a 19 year old were interviewed substantively and were held for 14 hours before the entire party were placed in detention. Ms D received no advice and had no idea that the interview was her main opportunity to provide full details of her claim. She stated that "during the interview I noticed that they didn't believe anything I was saying. I got the impression that they were dismissing anything I said. I felt they were contemptuous towards me". Comments she made regarding the family's ill-treatment and discrimination by the authorities were not followed up. The group was held in detention for a further five days and so had no opportunity to make further representations. She said "we had no chance...the children were tired, they were crying. It was such a long way from the airport". Her application was refused just 19 days later.[38]

The Short Procedure scheme has introduced an accelerated process for the consideration of certain asylum claims by the Home Office and lays the basis for differential treatment of asylum claims, not for individualised reasons, but depending on the nationality of the applicant or the port at which they arrived. Concerns have been raised by a number of bodies including the Asylum Rights Campaign (ARC),[39] that these changes will have a particularly serious impact on those who are traumatised or suffering the after-effects of persecution. This evidence suggests that procedural difficulties for women seeking asylum are considerably exacerbated under the Short Procedure scheme and that it may seriously impair the ability of a refugee to present her case.

Clearly in cases of gender-related persecution where limited information is available, the prospects for obtaining evidence relevant to the client's case are considerably jeopardised because the time allowed for the submission of further representations is restricted.[40] Similarly it may be impossible to obtain medical evidence or provide vulnerable individuals - including women who have been raped or sexually abused -

---

[37] Various aspects of the Short Procedure are altered by the Home Office on a regular basis and representatives should be familiar with these as and when they occur.
[38] Asylum Rights Campaign 1996, 52-53
[39] ibid.
[40] See this volume at 2.7

with access to medical care and counselling. There is a particular need to take account of the fact that an applicant may be suffering from sexually related torture, abuse or other forms of gender-related persecution, yet under the Short Procedure female applicants will be interviewed immediately and this will not usually be by female staff or interpreters unless specifically requested. The interviewing officer may be unaware that the applicant may have experienced sexual violence and will therefore not know to ask questions regarding this. If the representative is aware of such details, he or she should endeavour to make them known in order that an appropriate line of questioning is pursued. In addition, consideration should always be given by the representative to the possibility of submitting additional information or statements in support of the application.

2.4 A Note on the Self-Completion Questionnaire (SCQ)[41]

The Short Procedure means that many asylum seekers are no longer asked to set out, in their own words, their reasons for claiming asylum *with the exception* of those nationals who come from Iraq, Iran, Libya, Somalia, Liberia, Rwanda, Afghanistan, Palestine, the Gulf States (except Kuwait), Bosnia, Croatia and the former Yugoslavia.[42] For asylum seekers fleeing persecution from these countries, the SCQ can be used as a preparatory tool before the substantive interview takes place, and it is therefore important that the form is completed in a way that reflects women's experiences.

Wherever possible, representatives should assist their clients in the completion of the SCQ in order to ensure that all details relevant to the case are included in the form. In addition, representatives should be aware that there are several problems associated with the completion of SCQs which are specific to refugee women. The first of these reflects the point made in 2.2 above that where a woman arrives with a spouse or male relative, and makes a separate claim, it is the man who will frequently complete both questionnaires. As a result details relevant to the woman's claim may be omitted.

There is some evidence that women who have been involved in indirect political activity or to whom political opinion has been attributed will not include relevant information relating to their claim because of the nature of the questions asked on the SCQ which, as is suggested

---

[41] As with Short Procedures, this section is not exhaustive and cannot hope to be in the context of on-going procedural changes. See ILPA *Best Practice Guide to Asylum Appeals* 1997 for further information.

[42] This list of countries is likely to change.

elsewhere in this Handbook,[43] reflect a male-orientated process of asylum determination:

"If your claim is based on your political activities, you should supply details such as:

- the name of any political organisations with which you have been involved either in the UK or abroad

- when and how your first contact with them took place

- the nature of your involvement with them, both in the UK and abroad

You should include any evidence you have of your activities, such as membership cards, photographs, press articles etc."[44]

The information requested in Part C relating to the basis of the claim does not in any way allude to gender-related persecution and instead emphasises overt political activities, including the name of any political organisation with which the applicant has been involved and the nature of that involvement. Applicants should be encouraged to submit details of gender-related persecution in this section.

Where possible representatives and advisors should ensure that all details relevant to the client's application are submitted in the SCQ, not least because revealing such details at a later date may undermine the credibility of the applicant.[45]

2.5 The Standard of Proof

A refugee who claims asylum must show that their fear of persecution is well-founded. According to Hathaway the 'standard of proof' should be set at the criterion of a 'reasonable possibility' of persecution, and not at more strict criteria such as 'real and substantial danger' of persecution or the occurrence of persecution being 'more likely than not'.[46] In the UK the standard of proof to be applied to the assessment of the future

---

[43] See for example this volume at 5.4
[44] Extracted from Part C of the Self-Completion Questionnaire
[45] See this volume at 2.6 for further discussion of this issue
[46] Hathaway 1991, 75-80

likelihood of persecution has been laid down by the House of Lords in *Sivakumaran.*[47] That the appellant's fear of persecution is well-founded means that there has to be demonstrated a 'reasonable degree of likelihood' that she would be persecuted for a Convention reason if returned to her own country:

"In my opinion the requirement that an applicant's fear of persecution should be well-founded means that there has to be demonstrated a reasonable degree of likelihood that he will be persecuted for a Convention reason if returned to his own country."[48]

Through *Kaja*[49] this 'reasonable degree of likelihood' test has been extended to assessment of asylum appeals at all levels:

"Where the central feature for assessment is the reasonable likelihood of an event occurring and that event will have extremely grave consequences if it does occur, there is no inherent reason why the estimate must be based on facts more likely than not to have occurred...In both *Sivakumaran* and *Direk* there was reference to the relevance of the past to the estimate of the future. In both the estimate was based on a single estimate of 'reasonable likelihood'."[50]

Establishing that the fear of persecution is well-founded nonetheless remains problematic for many asylum seekers who often have no witness to the acts of violence against them and have no corroborative proof that the acts occurred. For many women this problem may be exacerbated because of the type of activity in which they were involved, or because serious harm has been inflicted within the family or community.

If there is no independent proof available, it will be necessary to rely on the testimony of the applicant alone, in which case it is critical that testimony is obtained which is believable, consistent and sufficiently detailed to provide a plausible and coherent account of the basis for the fear. The problems of reliance upon testimony alone

---

[47] *SSHD v Sivakumaran and others* [1988] Imm AR 147 (HL)
[48] ibid.
[49] *Koyazia Kaja v SSHD* [1995] Imm AR 1 (IAT)
[50] ibid.

in cases of female applicants highlight the importance of gender-sensitive information gathering.[51]

Representatives should be aware of the importance of their client's own testimony and they should also make every effort to gather additional evidence and information relating to both the situation for women in the applicant's country of origin and about the applicant's physical and mental health.[52]

It should also be noted that when an assessment is made by the decision maker as to whether the fear of persecution is well-founded, this will be based in significant part on general conditions in the applicant's country of origin but may not take into account the particular experiences of women. An assessment should also be made of the claimant's particular fear and of whether any changes in country conditions are meaningful and effective enough for her fear of gender-related persecution to be no longer well-founded:

"A change in country circumstances, generally viewed as a positive change, may have no impact, or even a negative impact, on a woman's fear of gender-related persecution."[53]

"Many cases of gender-based persecution occur at the hands of non-state agents of persecution whose actions are ignored or condoned by the authorities. Even where changes in the national legislation or other state of affairs have occurred, such agents of persecution are seldom brought to justice and there is no accountability by the state for the acts of persecution inflicted on the applicant."[54]

There have also been several recent appeal cases involving women from Sudan and Sierra Leone where the adjudicators have taken into account the additional likelihood of persecution simply by virtue of the applicant being returned to their country of origin. The implication is that for women the risk of return is even greater than for their male counterparts:

---

[51] See this volume at 2.2

[52] See this volume at 2.7

[53] CIRB *Guidelines on Women Refugee Claimants Fearing Gender-Related Persecution: UPDATE* November 1996, C.3 (Annex 5, 194)

[54] ADIMA *Guidelines on Gender Issues for Decision Makers* July 1996, paragraph 4.20 (Annex 6)

> "It also seems to be to be a fair point that the appellant returning to Khartoum by herself is likely to draw attention to herself in the light of the authorities' attitude towards women travelling alone."[55]

> "If she were to be returned to Sierra Leone she would be a woman on her own and it appears to me from the documentary evidence I have seen that she, as a women on her own, would be very vulnerable in that country."[56]

2.6 Credibility

> "Women refugee claimants face special problems in demonstrating that their claims are credible and trustworthy."[57]

Credibility is inextricably linked with the standard of proof and remains one of the most pervasive problems for almost all asylum applications made in the UK; many refusals are on the basis that the asylum seeker's credibility has been weakened due to inconsistencies in the application.[58] Whilst this problem is not unique to female applicants, there is evidence that women may experience particular problems in maintaining their credibility: procedural problems may undermine a claim even where a woman has been persecuted because of her direct involvement in political activity, for example where women are not given access to the determination process independently from their husbands or male relatives.[59] In addition, credibility may be particularly problematic for claims where the experience of persecution is in some way related to a woman's gender status.

---

[55] Appeal No. HX/75947/94 (5th May 1995) (unreported)

[56] Appeal No. HX/62851/95 (15th October 1996) (unreported)

[57] CIRB *Guidelines on Women Refugee Claimants Fearing Gender-Related Persecution: UPDATE* November 1996, D (Annex 5, 195)

[58] Refugee Council *The State of Asylum; A Critique of Asylum Policy in the UK* 1996

[59] See this volume at 2.1 and 2.6

2.6.1 Inability to Provide Information

"Women from certain cultures where men do not share the details of their political, military or even social activities with their spouses, daughters or mothers may find themselves in a difficult situation when questioned about the experiences of their male relatives."[60]

"A wife may be interviewed primarily to corroborate the stories told by her husband; if she is unaware of the details of her husband's experiences (for example, the number of her husband's military unit), the entire testimony may be discounted as lacking in credibility. Yet in many cultures, husbands do not share many details about military or political activities with their wives."[61]

In two recent cases in the Federal Court of Canada, the issue of a woman's place within her society and her lack of knowledge about the activities of male family members was addressed. In *Roble*[62] and *Montenegro, Suleyama,*[63] it was accepted that in both Somalia and El Salvador, a woman's knowledge of her husband's occupation or political involvement may be based entirely on what he has been willing to tell her.

2.6.2 Timing and Circumstances of the Application

"Credibility is what they focus on, any little thing. No proper reasons for refusals are given. There is a failure to look at things properly. There is a lack of care. Adjudicators have an unquestioning line that if asylum seekers do not put their case fully in the beginning, then the whole thing is tainted. Is it surprising a woman who has been raped does not tell an immigration officer this when she steps off the plane?"[64]

---

[60] CIRB *Guidelines on Women Refugee Claimants Fearing Gender-Related Persecution: UPDATE* November 1996, D (Annex 5, 195)

[61] UNHCR *Sexual Violence Against Refugees: Guidelines on Prevention and Response* 1995, paragraph 61

[62] *Roble v MEI* [1994] 2d 186 F.C.T.D

[63] *Montenegro, Suleyama v MCI* [1996] F.C.T.D., no. IMM-3173-94.

[64] Jane Coker 1995, cited in Refugee Council *The State of Asylum; A Critique of Asylum Policy in the UK* 1996, 33-34

Delay in applying for asylum is in some cases related to the issues discussed in 2.2 and is listed in the new Immigration Rules as one of the circumstances when adverse inferences may be drawn on an applicant's credibility:[65]

> **"If the dependent has a claim in [her] own right, it should be made at the earliest opportunity. Any failure to do so will be taken into account and may damage credibility if no reasonable explanation for it is given."[66]**

Although there are a number of reasons why victims of sexual violence in particular might not be forthcoming with information about their experiences at the outset, their reluctance to report such abuse can clearly have significant implications for the determination of their claims. This is reflected in IAT decisions including *Jamil*[67] which concerned a divorced Muslim woman from Pakistan subjected to abuse, rape and mental torture at the hands of the Pakistani police and her husband's family. In this case the Home Office Presenting Officer argued that the timing of the appellant's claim of sexual harassment was important and must undermine her claim; when the appellant had first arrived at Heathrow she made no mention of the violence to which she had been subjected. Experience has shown however that incidents may not come to light until refugees have been resettled and seek therapy which may be months or even years later:

> **"Sexual torture often produces a profound shame response. Humiliation and shame are perhaps desired goals of the perpetrator. This shame response is a major obstacle to disclosure. In working with people like this quite often the history of sexual trauma comes up later in the treatment contact, sometimes several months into the contact."[68]**

---

[65] Rule 341 of HC395 as amended (in particular by CM 3365). See also Macdonald and Blake *Macdonald's Immigration Law and Practice in the United Kingdom* 1995, 384 paragraph 12.26

[66] Rule 349 ibid.

[67] *Salma Jamil v SSHD*, IAT 25th June 1996 (13588) (unreported)

[68] Stuart Turner *Discrepancies and Delays in Histories Presented by Asylum Seekers: Implications for Assessment*, December 1996, paragraph 46 (unpublished)

Information disclosed later by the victim should not automatically be disregarded or considered to reflect negatively on the credibility of the applicant. It may be necessary for representatives to obtain psychological reports on the mental health status of their female clients to explain the delay in revealing information about gender-specific forms of persecution.[69]

"The fact that a woman failed to raise a gender-related claim of persecution on several occasions should not necessarily cast doubt on her credibility if it is raised at a later date and should not be responded to as if it does."[70]

2.6.3 Demeanour

"Think of all the fiction you have read; 'She looked at him with a steady eye', 'Not once did she falter', 'She spoke simply from the heart'; or conversely, 'She had a shifty, down-at-heel look', 'She could not hold my gaze', 'She shuffled anxiously and cleared her throat several times'. Many of our asylum seekers respond to direct questioning in the latter category, and for the genuine asylum seeker, there are reasons for this. In many authoritarian regimes and cultures, it is impolite, wrong, especially for a woman, to look one's superiors in the eye. The eyes must be cast down. This fact has been beaten into many a torture survivor."[71]

Insofar as representatives and asylum officers deal with people from a diversity of countries, cultures and backgrounds, cross-cultural sensitivity is required of all those involved in the determination process regardless of the gender of the applicant. However as is noted in the US guidelines, nowhere is this sensitivity more needed than in assessing credibility and 'demeanour'. By 'demeanour' what is meant is how a person handles himself or herself physically; for example, maintaining eye contact, shifts in posture and hesitations in speech, and trauma may have a significant impact on the ability to present testimony in a manner

---

[69] See this volume at 2.7.2

[70] ADIMA *Guidelines on Gender Issues for Decision Makers* July 1996, paragraph 3.27 (Annex 6)

[71] Gill Hinshelwood 'Interviewing Female Asylum Seekers', paper presented at the *UNHCR Symposium on Gender-Based Persecution* February 1996, Geneva 4 -5 (unpublished)

deemed 'credible'. However as the extract above suggests, the credibility problem which is associated with demeanour may be exacerbated for female applicants whose culture demands, for example, that they should avert their eyes when speaking to an authority figure as a sign of respect:

> **"In Anglo-American cultures, people who avert their gaze when answering a question, or seem nervous, are perceived as untruthful. In other cultures, however, body language does not convey the same message. In certain Asian cultures, for example, people will avert their eyes when speaking to an authority figure as a sign of respect. *This is a product of culture, not necessarily of credibility."*[72]**

In this context, the response of the applicant to questioning should be treated with caution, but representatives and advisors should be aware that demeanour is clearly an important aspect of an adjudicator's assessment of a woman's credibility:

> **"I have watched the appellant giving evidence with very great care indeed and I watched her demeanour. I must say that there were times when she was rather irritating in not answering the questions directly and forthrightly but I am convinced having watched her giving evidence that that was not because she wished to hide anything but it was because of her extreme nervousness."[73]**

> **"I personally believed everything that the appellant told me, she was giving her evidence particularly about the sexual acts under great strain and distress, it was certainly not an act, and at one stage, she said she felt physically sick and I am sure that that was the case, when the horrible memories of the acts which she complained of, were brought back to the forefront of her memory. At times, I wondered whether she would be able to continue with her evidence which she gave in a very flat and unemotional voice."[74]**

---

[72] INS *Considerations for Asylum Officers Adjudicating Asylum Claims From Women* June 1995, 7 (emphasis added). Expert evidence may be useful in cases refused for these reasons. See this volume at 2.7 for further information

[73] Appeal No. HX/66670/96 (22nd October 1996) (unreported)

[74] Appeal No. HX/75889/94 (23rd November 1995) (unreported)

2.7 Supporting Evidence[75]

"The general human rights background of the country in question is important in assessing the objective foundation for the fear. Where human rights reports substantiate that a real risk of ill treatment exists, a genuine fear of persecution in a country is likely to be well-founded if it relates to a Convention reason. At the least the burden of persuasion would shift to the determining authority to demonstrate powerful reasons to the contrary. Where after all the evidence has been placed before the tribunal of fact there remains doubt, the benefit of it should be given to the applicant."[76]

The process of verification is critical for the success of an asylum claim because it establishes both that the fear of persecution is well-founded and that the applicant's claim is credible. It remains the case however, that for women in particular this information may simply not be readily available. Because women refugees are frequently subjected to forms of persecution which differ from those of men, they may be unable to document their experiences. For example, they may not be able to provide membership cards or newspaper cuttings relating to their political involvement because they have been indirectly involved through a supporting role or because the political opinion has been imputed to them. In addition background reports and country information published by organisations such as Amnesty International and the US State Department have, until very recently, lacked an analysis of the position and status of women. Representatives should make every effort to obtain supporting information which can strengthen the credibility of their client's asylum claim.

2.7.1 Documentary Evidence and Country Reports

"The applicant's statements...cannot be considered in the abstract, and must be viewed in the context of the relevant background situation. A knowledge of conditions in the applicant's country of origin...is an important element in assessing the applicant's credibility."[77]

---

[75] See Annex 9

[76] Macdonald and Blake *Macdonald's Immigration Law and Practice in the United Kingdom* 1995, 382 paragraph 12.21

[77] UNHCR *Handbook* 1979, paragraph 42

Information about the human rights situation in the applicant's country of origin - both from the state's own sources and from non-governmental organisations - plays a vital role in refugee status determination. However, information which is relevant to the asylum cases of refugee women may not be readily available. Few refugee documentation centres have information on the position of women in a given country, on the incidence of sexual violence in that country, and on the consequences of returning to the country in question for a woman in the claimant's alleged position. This is an impediment to women whose claim to refugee status is related to their gender status, especially given that, in the absence of information, decision-makers will normally presume that there are no specific problems. Even if women who have fled their countries because of gender-related persecution are willing to reveal their experiences, they often have trouble substantiating them; women's stories may not appear credible and they may have more difficulties than men with comparable claims.[78]

> "Where a gender-related claim involves threats of or actual violence at the hands of government authorities (or at the hands of non-state agents of persecution where the state is either unwilling or unable to protect), the claimant may have difficulty in substantiating her claim with any 'statistical data' on the incidence of [sexual] violence in her country."[79]
>
> "It should be noted that violence against women, particularly sexual or domestic violence, tends to be largely under-reported or ignored in many countries. The absence of information on the above topics for any particular country should not necessarily be taken as an indicator that abuses of women's human rights do not occur."[80]

Given that the IND does not maintain country reports relating explicitly to gender issues, representatives should, in accordance with the UNHCR's *Guidelines on the Protection of Refugee Women*,[81] make

---

[78] Castel 1992, 55

[79] CIRB *Guidelines on Women Refugee Claimants Fearing Gender-Related Persecution: UPDATE* November 1996, C.2 (Annex 5, 194)

[80] ADIMA *Guidelines on Gender Issues for Decision Makers* July 1996, paragraph 3.6 (Annex 6)

[81] UNHCR *Guidelines on the Protection of Refugee Women* 1991, paragraph 73

themselves familiar with the status and experiences of women in the country from which their client has fled:

"Adequate research of the claims made in the application and an understanding of the situation in the country of origin of the applicant is important for the full exploration of the person's claims. Where gender-related claims are raised, or suspected, an understanding of the role, status and treatment of women in the country of origin is particularly important."[82]

In addition to examining issues directly related to the claim and the differential application of human rights for women, representatives should consider a number of issues when gathering information:

- **the position of women before the law**
  including their standing in court, the right to lay a complaint and give evidence, divorce and custody law, the right to own property and reproductive rights

- **the political rights of women**
  including the right to vote, to hold office and belong to a political party

- **the social and economic rights of women**
  including the right to marry the person of her choice, the right not to marry and the right to determine her own sexuality, the right to an education, a career, and a job or remunerated activities, the status of a widow or divorcee, and freedom of dress

- **the incidence and form of reported violence against women**
  the forms it takes (such as sexual abuse, honour killings, bride burning), protection available to women and the sanctions or penalties on those who perpetrate the violence

- **the consequences that may befall women on her return**
  in light of the circumstances described in her claim.[83]

---

[82] ADIMA *Guidelines on Gender Issues for Decision Makers* July 1996, paragraph 3.3 (Annex 6)
[83] See UNHCR *Guidelines on the Protection of Refugee Women* 1991, paragraph 73

It may also be useful to gather information about the cultural and social mores of the country with regard to the role and status of women, the family, the nature of family relationships, attitudes towards same sex relationships and attitudes towards 'foreign' influences.[84]

> **"In assessing gender-based persecution it is important to research the accepted norms of the relevant societies to determine how they operate both through legislation and in terms of actual practice in order to determine the degree of protection available to women."[85]**

Both representatives, and ultimately decision-makers, need to know about the prevalence of practices such as female infanticide and dowry deaths in different societies. At the same time, they need to be aware of the consequences for those women who fail to conform to mandatory dress codes, or for those who lose their virginity or become pregnant before marriage. The need for evidence regarding the failure of the state to provide protection will be particularly crucial to refugee claims based on experiences such as domestic violence and other types of harm in which the state is not directly implicated.[86] For example, does the state turn a blind eye to the punishment meted out to these women when family honour might be at stake or is the state able to provide protection to women in urban but not in rural areas? The difficulty, of course, is that limited country-specific material is available through the traditional sources of information for refugee claims. This is in large part due to the failure of many states to consider violence against women to be a serious problem, or one worth the assignment of resources sufficient to provide for the wide dissemination of research.

It may be necessary for advocates to build their own pool of resources through direct contacts with members of government departments, social services and academia. Where no country-specific information about gender-related issues is available, advocates should use general information about such issues to support, by extension, their client's claim. For example, the literature on domestic violence from many different countries makes reference to the inadequacy of police response.

---

[84] ADIMA *Guidelines on Gender Issues for Decision Makers* July 1996, paragraph 3.5
[85] ibid., paragraph 4.11
[86] Stairs and Pope 1990, 202-203

Given that in the absence of such information it will be very hard to establish the validity of a refugee woman's claim for asylum, a number of different methods can be adopted in order to gather supporting information:

- **Interviewing other women from the country of origin to verify the material collected in the interview;**

- **Gathering general information about the position of women in countries of origin from articles, newspapers, recent studies and reports;**

- **Accessing on-line information available on the Internet[87] or sources such as the UNHCR's RefWorld on CD-Rom;**

- **Contacting specialists and expert witnesses familiar either with the region or the gender issues involved.[88]**

What is clear from existing determinations is that when such efforts are made to obtain information, the woman is more likely to be successful in her application for asylum or in an appeal against a negative decision by the Home Office. The importance of adequate background information about the country of origin can be seen in the case of a woman from Algeria who applied for asylum because of the threat of *Mut'a* or temporary pleasure marriage:

"Having carefully perused all those documents I have referred to, I have no doubt in my mind that GIA members do select and target single women in Algeria for the purpose of enjoyment marriages... having carefully studied the background information about the country and having studied the current position of Algeria, I am satisfied that the appellant's fear was well-founded." [89]

---

[87] See Annex 9

[88] If an application is refused on grounds relating to the substance of the claim, the use of expert witnesses may prove invaluable at the appeal stage, in addition to documentary evidence relating to the situation of women in a particular country. See also ILPA *Directory of Experts on Conditions in Countries of Origin and Transit*, 2nd edition 1997

[89] Appeal No. HX/66670/96 (22nd October 1996) (unreported)

Expert evidence submitted can also lead to a reconsideration of the case prior to a hearing.

2.7.2 Medical Evidence

Clearly the extent to which medical evidence will be useful in supporting a claimant's testimony will depend largely upon the details of each claim, and it should be noted that even in cases of rape or sexual violence - unlike other forms of torture - there is generally no physical evidence unless the rape was a particularly brutal one or the woman was a virgin and has no children. Representatives should also be aware that there are cases where medical evidence has been dismissed by the adjudicator, as in the case of an Ethiopian woman who was raped by government soldiers:

> "It seems reasonable to suggest that they [the scars] could also be compatible with numerous innocent activities. Indeed the examiner appears understandably to have relied rather more on the appellant's emotional responses to examination which she claims were 'definitely those of an abused woman'...It is my view that the appellant's emotional response to the doctor was calculated and false...the appellants rape is a complete fabrication."[90]

This decision was subsequently overruled by the IAT:

> "The doctor giving the report is a very highly qualified and experienced psychiatrist retained by the Medical Foundation...In our view in his evaluation of the medical report [the adjudicator] was so dismissive of the potential weight of the report that it amounts to an error in law to say that it provided no independent support to her claim and that the rape claim was a fabrication."[91]

Reports from specialist organisations (in addition to GPs) which make an assessment of the refugee woman's physical and mental health can be critical to the successful outcome of refugee women's claims for asylum. In the case of a woman from Zaire, reports by the Black Women's Rape Action Project and Women Against Rape highlighted the traumatic

---

[90] Appeal No. HX/73584/94 (1995) (unreported)
[91] *Almaz Woldu Gimhedin v SSHD*, IAT 21st October 1996 (14019) (unreported)

effects on the applicant of horrific gang-rape by soldiers at gun-point, the threat to her life, and the murder and violence against close members of her family that she witnessed.[92] This report was instrumental in overturning the earlier refusal of the Home Office to accept that, in the light of these experiences, her life would be in danger if she returned to Zaire. If representatives consider that such information would be beneficial to the claims of their female clients they should ensure that a referral is made to the appropriate organisation at the earliest possible opportunity.[93]

2.8 A Note on the Appeals Process[94]

Given that over 90 percent of initial applications are refused by the Home Office, the appeals process has become increasingly important for those seeking asylum in the UK. The refusal to grant status to refugee women may be on credibility grounds such as those outlined above, on substantial issues of interpretation which are discussed in the following three chapters, or on a combination of the two. Since July 1993, all those whose asylum applications are considered substantively and refused have the right to appeal to a special adjudicator. Those whose appeals are dismissed have the right to apply for leave to appeal to the IAT against the determination, although not those who have been placed in the fast-track, accelerated appeals procedure. Legal Aid does not cover the cost of representation at the appeal hearing itself. Meanwhile although access to benefits for asylum seekers is complex, all asylum seekers refused since July 1996 will lose benefits.[95] Some asylum seekers awaiting appeal may suffer intense financial hardship for a period of between one and two years because of delays in the appellate process.[96] The situation is compounded by the fact that the Home Office can apply for leave to appeal to the IAT against a determination which is in favour of the asylum seeker. For those who have arrived in the UK with children and who are responsible for their care - usually women - the current system serves only to make them more vulnerable to exploitation and abuse.

---

[92] 'How asylum procedures failed Mrs. X and how the Short Procedure (SP) will lead to a further deterioration of standards', Hackney Community Law Centre and WAR press release, 1996

[93] See Annex 9 for sources of information and support

[94] This note is not intended to provide representatives with information on the mechanisms of the appeals process. See the ILPA *Best Practise Guide to Asylum Appeals* 1997 for information on appeal procedures.

[95] Seek expert advice and note the possibilities under the National Assistance Act (1948) and the Children Act (1989)

[96] Refugee Council 1996

Most, if not all, of the procedural problems facing refugee women which have been discussed in this chapter are likely to arise during the appeals process. In addition however there is also some evidence to suggest that rather than allowing gender-related cases to reach the courts where precedents could be established, the Home Office have awarded ELR to some female applicants. Clearly rights and benefits associated with ELR are significantly lower than those associated with full refugee status, especially regarding family reunion. In such cases the representative in consultation with his or her client will need to decide whether to challenge the grant of ELR. Although the remainder of this Handbook will argue for the need to develop a body of case law on the gender-related persecution claims, proceeding with an appeal against a refusal to upgrade should be considered very carefully because of the dangers of curtailment or non-renewal of ELR. Representatives should be especially aware of the potential damage of a negative finding on credibility.

It is also apparent that for many of the reasons discussed in this chapter, women may be less willing than men to proceed further and may be content to settle for ELR although it limits the possibility of family reunion. There are practical and financial reasons for this reluctance including anxieties about reliving the events as well as fears about publicity. The following testimony from a Middle Eastern woman forced to undergo hymen reconstruction because she was no longer a virgin illustrates the concerns of many female asylum seekers:

"They [the Home Office] made a deal and told me to take one year Exceptional Leave to Remain...In the end I accepted it. Had I won this case I would have been the first woman and that's what they wanted to avoid. I really wanted to win my case and open things up but I didn't want to fight anymore. If I carried on I would have been famous but scandalised. A lot of personal problems would come out. All my private life would come out, and names. I would help a lot of women but then I would pay the price...maybe even a bullet on the street. I care for my friends, my family and my reputation."[97]

---

[97] Interview with the author, November 1996

2.9 Campaigning

In addition to the legal process, campaigning may be essential, and representatives should utilise all available means to fight the removal of their client. Timing of the launch of a campaign is critical and advisors should have a strategy in mind in the early stages of the case. Successful campaign strategies undertaken by representatives have included:

- **Utilising existing campaign networks and anti-deportation campaigns;[98]**

- **Obtaining resolutions in support of the campaign from branches of political parties, trade unions and anti-racist organisations;**

- **Approaching parliamentarians and prominent individuals for support;**

- **Contacting women's organisations, faith groups and refugee community organisations;**

- **Contacting refugee charities to see if they can support a point of issue;**

- **Raising awareness through public meetings, colleges and workplaces;**

- **Accessing family, school and local community support networks;**

- **Utilising media networks to gain sympathetic coverage.**

Southall Black Sisters, a black women's organisation specialising in the needs of Asian women, and Women Against Fundamentalism have launched a number of successful campaigns on behalf of refugee women. The following case study is just one example of how campaigning can be extremely effective:

---

[98] See Annex 9 for details

The campaign to prevent the removal of Ms J started in March 1990 when Ms J was suddenly picked up by police and detained in Harmondsworth Detention Centre. She was not with her young children at the time, one of whom was still being breast fed, and was to be removed without them. This was despite the fact that her legal representatives had made representations which were pending a decision. Southall Black Sisters (SBS) and Women Against Fundamentalism (WAF) launched a campaign to obtain her release from detention and prevent her immediate removal. They contacted her solicitor and MP who made representations on her behalf. They also contacted the press, who contacted the Home Office, IND and the detention centre. *The Independent* newspaper covered the story. This pressure led to Ms J's release from detention and she was allowed to remain until a decision had been made in her case. In the meantime SBS and WAF continued to build up public support and produced a campaign leaflet asking for help. As a result of this campaign Ms J was granted ELR.[99]

---

[99] Case study provided by Southall Black Sisters and Women Against Fundamentalism. For further details of Ms J's asylum claim see this volume at 3.1. See Annex 9 for contact addresses.

Chapter 3 'PERSECUTION' AND THE MEANING OF 'SERIOUS HARM'

> "Increased emphasis on the role of gender in persecution is not intended to alter the ordinary meaning of persecution. Rather it is intended to ensure that all of the applicant's claims of persecution are fully considered."[1]

Refugee women may have been subjected to *forms* of abuse, such as torture, beating or arbitrary detention which are not specific to their gender. There are also many *forms* of serious harm arising in asylum claims which are unique to, or more commonly affect, women including rape, sexual abuse, female genital mutilation, bride burning, forced marriage, violence within the family, forced sterilisation and forced abortion. However "persecution has not been widely interpreted to include these generally female-specific experiences."[2] This chapter is concerned with the meaning of 'serious harm' in Hathaway's definition of 'persecution'; does the treatment to which the applicant was subjected in the past or which the applicant fears amount to persecution?

The UNHCR *Handbook* recognises that there is no universally accepted definition of 'persecution', but from Article 33 of the Convention it may be inferred that a 'threat to life or freedom' on one of the five enumerated grounds is always persecution.[3] The *Handbook* further acknowledges that "[o]ther serious violations of human rights - for the same reasons - would also constitute persecution."[4] Meanwhile in a recent and highly significant Canadian case, the judge concluded that "underlying the Convention is the international community's commitment to the assurance of basic human rights..."[5] Given that all existing definitions of persecution share the notion that violations of basic human rights constitute persecution, it is necessary to examine the human rights protected under international law.

The process of identifying every abuse of human rights against internationally agreed standards of human rights allows proper

---

[1] ADIMA *Guidelines on Gender Issues for Decision Makers* July 1996, paragraph 4.4 (Annex 6)
[2] Kelly 1994, 523
[3] UNHCR *Handbook* 1979, paragraph 51
[4] ibid.
[5] *Canada (Attorney General) v Ward* [1993] 2 SCR 689

consideration of all forms of serious harm a person may face including those harms that are gender-specific.

Hathaway proposes that we move away from any intuitive reasoning about what persecution is and try to substantiate our reasoning by basing it on very objective indicators. Arguing that "[o]ur basic international legal obligations are the appropriate common denominators,"[6] he grounds his definition of 'serious harm' in human rights agreements containing standards accepted as legitimate by virtually all states; the *Universal Declaration of Human Rights*, the *International Covenant on Civil and Political Rights* and the *International Covenant on Economic, Social and Cultural Rights*. On the basis of these international agreements he establishes a hierarchy of rights:

Examples of Level 1 Rights: freedom from torture or cruel, inhuman or degrading treatment; freedom from slavery; freedom of thought, conscience and religion

Examples of Level 2 Rights: freedom from arbitrary arrest or detention; equal protection of the law; fair criminal proceedings; family privacy; freedom of internal movement; freedom of opinion, expression, assembly, and association; rights to vote; access to public employment

Examples of Level 3 Rights: right to work; right to essential food, clothing and housing, health care; basic education; cultural expression

Examples of Level 4 Rights: private property; protection from unemployment.[7]

According to Hathaway, "persecution is most appropriately defined...in relation to...the core entitlements which [have] been recognised by the international community". The types of harm to be protected against include the breach of any right within the first category, a discriminatory

---

[6] Hathaway 1990, 11
[7] See also Kelly 1994, 521-22

or non-emergency abrogation of a right within the second category, or the failure to implement a right within the third category which is either discriminatory or not grounded in the absolute lack of resources.

For the purposes of this Handbook therefore, the definition of 'serious harm' follows Hathaway who defines persecution within a human rights paradigm as "the sustained or systematic violation of basic human rights demonstrative of a failure of state protection."[8] Within this framework certain human rights are considered so fundamental as to be non-derogable such that any violation of those rights is considered egregious. Genocide, slavery, assassination, torture, arbitrary arrest and detention are among the human rights violations that are the most widely accepted as prohibited conduct. In addition to the human rights instruments identified above, the ECHR which created a European Commission as well as a European Court of Human Rights, sets up an effective system for the protection of human rights at the international level.[9] In cases of *refoulement* or other forms of removal, the person concerned may invoke Article 3 of the Convention which states that "no one shall be subjected to torture or to inhuman or degrading treatment or punishment."[10]

This framework for the assessment of 'serious harm' has been accepted in UK case law. In *Jonah*,[11] it was held that 'persecution' in the context of Article 1(A) of the Convention should be given its ordinary meaning of 'to pursue with malignancy or injurious action". In *Gashi and Nikshiqi*,[12] the IAT in allowing the appeals of both appellants used Hathaway's framework to assess the level of harm and concluded that "[t]here seems to be no doubt that [persecution] includes not only the first category but the second category as well and some aspects of the third category". The submissions by the UNHCR appear to have been significant for the Tribunal's determination on this issue:

---

[8] Hathaway 1991, 104-105
[9] See ECRE *Asylum in Europe: An Introduction* 1993 and Annex 2
[10] See for example *Soering v United Kingdom* 14038/88 [1989] 11 EHRR 439 (E Ct HR), *Chahal v United Kingdom*, E Ct HR 15th November 1996 (70/995/576/662) (unreported) and *D v United Kingdom*, E Ct HR 12th May 1997 (146/1966/767/964) Times Law Report
[11] *R v IAT ex p Jonah* [1985] Imm AR 7 (QBD)
[12] *Urim Gashi and Astrit Nikshiqi v SSHD*, IAT July 1996 (13695) (unreported)

> "We close by referring to one particular paragraph in [the] submission on behalf of UNHCR which we think encapsulates the dangers in failing to treat the Convention as a practical and living tool which the signatories co-operate with to provide that substitute protection of the more basic fundamental human rights [that] "the term 'persecution' cannot be seen in isolation from the increasingly sophisticated body on international law on human rights generally. In recognition of the adaptable nature of the refugee definition to meet the ever changing needs of protection, UNHCR recognises an important link between persecution and the violation of fundamental human rights."[13]

Macklin and others suggest however that conventional typologies of human rights continue to exclude the experiences of women.[14] Inclusion of the *Convention on the Elimination of All Forms of Discrimination Against Women* (CEDAW), the *UN Declaration on the Elimination of Violence Against Women* and the *UN Platform for Action* in a reformulation of Hathaway's hierarchy, would go some way towards ensuring that gender-specific human rights violations are recognised.[15] These efforts, and others at the inter-governmental and non-governmental level, have started to focus attention on gender-specific human rights abuses perpetrated against women. In documenting these violations, they have both called attention to their occurrence and have served to bring the issues into the discourse on international human rights. As this chapter will demonstrate, however, the definition of what constitutes 'serious harm' in the context of 'persecution' continues to reflect a gendered conceptualisation of human rights which can serve to exclude the experiences of women seeking asylum.

The *form* of the harm or punishment may be selected because of the gender of the victim, but decision makers should assess whether an instance of harm amounts to persecution on the basis of the *general principles* which are set out above and examined in detail in this chapter.

---

[13] *Urim Gashi and Astrit Nikshiqi v SSHD*, IAT 22nd July 1996 (13695) (unreported)
[14] See Macklin 1995
[15] See this volume at 3.7 and Annex 3

3.1 Sexual Violence Including Rape

The occurrence of sexual violence in refugee producing situations has been well-documented and would appear to be a major factor in forced migration although as the UNHCR acknowledges, the true scale of sexual violence against refugee women is unknown because numerous incidents are never reported.[16] Sexual violence including rape occurs in a variety of different situations. It may be explicitly politically motivated (for example as a method of interrogation or as part of a process of 'ethnic cleansing') or can occur in situations of generalised violence such as civil war. Women who are on their own may be particularly vulnerable to this kind of abuse as are women detained on political grounds, either because of their own activities, or because of the activities of absent husbands or other family members.

> **Mrs S is a Ugandan citizen. Her father was a member of the UPC and her grandfather was one of the founder members of the party. UPC meetings also used to be held in her husband's building and he used to entertain party members whenever they came to a conference. As a result of the political activities of her male family members, Mrs S was herself arrested. She was taken to the local barracks where she was tortured and raped. She was kept in a cell with three or four other women and each of them was tortured and raped in front of the others. They would be urinated on and made to drink the urine, and when Mrs S refused to do this, she was pushed against a piece of broken glass and her leg injured to the extent that she could not walk.[17]**

Whilst the reasons or *grounds* leading to the use of sexual violence including rape are clearly critical in the context of an asylum claim - and are discussed in Chapter 5 - what is of concern in this section is sexual violence including rape as a gender-specific *form* of persecution. Sexual violence can include, *but is not limited to*:

---

[16] UNHCR *Sexual Violence Against Refugees; Guidelines on Prevention and Response* 1995. See also Spijkerboer 1994

[17] Appeal No. HX/70880/96 (10th February 1997) (unreported). The appellant's appeal was refused but the adjudicator made a recommendation that ELR be granted given the horrific nature of her experiences.

- rape;
- mechanical or manual stimulation of the erogenous zones;
- the insertion of objects into the body openings (sometimes with objects made of metal to which an electrical current is later connected);
- the forced witnessing of sexual acts;
- forced masturbation or to be masturbated by others;
- fellatio and oral coitus;
- a general atmosphere of sexual aggression and threats of the loss of the ability to reproduce and enjoyment of sexual relations in the future.[18]

Examples from UK cases also include the use of high-power water jets directed at the vagina, being forced to watch others (including children) being sexually abused or raped, being watched by others, and forced prostitution.

Sexual violence including rape involves the infliction of both physical and psychological suffering upon the victim. It may also carry traumatic social repercussions, which may be affected by a woman's cultural origins or social status. In some countries women who have been raped in custody are unwilling to report the abuse; some may feel degraded or ashamed or fear that they would suffer social stigma should they disclose what has been done to them. It has been suggested that the key to understanding the injury of sexual violence including rape is to recognise that although in many cases the insult may have been intended *for* men *through* women, it is internalised *by* women.[19] This happens in three ways. Firstly, women bear the physical injury. Secondly, they blame themselves for being raped and feel ashamed. Thirdly, in cultures where men view rape as a stain on their honour and that of the family, women internalise this guilt. In many cultural contexts therefore, the experience of sexual violence may lead to the woman being ostracised by both her family and the community. She may be unable to marry or stay married or may be 'married off'. In some societies, a woman who has been raped may also be perceived as a culprit and consequently may be liable to punishment by the state.

---

[18] UNHCR *Guidelines on the Protection of Refugee Women* 1991, paragraph 59
[19] Thompkins 1995

Ms J is a 27 year old woman from Pakistan. When she was 20 years old, she was raped by the man who is now her estranged husband. She knew she could not return to her family as she would have been punished severely, publicly castigated and treated like a social outcast for having dishonoured her family and brought shame to her community. Moreover, she knew that it was impossible to prove rape, as she would have to produce four independent male witnesses to testify that she had been raped. This is required by law. The couple were arrested under *Hudood* laws and accused of *Zina* (sex outside marriage). So she had no choice but to marry the man who had raped her, who later sponsored her to come to the UK as a visitor. As soon as Ms J entered this country, her husband took away her passport and all other documents. He subsequently subjected her to intense abuse and she lived in constant fear of him. In the end he reported her to the Home Office who then treated her as an illegal entrant. In Pakistan, Ms J will either face death by stoning or up to ten years imprisonment and thirty lashes for *Zina*. Her claim for asylum must therefore be seen in the context of Pakistan's discriminatory treatment of women. It was argued by the Home Office however that "the avoidance of alleged crimes in another country cannot confer upon her any entitlement to stay here". After a vigorous campaign Ms J was granted ELR.[20]

3.1.1 Sexual Violence as Cruel, Inhuman and Degrading Treatment

Sexual violence including rape can have serious physical, social, intellectual and psychological consequences. Physical consequences can include HIV infection, STD's, mutilated genitalia, pregnancy, miscarriage of an existing foetus, menstrual disorder, severe abdominal pain and self-mutilation as a result of psychological trauma. The UNHCR also notes in its publication entitled *Sexual Violence Against Refugees; Guidelines on Prevention and Response* that "[w]here women have undergone extreme forms of female genital mutilation, they may suffer extensive injuries if their genitalia are reopened by a sharp

---

[20] Southall Black Sisters *Evidence to the Home Affairs Select Committee*, November 1992 (available from the Home Affairs Select Committee or SBS). Ms J was ignorant of British immigration laws and simply followed the advice of her husband, who told her to tell immigration that she was visiting the UK rather than joining her husband. See also this volume at 2.9 for details of her campaign to stay in the UK with her children.

instrument or by the force of penetration itself".[21] Even if physical injury is minimal, all victims experience psychological trauma. This may lead to difficulties for the representative in 'finding out' about the harm itself.[22] Moreover as was previously suggested, the social consequences of sexual violence can range from rejection by the spouse and immediate family members, to stigmatisation or ostracism by the wider community to severe punishment and/or deprivation of education, employment and other types of assistance and protection which may rise to the level of serious harm.[23] Where a rape victim may be killed or banished, or considered to have no alternative but to marry her attacker or become a prostitute these should be considered as additional human rights violations. According to the UNHCR, in cases where the return to the country would have one of these results, and where no other basis for her recognition has been identified, the applicant may be considered a refugee *sur place*.[24]

> **"Some decision makers have proven unable to grasp the nature of rape by state actors as an integral and tactical part of the arsenal of weapons deployed to brutalise, dehumanise, and humiliate women and demoralise their kin and community."[25]**

Sexual violence including rape should be one of the least controversial examples of 'serious harm' in the context of a definition of persecution. However this has not always been the case. Such acts have been characterised as the random expression of spontaneous sexual impulses by a military officer toward a woman, or as the common (and by implication acceptable) fate of women caught in a war zone.[26] The UNHCR suggests that this shows a lack of awareness and maintains that it is important to understand that sexual violence is a serious violation of an individual's personal security and integrity.[27]

---

[21] UNHCR *Sexual Violence Against Refugees; Guidelines on Prevention and Response* 1995, 6. See also this volume at 3.3

[22] See this volume at 2.2

[23] See this volume at 3.2

[24] UNHCR *Sexual Violence Against Refugees; Guidelines on Prevention and Response* 1995, 68

[25] Macklin 1995, 226

[26] See also this volume at 4.2.6

[27] UNHCR *Sexual Violence Against Refugees; Guidelines on Prevention and Response* 1995

"Severe sexual abuse does not differ analytically from beatings, torture, or other forms of physical violence that are commonly held to amount to persecution. The appearance of sexual violence in a claim should not lead adjudicators to conclude automatically that the claim is an instance of purely personal harm."[28]

There is no difference between the sexual violence used against women, and the torture inflicted upon men. Indeed Hathaway himself finds that "[t]he threat of rape, for example, is a sufficient basis for persecution" and cites a Canadian precedent which labels rape as "persecution of the most vile sort."[29] There can be no doubt therefore that sexual violence and rape fulfil the necessary criteria for 'serious harm' in a human rights framework. This unanimity seems to be inescapable in the light of international law:

Sexual violence including rape is a grave violation of the fundamental human right to security of person, including the right not to be subjected to torture or other cruel, inhuman or degrading treatment or punishment. This right has been laid down in, *inter alia*:

- Articles 3 and 5 of the Universal Declaration of Human Rights (General Assembly Resolution 217A (III));

- Article 7 of the International Covenant on Civil and Political Rights (General Assembly Resolution 2200 A (XXI));

- The Convention against Torture and Other Cruel, Inhuman or Degrading Treatment or Punishment (General Assembly Resolution 39/46).[30]

---

[28] INS *Considerations for Asylum Officers Adjudicating Asylum Claims from Women* June 1995. Establishing the persecution ground is in some cases the most serious problem facing women as refugee claimants and one which will be discussed in detail in Chapter 5.

[29] Hathaway 1995, 112

[30] See for example *Kisoki* Committee Against Torture Sixteenth Session *Communication No. 41/1996*, 13th May 1996. Contact the AIRE Centre for further information (Annex 9)

These rights are so fundamental that no circumstance whatsoever justifies their derogation under international law.[31] Refugee law doctrine is unanimous therefore in its opinion that sexual violence including rape constitutes an act of serious harm and there is solid support for this position in the gender guidelines which have been produced by Canada, the United States and Australia:

"The fact that violence, including sexual and domestic violence, against women is universal is *irrelevant* when determining whether rape, and other gender-specific crimes constitute forms of persecution."[32]

"Rape and other forms of sexual assault...clearly come within the bounds of torture as defined by the Convention Against Torture (CAT). Furthermore, sexual violence amounts to a violation of the prohibition against cruel, inhuman or degrading treatment, the right to security of person and in some instances the right to life, as contained in a variety of national instruments."[33]

Rape and other forms of sexual abuse violate the prohibitions of violence to person, cruel treatment and torture, and degrading treatment contained in the four Geneva Conventions of 1949. International humanitarian law also explicitly prohibits rape. Article 27 of the *Fourth Geneva Convention* of 1949 states; "women shall be especially protected against any attack on their honour, in particular against rape, enforced prostitution, or any other form of indecent assault". This provision is reiterated in Additional Protocols I and II:

"Sexual violence is a gross violation of fundamental human rights and, when committed in the context of armed conflict, a grave breach of humanitarian law."[34]

---

[31] See for example the UNHCR's *Note on Certain Aspects of Sexual Violence Against Refugee Women* [A/AC.96/822], 1993

[32] CIRB *Guidelines on Women Refugee Claimants Fearing Gender-Related Persecution: UPDATE* November 1996, Section B (Annex 5, 192)

[33] ADIMA *Guidelines on Gender Issues for Decision Makers* July 1996, paragraph 4.6 (Annex 6)

[34] UNHCR *Sexual Violence Against Refugees; Guidelines on Prevention and Response* 1995, 1

The concept of 'serious harm' as a critical component of the central phrase a 'well-founded fear of persecution', must be interpreted to include refugee women's experiences of sexual violence. However, problems for many female asylum seekers who have suffered such abuse may also arise because of difficulties in establishing a failure of state protection,[35] or in providing 'proof' or 'evidence' that the rape has taken place and maintaining 'credibility'. These problems are exacerbated because of the difficulties of 'finding out' about sexual violence including rape which were discussed in detail in Chapter 2.

3.1.2 Case Law
Canada
Canadian tribunals have explicitly found that threats of rape and rape itself "are degrading and constitute quite clearly an attack on the moral integrity of the person and, hence, persecution of the most vile sort". In *Smith*[36] the CRDD, referring to the UDHR and the Convention on Consent to Marriage, also arrived at the conclusion that the forced marriage of a fifteen-year-old Zimbabwean girl to a polygamous man, followed by years of physical and sexual brutality, amounted to persecution.

United States
In the United States, serious physical harm has consistently been held to constitute persecution. Rape and other forms of sexual violence can clearly fall within this rule. For example in *Lazo-Majano*,[37] in which a Salvadoran woman was raped and brutalised by an army sergeant who denounced her as subversive, it was ruled that the applicant had been 'persecuted' within the terms of the Convention.

United Kingdom
Recognition of sexual violence as 'serious harm' in the UK has been inconsistent, and in some cases rape has been dismissed as irrelevant to the UN Convention. For example in the case of a Kenyan woman who was arrested and detained and tortured twice by the authorities because of her involvement with the Safina party, the letter from the Home Office refusing her claim states that "rape is a criminal matter and as such not the basis of a claim to asylum under the 1951 United Nations Convention". By contrast however sexual violence including rape as a

---

[35] See Chapter 4
[36] *Smith v Canada (MEI)* (19 Feb 1993)
[37] *Lazo-Majano v INS* [1987] 813 F.2d 1432, 1434 (9th Circuit)

violation of fundamental human rights has been recognised in several recent appeal cases.

In the case of a Kurdish woman from Turkey who had been gang-raped by Turkish police, the special adjudicator upheld her right to asylum in the UK noting that "the maltreatment and sexual abuse [she suffered] were acts of persecution."[38]

A Kenyan woman, detained and repeatedly raped by police officers because of her alleged political opposition, has been recognised as a Convention refugee.[39]

It should be noted that the circumstances in each of these cases were such that both state responsibility and the grounds of the persecution were clear. However, even where the grounds of the persecution are not accepted, there appears to be growing recognition among adjudicators of the implications of the sexual violence for the appellant, which may lead to a recommendation that ELR be granted. For example, in dismissing the appeal of a woman from Ghana raped and tortured because of the political activities of her father and husband, the adjudicator made the following comments:

"I believe it would be quite wrong to return the appellant if she were medically unfit. That includes her psychological well-being. Rape is an appalling abuse leaving its mark for many years and which, if not dealt with by expert counselling at an early stage can leave emotional scars so deeply embedded that call for the most compassionate treatment. I thus recommend no steps be taken to remove the appellant until her medical condition permits and that her overall circumstances be given the most compassionate consideration."[40]

---

[38] See Appeal No. HX/73695/95 (17th May 1996) (unreported)

[39] See Appeal No. HX/70880/96 (10th February 1997) (unreported). Whilst the determination of the adjudicator does not explicitly refer to the rape as persecution, implicit within the decision is a recognition that sexual violence including rape constitutes a violation of fundamental human rights.

[40] See Appeal No. HX/73663/94 (27th October 1995) (unreported)

3.2 Social Mores and Discrimination

"Gender-based persecution is sometimes more subtle than other forms. It can take the form of restrictions on the way a woman behaves or it can involve forcing her to act in a certain way."[41]

In many countries, women are subjected to discriminatory treatment and social mores which are enforced through law or through the imposition of cultural or religious norms which restrict their opportunities and rights.

Social mores and discrimination are seen in, *but are not limited to:*

- **Legislated Discrimination,** for example Pakistan's *Hudood* laws or restrictions on women's movements and/or activities in Afghanistan

- **Dress Codes**

- **Employment or Education Restrictions**

- **Behavioural Restrictions,** for example, not going out in public without a male 'protector'

- **The Consequences of Divorce, Separation or Widowhood**

- **'Honour Killings'**

Discrimination or social mores as 'serious harm' is particularly clear in cases where the *level of punishment for violating gendered discriminatory norms* rises to the level of persecution. In some cases the penalty imposed by the state for non-compliance with a discriminatory law might be disproportionately severe. Neal cites Iranian law that makes women's failure to wear the *chador* a criminal act punishable by seventy-five lashes as an example of this.[42]

---

[41] ADIMA *Guidelines on Gender Issues for Decision Makers* July 1996, paragraph 4.10 (Annex 6)

[42] Neal 1988

"The status of women in some societies may be restricted and dictated by legal, social or religious mores. The restrictions will vary from mere inconvenience to oppression. In addition a broad range of penalties may be imposed for disobeying restrictions placed on women."[43]

There are many examples where women are punished for transgressing social mores or for finding themselves in circumstances deemed socially and culturally unacceptable. The severity of the punishment violates all recognised international human rights principles and clearly constitutes 'serious harm' within the meaning of 'persecution'.

Mrs M came to the UK from Pakistan for medical treatment during her second pregnancy. Whilst she was here her husband claimed that her first child was not his son and that because she had given birth to a girl she had brought shame upon him and his family. Mrs M became convinced that he would murder her if she returned to Pakistan after he wrote a letter to the authorities in the UK requesting that they send her back and suggesting she should be arrested at the Pakistani airport and punished by stoning to death under the law, before her feet touched the purity of the soil in Pakistan. In refusing her claim for asylum on the basis that it did not fall within the Convention, the adjudicator accepted the appellant would suffer ostracism if not punishment on her return to Pakistan by reason of the vindictive action taken by her husband in the context of society where the appellant would be regarded as having transgressed the norms associated with wives in particular and women in general in Pakistan.[44]

A further example is where women who have been sexually abused face harsh punishment because it is a condition of marriage that a woman be a virgin. The inability to fulfil this condition seriously jeopardises her honour and that of her family. To save face, the family may disown the woman or she may be killed by her father or brother ('honour killings'). Although such practices may not be officially sanctioned by the state, the authorities may be unable or unwilling to stop them. Similarly women

---

[43] ADIMA *Guidelines on Gender Issues for Decision Makers* July 1996, paragraph 4.9 (Annex 6)

[44] Appeal No. HX/75169/94 (2nd January 1996) (unreported)

who are divorced or separated, whether or not by agreement, may be subjected to a whole range of discriminatory measures which can amount to 'serious harm'.[45]

> **Ms S arrived in the UK from Fiji in 1988 to join her husband, but the marriage broke down after she was abused and ill treated by both her husband and in-laws. In 1989 the police told her that the Home Office had refused her application to remain here and that she was liable for deportation because her marriage had broken down within the first 12 months (the 'one year rule'). An application for asylum was made on the basis that she would experience violence and even possible death from her father and brothers, and ostracism/ harassment from the wider Hindu community if she returned to Fiji following the breakdown of her marriage. Ms S twice attempted to commit suicide rather than return. She was eventually granted ELR.[46]**

In addition to the issues outlined above, there is also an argument which holds that in certain cases persecution is not a punishment that the woman endures for having violated the norm, but rather the imposition of the law or norm in and of itself.[47]

> **"[The appellant's] clothing, manner of dress and behaviour were also the subject of close scrutiny to ensure that she acted within the confines of the new Islamic dress and behaviour code imposed by the Khomeini regime. The relentless pressure and harassment eventually took their toll and the situation became unbearable...The appellant felt as if she was being tortured to death."[48]**

Critical to the formulation of these claims is the fact that the applicant must establish that the government is the source of the persecutory measure or that the government is unwilling or unable to protect her from the persecution. When the treatment is through discriminatory statutes or laws which may be gender-neutral but are applied in a manner which

---

[45] See also Chapters 4 and 5 for more detailed analysis of the implications of this for establishing state culpability and the persecution ground

[46] Case study provided by Southall Black Sisters

[47] See for example Kelly 1993

[48] New Zealand Refugee Status Appeals Authority, Appeal No. 2039/93 (12th February 1996)

target women and which are enforced by the government, state involvement is clear.[49] However when the discriminatory practice is not applied by the government, but through cultural norms which discriminate against women - such as those which forbid them to study or hold certain professions - the applicant must demonstrate both the existence of the norms and the failure or inability of the government to protect her from its imposition. The issue of the failure of state protection in the context of social mores and discrimination is examined in more detail in Chapter 4.

3.2.1 Discrimination as 'Serious Harm'

Social mores and discrimination can in themselves constitute 'serious harm' rising to the level of 'persecution'.

Of specific concern here is the issue of whether or not social mores and discrimination themselves fulfil the criteria of 'serious harm'. Although the legal obligation to eliminate all forms of discrimination against women is a fundamental tenet of international human rights law, the level of discrimination sufficient to rise to the level of 'serious harm' is not a point on which states readily agree. The UNHCR *Handbook* specifically addresses the issue of discrimination in the context of the definition of 'persecution'[50]. If measures of discrimination lead to consequences of a substantially prejudicial nature for the person concerned then 'serious harm' can be said to have occurred:

"Where measures of discrimination are, in themselves, not of a serious character, they may nevertheless give rise to a reasonable fear of persecution if they produce, in the mind of the person concerned, a feeling of apprehension and insecurity as regards [her] future existence. Whether or not such measures of discrimination in themselves amount to persecution must be determined in the light of all the circumstances. A claim to fear of persecution will of course be stronger where a person has been the victim of a number of discriminatory measures of this type and where there is thus a cumulative element involved."[51]

---

[49] Kelly 1994
[50] UNHCR *Handbook* 1979, paragraphs 54 and 55.
[51] ibid., paragraph 55

The UNHCR *Handbook* cites the examples of serious restrictions on the right to earn a livelihood, the right to practice his or her chosen religion and his or her access to normally available educational facilities as examples of discrimination rising to the level of persecution.

The UNHCR's *Guidelines on the Protection of Refugee Women* (1991) do not clarify this issue any further insofar as they do not distinguish persecution from 'mere' discrimination. Other authors by contrast are very much clearer and locate discrimination within Hathaway's framework. For example, in addition to the punishment inflicted for failing to abide by social mores, it can be argued that a policy compelling women to wear the veil violates her 'first order' freedom of religion or conscience. The premise is that if the law discriminates by selectively abrogating fundamental human rights of designated groups, the law itself persecutes. In principle, it should not matter that it would be relatively 'easy' for the claimant to obey the law (and thus avoid prosecution) by wearing a veil, if in doing so she must forsake a protected freedom.[52] More often however the wearing of the veil constitutes only one element in a plethora of rules, policies and customs circumscribing the lives of women from particular countries. Therefore, in a claim based on discriminatory treatment and/or social mores, the decision-maker must evaluate all the circumstances, including the type of right or freedom denied, the manner in which the right is denied, the seriousness of the harm to the applicant, and any non-persecutory justification for the discriminatory treatment. Any harm to a right lower than level 1 or 2 may be persecutory if the harm is systematic or cumulative and seriously affects the integrity of the applicant.[53]

> **"The Authority should...consciously strive both to recognise and to give proper weight to the impact of discriminatory measures on women."[54]**
>
> **"Discrimination can affect gender-based groups to different degrees...various acts of discrimination, in their cumulative effect, can deny human dignity in key ways and should properly be recognised as persecution for the purposes of the Convention."[55]**

---

[52] Macklin 1995, 230
[53] Hathaway 1991
[54] New Zealand Refugee Status Appeals Authority, Appeal No. 1039/93 (13th February 1995)
[55] New Zealand Refugee Status Appeals Authority, Appeal No. 2039/93 (12th February 1996)

3.2.2 Case Law
United States

In *Fatin*[56] the Third Circuit considered whether an Iranian woman faced with having to wear the traditional Islamic veil and to comply with other harsh rules imposed on women in Iran risked 'persecution' as the Board has defined it. The applicant asserted that the routine penalty for women who break the moral code in Iran is "74 lashes, a year's imprisonment, and in many cases brutal rapes and death". These, the court states, would constitute persecution. The court went on to note that "the concept of persecution is broad enough to include governmental measures that compel an individual to engage in conduct that is not physically painful or harmful but is abhorrent to that individual's deepest beliefs."[57] Having to renounce religious beliefs or to desecrate an object of religious importance might, for example, be persecution if the victim held strong religious beliefs.

Fisher[58] also concerned an Iranian woman whose claim was based on the failure to conform to fundamentalist religious and cultural norms. The court emphasised that persecution should not be evaluated "solely on the basis of the physical sanction". Citing *Fatin*, the court also stated that "when a person with religious views different from those espoused by a religious regime is required to conform to, or is punished for failing to comply with laws that fundamentally are abhorrent to that person's deeply held religious convictions, the resulting anguish should be considered in determining whether the authorities have engaged in extreme conduct that is tantamount to persecution."[59]

United Kingdom

Case law relating to discrimination as 'serious harm' is clearer in cases of persecution which are not gender-specific. For example, in *Chiver*[60] the IAT ruled that discrimination could constitute 'serious harm' where the respondent, a Romanian, had suffered serious discrimination in being barred from employment and state benefits because of his political opinions.

---

[56] *Fatin v INS* [1993] 12 F.3d 1233 (3rd Circuit)
[57] ibid.
[58] *Fisher v INS* [1994] 37 F.3d 1371 (9th Circuit)
[59] ibid.
[60] *SSHD v Adrian Ghorghe Chiver*, IAT 24th March 1994 (10758) (unreported)

> **"We agree with the adjudicator that persecution...will be shown if the appellant establishes a reasonable likelihood that he will be unable to obtain employment."[61]**

More recently in *Gashi* and *Nikshiqi*,[62] the IAT referred to Hathaway's human rights framework which was discussed in 3.1 and accepted that human rights violations below level 1, can also constitute 'serious harm' within the meaning of 'persecution':

> **"We do not think that when the Convention was drafted it was intended to include the right to be free of arbitrary deprivation of property or to be protected against unemployment (Professor Hathaway's fourth category)...However there seems to be no dispute that it includes not only the first category but the second category as well and some aspects of the third category."[63]**

By contrast in cases of gender-specific discrimination, there has sometimes been a failure on the part of adjudicators to recognise general human rights as women's right. For example, in *Islam*,[64] the IAT stated that "we do not think that the purpose of the Convention is to award refugee status because of disapproval of social mores or conventions in non-western societies". However in both the earlier case of *Gilani*[65] and the more recent case of *Ahmady*,[66] there has been recognition that gender-specific treatment of women in the Iranian context rises to the level of 'serious harm':

> **"We accept the penalties which can be imposed for transgressing against the 'social mores' of dress and behaviour can amount to persecution and indeed in Iran may amount to persecution."[67]**

---

[61] *SSHD v Adrian Ghorghe Chiver*, IAT 24th March 1994 (10758) (unreported)

[62] *Urim Gashi and Astrit Nikshiqi v SSHD*, IAT 22nd July 1996 (13695) (unreported)

[63] ibid.

[64] *Shahanna Sadiq Islam and others v SSHD*, IAT 2nd October 1996 (13956) (unreported)

[65] *Mashid Mahmoudi Gilani v SSHD*, IAT 3rd June 1987 (5216) (unreported)

[66] *Abdollah Fathi and Mashid Ahmady v SSHD*, IAT 1st December 1996 (14264) (unreported)

[67] *Shahanna Sadiq Islam and others v SSHD*, IAT 2nd October 1996 (13956) (unreported)

"The next question then is whether the treatment amounts to persecution. I think that the cumulative effect of her being arrested because of her failure to observe the dress laws, the fact that she has been dismissed from her employment for the same reason and that she has been harassed on occasions by security forces might well amount to persecution."[68]

3.3 Female Genital Mutilation (FGM)[69]

"Nafisa, a six year old Sudanese girl, is petrified. She is about to have her external sexual organs cut away without anaesthetic as her aunt Zeinab watches in despair. For the past year Zeinab has been trying to persuade the girl's mother and sister to spare her from this agony, known as female genital mutilation. She has been through it herself. At the age six she had the covering of her clitoris removed. When she was fifteen her entire clitoris was removed, along with her labia. The vulva was stitched together, leaving just a small hole for the passage of urine and menstrual blood. She still remembers the pain."[70]

The World Health Organisation estimates that over 110 million women and girls have undergone FGM and that every year around 2 million mutilated girls are added to this number. FGM in a variety of its forms is practised in more than 20 African countries although the gravity of the mutilations varies from country to country. Infibulation is reported to affect nearly all the female population of Somalia, Djibouti and the Sudan (except the non-Moslem population of southern Sudan), southern Egypt, Ethiopia, Eritrea, northern Kenya, northern Nigeria and some parts of Mali. In also occurs in various forms in Southern Algeria, Upper Volta, Ghana, the Gambia, Liberia, Cote d'Ivoire, Mozambique and Togo. Outside Africa, excision is also practised by some populations in

---

[68] *Abdollah Fathi and Mashid Ahmady v SSHD*, IAT 1st December 1996 (11544) (unreported). This comment was made by the initial adjudicator who had refused her appeal on the grounds that the persecution suffered was not for a Convention reason

[69] Female Genital Mutilation has often been referred to as female circumcision and compared to male circumcision. However, such a comparison is often misleading. Both rituals include the removal of well-functioning parts of the genitalia and are quite unnecessary. Both rituals also serve to perpetuate customs which seek to regulate and keep control over the body and sexuality of the individual. However, FGM is far more drastic and damaging than male circumcision.

[70] UNICEF *Children First; Lifting the Veil on Female Genital Mutilation* 1995

Oman, South Yemen, Saudi Arabia, Iraq, Jordan and in the United Arab Emirates. Circumcision is practised by the Muslim populations of Indonesia and Malaysia and Bohra Muslims in India, Pakistan and East Africa.[71] **Even though FGM is practised mostly among Islamic countries, it is not an exclusively Islamic practice. FGM is a cross-cultural and cross-religious ritual.**

FGM is mostly carried out in unsanitary conditions using unclean sharp instruments such as razor blades, scissors, kitchen knives and pieces of glass. These are frequently used on several girls in succession causing infection and the transmission of viruses including HIV. Antiseptic techniques and anaesthesia are generally not used. The procedure is generally performed between the ages of three and ten years although it may be carried out during infancy, adolescence, on marriage or during a first pregnancy. In the context of women claiming asylum it is also important to recognise that the age varies with the type of the ritual and the customs of the local village or region with the result that even adult women may perceive FGM as a form of persecution or they may fear the consequences for their children. The term FGM covers three main forms of female genital mutilation:

- **Circumcision**
    - removal of the prepuce ("hood") and/or the tip of the clitoris
    - known in Muslim countries as 'Sunna' (tradition)
    - this, the mildest type, affects only a small proportion of the millions of women who undergo FGM

- **Clitorodectomy or Excision**
    - consists of the removal of the entire clitoris (both prepuce and glands) and the removal of the adjacent labia

- **Infibulation**
    - the most extreme form
    - In countries such as the Sudan, Somalia and Djibouti, 80-90 percent of all FGM is infibulation
    - consists of the removal of the clitoris, the adjacent labia (majora and minora), and the joining of the scraped sides of the vulva across the vagina, where they are secured with thorns or sewn with catgut or thread. A small opening is kept to allow passage of urine and menstrual blood.[72]

---

[71] See Minority Rights Group *Female Genital Mutilation; Proposals for Change* 1992
[72] ibid. See also Toubia 1995

Although reasons given for FGM vary from one culture to another, the most common justifications include the assumption that not having undergone the operation leaves a girl not only 'unclean' but 'masculine', in that she retains a vestige of a male sex organ. She is thus thought to be sexually aggressive (therefore unlikely to remain a virgin before marriage or faithful within marriage), and otherwise lacking in feminine virtues such as passivity and submission. As a result the overriding fear among mothers is that a girl who has not undergone the procedure will be unable to find a husband or have children and will subsequently end up as a social outcast. Family honour, custom, cleanliness, protection against spells, assurance of virginity and faithfulness to the husband are also given as reasons for the practice.

The World Health Organisation has appealed for an end to the practice of FGM and in 1994 specifically urged all Member States "to establish national policies and programmes that will effectively, and with legal instruments, abolish female genital mutilation…and other harmful practices affecting the health of women and children."[73] Significantly however, and despite the fact that FGM is currently illegal in many countries in Africa and the Middle East, this has not reduced the number of girls that are mutilated every year. The governments of these countries have not established mechanisms for monitoring the spread and practice of FGM nor have laws been properly enforced. This fact is of critical importance in establishing whether state protection is available for women in these countries.[74]

3.3.1 A Violation of Women's Human Rights

"The removal of the clitoris and also frequently the labia, with or without infibulation, is not only much more serious in medical terms but it also represents a severe physical and psychological mutilation, constituting a direct attack on women's sexuality."[75]

FGM raises numerous human rights issues, including reproductive and sexual rights, the protection from violence, women's rights, the right to health, the right to freedom from cruel inhuman and degrading treatment and children's rights. Beyond the obvious initial pain of the operations,

---

[73] See Minority Rights Group 1992
[74] See Chapter 4 of this volume
[75] Winter 1994, 941

FGM has long-term physiological, sexual and psychological implications. The unsanitary environment under which FGM often takes place can result in infection of the wound and transmission of viruses such as hepatitis and HIV. Some of the other health consequences of FGM include primary fatalities as a result of shock, haemorrhage, tetanus or septicaemia. Long-term complications include sexual frigidity, genital malformation, delayed menarche, chronic pelvic complications, recurrent urinary retention and infection and an entire range of obstetric complications due to obstruction of the birth canal by scar tissue. There is often severe tearing of the perineum.

The long term implications of FGM for refugee women should *always* be emphasised by those representing female refugees for whom FGM forms part of the claim for asylum.

This is critical to counter-act any suggestion that because FGM has already happened, or only happens once in a woman's lifetime, there is no 'well-founded fear' of persecution should she be returned. It should be noted for example that an infibulated woman must be cut open to allow intercourse on the wedding night and is closed again afterwards to secure fidelity to the husband.

"I don't remember anything of my excision or infibulation which were done to me when I was very young. It was only when I was 20, just before my marriage, that I became aware of my condition. I grew up in a closed society, where sex and sexuality were taboo subjects. When I became conscious of my excision and infibulation, I was overcome with a feeling of revulsion. What should I do I asked myself. For me, there was no question of letting myself be 'opened' with a knife on the day of my marriage as is the custom for all women who are both excised and infibulated."[76]

In some cases an infibulated mother must undergo another operation whereby she is 'opened' to ensure the safe birthing of her child. Labour is often prolonged and may result in foetal asphyxia with the risk of neonatal brain damage and death.[77] In such cases it is common to re-infibulate the woman after delivery. The pain and other sufferings that

---

[76] Extracted from Awa Thiam *La Parole aux Negresses* 1978, cited in Minority Rights Group 1993, 24

[77] See Toubia 1995, 227-230 for further information

may result from FGM can therefore affect the victim's whole life. Some forms of FGM may also be at least partly undone, with the result that a woman suffers less. If the woman is denied this possibility, this may amount to persecution.

Women on whose bodies FGM has already been carried out do not *per se* fall outside the scope of the refugee definition.

There is a powerful argument that female genital mutilation is a violation of women's fundamental human rights at a non-derogable level. FGM as described by Charlotte Bunch[78] and others constitutes 'cruel, inhumane and degrading treatment' - a level 1 human rights violation - as prohibited in Article 5 of the *Universal Declaration of Human Rights* and a number of international instruments concerned with the protection of women's human rights.[79] This position is supported by a wide-range of governmental and non-governmental organisations:

"FGM, which causes severe pain as well as permanent physical harm, amounts to a violation of human rights, including the rights of the child, and can be regarded as persecution. The toleration of these acts by the authorities, or the unwillingness of the authorities to provide protection against them, amounts to official acquiescence. Therefore, a woman can be considered as a refugee if she or her daughter/daughters fear being compelled to undergo FGM against their will; or, she fears persecution for refusing to undergo or allow her daughters to undergo the practice."[80]

"[FGM] should be construed as a definite form of violence against women which cannot be overlooked nor be justified on the grounds of tradition, culture or social conformity."[81]

In the UK, Ann Widdecombe (then Home Office Minister) made a number of comments during the penultimate debate of the then Asylum and Immigration Bill, which accepted enforced female genital mutilation, as well as forced sterilisation and abortion, as probably always

---

[78] Bunch, 1990
[79] See this volume at 3.7
[80] Letter to the Refugee Legal Centre from UNHCR 1994 (unpublished)
[81] UN Special Rapporteur on Violence Against Women 1994 (unpublished)

constituting torture.[82] As a result the Asylum Policy Unit has given explicit instructions to Immigration Officers which recognise that female genital mutilation is a form of torture:

"**Current guidance on the consideration of claims involving allegations of torture stresses that torture can take many forms. But caseworkers are reminded that acts of forcible abortion, forcible sterilisation or acts involving genital mutilation are likely always to constitute torture. Applications involving such claims must therefore be considered in line with current guidelines for the consideration of asylum claims involving allegations of torture. It follows therefore, that a claim cannot be certified under paragraph 5 of Schedule 2 to the 1993 Act, as inserted by Section 1 of the 1996 Act, for the purpose of engaging the accelerated appeal procedure, if the evidence establishes a reasonable likelihood that the applicant has been subjected to forcible abortion, sterilisation, genital mutilation, or any other act of torture in the country or territory to which it is proposed the applicant should be returned."[83]**

It should be noted however that in the UK context establishing the persecution ground may be one of the most serious problems facing women whose claims are based wholly on female genital mutilation, because women generally are not recognised as members of 'a particular social group'.[84]

3.3.2 Case Law
Canada
One aspect of the claim for asylum made by a Somali woman and her two children, was the mother's fear that, if returned to Somalia, her daughter would have to face the danger of being subjected to the custom of FGM. The Court ruled that forcing a minor female to undergo FGM would grossly infringe her rights as secured in international human rights instruments, and recognised that the state in Somalia does not protect minor females from suffering this treatment.

---

[82] House of Commons considerations of Lords amendments 15.7.96, *Hansard* Cols. 822-825. See also Baroness Blatch, House of Lords reports 20.6.96, *Hansard* Cols. 476-477. These statements can also be found in ILPA *The Asylum and Immigration Act 1996: A compilation of ministerial statements made on behalf of the government during the Bill's passage through Parliament* 1996
[83] Asylum Policy Unit Internal Memo *APT 13/96*
[84] See this volume at 5.5.1

> "The minor female claimant's fear of persecution is related to the widespread practice of female genital mutilation (FGM) to which young girls in Somalia are subjected...in our view, this minor claimant's right to personal security would be grossly infringed if she were forced to undergo female genital mutilation in contravention of Article 3 of the Universal Declaration of Human Rights."[85]

The Board held that FGM, as practised in Somalia, grossly infringes minor females' rights contained in Article 3 of the Universal Declaration of Human Rights. This treatment also violates the specific rights included in Articles 19, 24 and 37 of the Convention on the Rights of the Child. Female genital mutilation may therefore be seen as a 'torturous custom'.

United States
In an important recent case in the United States a 19 year old woman, Fauziya Kasinga, who fled from Togo to avoid FGM was granted asylum by the US Board of Immigration Appeals, the highest administrative tribunal in the US immigration system.[86] Kasinga had escaped FGM as a young girl due to her influential father's opposition to the practice. Upon his death, when Kasinga was 15, her aunt assumed control of the house according to tribal custom and arranged for Kasinga to marry a man more than twice her age and undergo FGM.

France
In France, the Refugee Appeal Commission has accepted that FGM may amount to persecution and that women wishing to avoid FGM can be considered as members of a 'particular social group'. This is reflected in *Aminata Diop*[87] where the applicant claimed refugee status after she left Mali because of mistreatment by her family for refusing to undergo FGM,[88] although the Commission did not grant her refugee status for failure to adequately document her claim.

---

[85] *Farah v Canada (MEI)* (13 July 1994)
[86] For further details see *The Independent* 06.05.96, *The New York Times* 22.06.96 and *The Guardian* 06.07.96. See also *Feminist News*, 14th June 1996 online at http://www.feminist.org/news/newsbyte/june96
[87] CCR 164078 (18th August 1991)
[88] There are two possible approaches to the issue of FGM;
   (1) that the act itself constitutes 'serious harm';

United Kingdom

There is no case law in the UK where female genital mutilation has been the principal basis for a claim to asylum although following the statement of the Asylum Policy Unit recognising that it constitutes torture,[89] representatives may be more willing to argue for their clients on this basis, including ensuring that any female applicant who has experienced FGM is not subjected to accelerated procedures for determination of their claims. It should not be difficult to 'prove' that the client has been subjected to FGM even given time constraints.

Whilst there is no case law specifically pertaining to FGM, there appears nonetheless to be some sensitivity to this issue among adjudicators especially in cases where the appellant has young female children. In the recent case of an Eritrean woman, for example, the adjudicator recognised the dangers facing the appellant's children if she were returned to Eritrea although the principal basis for the claim was her and her husband's involvement within the Eritrean Liberation Front:

> **"I also see that female genital mutilation, which is widely considered by international health experts as damaging to both physical and psychological health, is practised extensively on girls at an early age. The government, through the Ministry of Health and National Union of Eritrean Women, is actively discouraging this practice but it still exists. I am very conscious of the fact that the appellant has three young daughters."[90]**

The argument that female genital mutilation without a woman's consent constitutes cruel, inhuman and degrading treatment is so strong that even where the claim cannot be framed within the UN Convention, leave to remain should be allowed on compassionate and humanitarian grounds.

---

(2) that the refusal to allow FGM to be performed by the woman, either for herself or on behalf of her children, has consequences which rise to the level of persecution. Much will depend on the individual case, but it should be noted that each of these lines of argument has different implications for the presentation of the grounds for the asylum claim.

[89] See this volume at 3.3.1

[90] Appeal No. HX/76443/95 (4th December 1996) (unreported)

3.4 Violence Within the Family [91]

Violence within the family is a widespread and often gender-specific form of abuse which can constitute 'serious harm' and, in some cases, rise to the level of persecution. Yet despite the fact that the abuse of women by their male partners and family members is among the most common and dangerous forms of gender-specific violence and although such violence has begun to be recognised as a human rights concern - for example in the *Declaration on the Elimination of Violence Against Women*[92] - it nonetheless remains on the margin. This results primarily from the fact that it tends not to be viewed as violence at all; it is seen as 'personal', 'private' or a 'family matter', its goals and consequences are obscured, and its use justified as chastisement or discipline.

> **"[Violence within the family] is still considered different, less severe, and less deserving of international condemnation and sanction than officially sanctioned violence."[93]**

In describing forms of violence which occur within the family, Copelon draws comparison with other recognised methods of torture.[94] This form of violence commonly involves some form of, usually escalating, physical brutality and can include beating with hands or objects, biting, spitting, punching, kicking, slashing, stabbing, strangling, scalding, burning and attempted drowning. Sexual abuse including rape are likewise common concomitants of violence within the family and take many different forms. As in other contexts, sexual abuse including rape, which may do less physical damage than beatings, is often experienced by women as the gravest violation. Meanwhile in confining women to the home they become isolated from friends, family and others. Their lives and those of their loved ones are threatened and they are made to fear for the loss of their children.

Analytically therefore, violence within the family, as with any other form of violence, should be considered as a violation of fundamental human rights within the *Universal Declaration of Human Rights*.

---

[91] Violence within the family is a broader term than either domestic or intimate violence. For example, it also refers to the abuse inflicted by fathers on their daughters. This abuse may or may not be sexual.

[92] See this volume at 3.7 and Annex 3

[93] Copelon 1994, 117

[94] See this volume at 3.1

"When stripped of privatisation, sexism and sentimentalism [violence within the family] is no less grave than other forms of inhumane and subordinating official violence, which have been prohibited by treaty and customary law and recognised by the international community as *jus cogens*, or peremptory norms that bind universally and can never be violated."[95]

"This conduct, virtually *de facto*, constitutes serious violations of internationally recognised human rights."[96]

The nature and the degree of the harm perpetrated in the course of such violence constitute a serious, if not egregious, violation of women's human rights. Moreover even if the acts are considered to be neither torture nor gross human rights violations, forms of violence within the family *at a minimum* constitute serious abuse of a woman's human rights and as such rise to the level of persecution.

"The process of battering - whether physical or psychological or both - often produces anxiety, depression, debility and dread as well as the same intense symptoms that comprise the post-traumatic stress disorders experienced by victims of official violence as well as by victims of rape."[97]

However in the UK case of *Ranjbar*,[98] the Secretary of State appealed against the decision of the adjudicator to allow the appeal of a young Iranian woman who had been severely beaten by her father:

"She [the appellant] is a member of a particular social group, namely those who are subject to physical attack as the result of being female children of a person who expresses his institutionalised attitude to women in the form of *physical attacks which fall within the category of inhuman or degrading treatment."* [99]

---

[95] Copelon 1994, 114
[96] Goldberg 1993, 583
[97] Copelon 1994, 118
[98] *SSHD v Fatemah Fironz Ranjbar*, IAT 28th June 1994 (11105) (unreported) (emphasis added)
[99] ibid.

The grounds of appeal against this decision which were accepted by the IAT, included not only that this type of violence is not condoned by the authorities and that gender is too broad a category to be recognised as a 'particular social group',[100] but also that the harm inflicted was not serious enough to rise to the level of persecution:

> **"The degree of hostility and repression...the respondent has suffered does not, in our view, amount to persecution...We confine ourselves to the conclusion that the degree of ill-treatment the respondent claims to have suffered, solely within the small family, is not persecution within the meaning of the Convention."**[101]

This case highlights some of the problems associated with claims for asylum by refugee women involving violence within the family. It should be noted that in addition to a failure to recognise the level of harm inflicted as a serious violation of women's fundamental human rights, one of the most serious problems in framing such cases within the Convention lies in establishing state accountability. This issue will be addressed in detail in Chapter 4. Moreover cases of violence within the family are not typically seen to fall within one of the enumerated grounds, a problem which is discussed in Chapter 5.

3.5 Marriage Related Harm

Marriage related harm is harm associated with, *but not limited to:*

- **Forced Marriage**
- **Child Marriage**
- **'Dowry Death' or Bride Burning**
- **'Honour Killings'**
- ***Sati***[102]
- ***Mut'a* or Temporary Pleasure Marriage**
- **Mixed Marriages**
- **Difficulties in Obtaining Custody of Children**[103]

---

[100] See also this volume at 5.5.1

[101] Goldberg 1993

[102] The custom of *sati*, which involves the burning or burying alive of a widow along with the body of her deceased husband, persists despite the introduction of the Commission of Sati (Prevention) Act in 1987.

[103] Many of these issues overlap considerably with other forms of persecution through

One of the most dramatic forms of violence against women in India and Bangladesh is what has come to be known as 'dowry death' (rather than murder). Although the institution of dowry was legislatively abolished in 1961 in India and in 1980 in Bangladesh, the giving and accepting of dowry persists. 'Dowry death', also known as bride burning, occurs when a wife and her family cannot meet the demands of her husband and/or his family for additional money or property or when a husband wishes to gain an additional dowry by remarrying. He and his family begin physically and psychologically abusing his bride, and the abuse, if it does not drive the wife to suicide, may result in her 'death' by burning, with the husband claiming that the wife caught fire while cooking on a kerosene stove. More than 5,000 'dowry deaths' occur every year. Many cases are not reported, but those which are brought to court tend to linger for months or even years, and the accused are usually acquitted due to lack of evidence. If a woman flees, the problems in acquiring state protection are critical in establishing culpability of the state.[104]

Ms C is from India. She joined her husband, a British citizen, in the UK in 1989. Her marital problems began soon after her arrival in the UK, when her in-laws criticised her for providing insufficient dowry. She then suffered physical violence, mental cruelty and verbal abuse from her in-laws, and sexual and physical abuse from her husband and decided to return to India to join her family. Once again she was subjected to threats from her husband's family, who said they would pressure her husband into divorcing her if she did not return to him and provide more dowry. Her family also pressurised her into returning to the UK to attempt a conciliation, but when she did she was subjected to hostility and finally abandoned. She divorced her husband in 1993 and subsequently remarried a British citizen. She is presently appealing against a deportation order. If she returns to India, she fears social persecution as a 'twice divorced' woman as she divorced her first husband and would be separated from the second. She could also face further threats from in-laws for failing to provide more dowry.[105]

gendered social mores and discrimination which are discussed in this volume at 3.2
[104] See Chapter 4
[105] Case study provided by Southall Black Sisters

Even more common is forced marriage which may often involve children and is a form of abuse that is often not recognised. In many cases of women who refuse to agree to such arrangements, it will be the punishment inflicted as a refusal to abide by discriminatory social mores, rather than the marriage itself, which will rise to the level of 'serious harm'.[106]

"Many societies practice arranged marriage and this in itself may not be a persecutory act. However, the consequences of defying the wishes of one's family when viewed against the background of the State's failure to protect a person should be carefully considered."[107]

The repercussions for women of divorcing their husbands or entering into mixed marriages may be equally devastating. Meanwhile in countries such as Algeria, women face *Mut'a*, or 'temporary pleasure marriage', in which a man may marry a woman for just three hours before passing her to male friends or relatives for their enjoyment. There have recently been a number of reports about single women being abducted, raped and even killed after entering into temporary pleasure marriages. In Iran this practice is known *Siqa'a* and is condoned and lawful.[108]

Clearly there are many situations where harm inflicted either as a result of marriage or because of a refusal to conform to prescribed norms of behaviour constitutes cruel, inhuman or degrading treatment. In addition, however, there are articles within the *Universal Declaration of Human Rights* which indicate that there are certain rights around the institution of marriage which may be utilised in some cases to argue that the marriage itself deprives a woman of her fundamental rights and freedoms. Article 16 of the *Convention on the Elimination of All Forms of Discrimination Against Women* (CEDAW) also explicitly details the content of women's equal rights within the family, regarding entry into marriage, choice of spouse and rights within marriage. This article also prohibits child marriages.[109]

---

[106] See this volume at 3.2

[107] ADIMA *Guidelines on Gender Issues for Decision Makers* July 1996, paragraph 4.10 (Annex 6)

[108] For further information see Mahnaz Afkhami and Erika Friedl (eds) *In the Eye of the Storm; Women in Post-Revolutionary Iran* 1994

[109] See this volume at 3.7.1 and Annex 3

Article 16/1
"Men and women of full age, without any limitation due to race, nationality or religion, have the right to marry and found a family. They are entitled to equal rights as to marriage, during marriage and at its dissolution."

Article 16/2
"Marriage shall be entered into only with the free and full consent of the intending spouses."

3.6 Reproductive Rights Including Forced Sterilisation and Abortion
A further form of gender-specific 'serious harm' is that which can result from compulsory demographic policies. In China, sterilisation is compulsory for couples with two children and local authorities may also require women to have an abortion if she is pregnant without their consent.

Forced sterilisation and abortion is an infringement of the basic right not be treated inhumanely or degradingly, of the right to private and family life, and of the right to marry and have a family.

Cheung[110] provides a clear and forceful judicial statement concerning the practice of forced sterilisation of women amounting to persecution under the definition of refugee in the Canadian Immigration Act (which is the same definition as found in the 1951 Convention). In addition Ann Widdecombe has made the following policy statement which resulted in an internal memo which deals specifically with this issue being issued to immigration officers by the Asylum Policy Unit.[111]

"I stress that...I utterly accept that forcible abortion, sterilisation, genital mutilation and allied practices would almost always constitute torture. In fact, they would probably always constitute torture...We would regard enforced abortion as torture, as we would enforced mutilation or sterilisation."[112]

---

[110] *Cheung v Canada (MEI)* [1993] 2 FC 314 (FCA)
[111] See this volume at 3.3.1 and footnotes 83-84
[112] House of Commons considerations of Lords amendments 15.7.96, *Hansard* Cols. 822-825. See also Baroness Blatch, House of Lords reports 20.6.96, *Hansard* Cols. 476-477. These statements can also be found in ILPA *The Asylum and Immigration Act 1996: A compilation of ministerial statements made on behalf of*

3.7 International Instruments for the Protection of Women

In addition to the 1951 Convention and the 1967 Protocol relating to the status of refugees, a number of rights and principles with regard to the equality, security, liberty, integrity and dignity of all human beings - including women - can be referred to in representations of gender-specific asylum claims. Central among these are the *International Covenant on Civil and Political Rights*, the *International Covenant on Economic, Social and Cultural Rights* and the *Convention against Torture and Other Cruel, Inhuman or Degrading Treatment or Punishment*.[113] In addition the following international instruments and documents contain gender-related provisions that recognise and promote the principle that women's rights are human rights and that women's rights are universal. Such international declarations are intended to ensure the protection of women and can be utilised by representatives.

3.7.1 The Convention on the Elimination of All Forms of Discrimination Against Women (CEDAW) (1979)[114]

In 1992 the Committee on the Elimination of Discrimination Against Women issued a recommendation (General Recommendation No. 19) dealing exclusively with violence against women. The Committee stated that gender-based violence is a form of discrimination which seriously inhibits a woman's ability to enjoy rights and freedoms on an equal basis with men. CEDAW is the most comprehensive international human rights instrument for women. It prohibits actions by states which are discriminatory and requires states to take affirmative steps to eradicate discriminatory treatment of women, and as such may be particularly useful in establishing state culpability.[115]

In 1990 the UNHCR Executive Committee affirmed the linkage between a violation of the rights guaranteed under CEDAW and persecution for purposes of the Refugee Convention, stating that severe discrimination prohibited by CEDAW can form the basis for the granting of refugee status.[116] It should be noted however that CEDAW says little about issues such as reproductive rights except to confirm women's

---

the government during the Bill's passage through Parliament 1996. See this volume at 3.3.1 for the APU policy response.

[113] See Annex 1

[114] See Annex 3

[115] See Chapter 4

[116] UNHCR *Note on Refugee Women and International Protection* EC/SCP/59 (28th Aug. 1990), 5

rights to family planning information, counselling, and services and to have equal rights with men to decide on the number and spacing of their children.

Article 1

"For the purposes of the present Convention, the term 'discrimination against women' shall mean any distinction, exclusion or restriction made on the basis of sex which have the effect or purpose of impairing or nullifying the recognition, enjoyment or exercise by women, irrespective of their marital status, on a basis of equality between men and women, of human rights and fundamental freedoms in the political, economic, social, cultural, civil or any other field."[117]

3.7.2 The Declaration on the Elimination of Violence Against Women (1993)[118]

This is the first set of international standards dealing specifically with violence against women and recognises that some groups of women, including refugee women, are especially vulnerable to violence. It affirms that violence against women constitutes a violation of the rights and fundamental freedoms of women and impairs or nullifies their enjoyment of those freedoms and rights.

Article 1

"The term 'violence against women' means any act of gender-based violence that results in, or is likely to result in, physical, sexual or psychological harm or suffering to women, including threats of such acts, coercion or arbitrary deprivation of liberty, whether occurring in public or in private life."

---

[117] See Annex 3
[118] ibid.

Article 2

Includes violence encompassing, *but not limited to:*

- physical, sexual and psychological violence occurring in the family, including battering,[119] dowry-related violence,[120] female genital mutilation[121] and other practices harmful to women;

- physical, sexual and psychological violence occurring within the general community including rape, sexual abuse and sexual harassment and intimidation;[122]

- physical, sexual and psychological violence perpetrated or condoned by the State, wherever it occurs.

Article 3

"Women are entitled to the equal enjoyment and protection of all human rights and fundamental freedoms in the political, economic, social, cultural, civil or any other field including the right to be free from all forms of discrimination."[123]

3.7.3 UN Platform for Action (1995)[124]

In addition to Article 113, which reiterates the provisions made in Article 2 of the Declaration on the Elimination of Violence Against Women above,[125] the following articles are particularly relevant to cases of women fleeing gender-specific forms of persecution:

Article 114

"Other acts of violence against women include violation of the human rights of women in situations of armed conflict, in particular murder, systematic rape, sexual slavery and forced pregnancy."

---

[119] See this volume at 3.4
[120] See this volume at 3.5
[121] See this volume at 3.3
[122] See this volume at 3.1
[123] See this volume at 3.2
[124] See Annex 3
[125] ibid.

Article 115

"Acts of violence against women also include forced sterilisation and forced abortion, coercive/forced use of contraceptives, female infanticide and prenatal sex selection."

Article 224

"Any harmful aspect of certain traditional, customary or modern practices that violates the rights of women should be prohibited and eliminated."[126]

Articles 135, 136 and 147 refer specifically to the protection and assistance needs of refugee and displaced women and can be used to remind governments of their international obligations to protect women fleeing gender-specific forms of 'serious harm'[127].

---

[126] See Annex 3 for further details
[127] ibid.

Chapter 4 THE FAILURE OF STATE PROTECTION

In the context of Hathaway's framework, 'persecution' is defined as 'serious harm' and the 'failure of state protection'. It has already been suggested that in many instances the problems with the Convention definition arise not from its substance but from the way it is interpreted by both representatives and decision makers. Whilst the definition by states of 'serious harm' has proved problematic in cases of gender-specific persecution,[1] even more critical to the claims of many refugee women seeking asylum in the UK is the specific but related issue of state protection.

The concept of state responsibility, as outlined clearly elsewhere,[2] defines the limits of a government's accountability for human rights abuses under international refugee law, which was formulated as a back-up to, and not a replacement of, the state machinery for protection; it was meant to come into play only in situations where that protection was unavailable, and then only in certain situations. In this context, refugee law reinforces the primacy of the state.[3] Insofar as it is established that meaningful state protection is available to the claimant, a fear of persecution cannot be said to exist.

A person seeking to establish eligibility for asylum must therefore demonstrate more than a well-founded fear of 'serious harm'. In order to constitute persecution, such harm must be at the hands of the state or a force that the state cannot or will not control. The failure of state protection is apparent in the following situations:

- **If serious harm has been committed by the authorities or by organisations informally related to them;**

- **If serious harm has been committed by others and the authorities are *unwilling* to give protection, because they support the actions of the private persons concerned, because they tolerate them or because they have other priorities;**

- **If serious harm has been committed by others, and the authorities are *unable* to give effective protection.[4]**

---

[1] See Chapter 3
[2] See for example Thomas and Beasley 1993
[3] Goldberg 1993
[4] Hathaway 1991

The state may be said to have failed in its duty to protect when it is actively involved in the persecution (through legislature, police officials and the military), where it offers active assistance to, or condones, persecution through a non-state agent, or where it is unable to offer effective protection.

Representatives should be aware however that in recent years a number of countries have narrowed their interpretation of the Convention and have restricted their application of the concept of agents of persecution.[5] In some cases states have been held responsible for 'serious harm' only when their designated agents are directly implicated in persecutory measures; states have not been considered responsible if they have maintained a legal and social system in which violations of physical and mental integrity are endemic. This derogation from international obligations and standards can clearly be seen in an Act adopted by the member states of the European Union pursuant to Title VI of the Treaty setting out their Joint Position as at 4th March 1996 on the meaning of the term 'refugee'.[6] Section 5.2 of this Act deals specifically with persecution by third parties (non-state agents):[7]

"Persecution by third parties will be considered to fall within the scope of the Geneva Convention where it is based on one of the grounds in Article 1A, is individual in nature and is encouraged or permitted by the authorities. Where the official authorities fail to act, such persecution should give rise to individual examination of each application for refugee status, in accordance with national judicial practice, in the light in particular of whether or not the failure to act was deliberate."[8]

---

[5] See UNHCR *An Overview of Protection Issues in Western Europe: Legislative Trends and Positions Taken by UNHCR* European Series No 3, 27-30 1995

[6] Council of the European Union *Joint Position Defined by the Council on the Basis of Article K.3 of the Treaty on European Union on the Harmonised Application of the Definition of the Term 'Refugee' in Article 1 of the Geneva Convention of 28th July 1951 Relating to the Status of Refugees.*

[7] This provision was recently cited in *Lazarevic, Radivojevic, Adan and Nooh v SSHD*, Court of Appeal 13th February 1997 (unreported)

[8] It should be noted that the Danish and Swedish delegations did not agree with this point: "In relation to the question of origins of persecution, Denmark and Sweden are of the opinion that persecution by third parties falls within the scope of the 1951 Geneva Convention where it is encouraged or permitted by the authorities. It may also fall within the scope of the Convention in other cases, when the authorities

In order to respond to the experiences of women as asylum seekers, the concept of state responsibility, as adopted in the determination process, must reflect existing international obligations to protect against systematic abuse based on gender. Demanding that international refugee law reconceptualise human rights abuse to include that which has largely been deemed 'private' may face opposition from states trying to narrow the existing interpretation. However some states, most notably Canada, the United States and Australia, have explicitly recognised state liability for private actions and this is reflected in their case law. In addition there are a number of other human rights documents such as the *UN Convention on the Elimination of All Forms of Discrimination Against Women* and the *UN Platform for Action* which explicitly articulate an obligation on the part of the state to protect against the conduct of private actors.[9]

In this context, the argument that there has been 'a failure of state protection' for refugee women fearing serious harm which is not directly at the hands of the state, is clear. It will be necessary however for the representative to *prove* that state protection was not available for his or her client through research and through the use of expert evidence to substantiate the claim.[10]

"In determining whether the state is willing or able to provide protection to a woman fearing gender-related persecution, decision-makers should consider the fact that the forms of evidence which the claimant might normally provide as 'clear and convincing proof' of state inability to protect, will not always be either available or useful in cases of gender-related persecution."[11]

"In assessing gender-based persecution it is important to research the accepted norms of the relevant societies to determine how they operate both through legislation and in terms of actual practice in order to determine the degree of protection available to women."[12]

---

prove unable to offer effective protection".

[9] See this volume at 4.6 and Annex 3

[10] See this volume at 2.7

[11] CIRB *Guidelines on Women Refugee Claimants Fearing Gender-Related Persecution: UPDATE* November 1996, C (Annex 5, 194)

[12] ADIMA *Guidelines on Gender Issues for Decision Makers* July 1996, paragraph 4.11 (Annex 6)

4.1 Persecution by the State or an Agent of the State

The UNHCR *Handbook* comments that "persecution is normally related to action by the authorities of the country."[13] According to *Macdonald* the authorities of a country will include regional or local government or parties which control the state.[14] Cases of sexual violence (including rape) against women, often involve the security forces or other public officials yet such is the extent of the public/private dichotomy in the interpretation of refugee law, that even acts committed by the authorities are not attributed to them and are dismissed as 'private'.[15] It is also evident that there are a variety of situations in which 'serious harm' in a form other than direct physical attack is inflicted upon women by gender-based discrimination enforced through law.

The representative must establish whether a reasonable basis exists for regarding the act of persecution as a 'public' one that can be attributed to the state. If they do not consider the state to be directly implicated, then they must determine whether the state has been *unwilling* or *unable* to provide protection.[16]

4.1.1 Sexual Violence Including Rape

Women are sexually assaulted by agents of the state in a variety of circumstances. Women detained for political reasons may be sexually abused or raped (along with other forms of torture) with specific sanction by, or the tacit approval of, the authorities. Women imprisoned or detained for non-political reasons may be subjected to sexual violence including rape for the amusement of their captors. Civilian women may be raped by government or opposition militia as part of a campaign to terrorise the local populace, punish politically active males by proxy or 'reward' victorious combatants.[17]

Several recent feminist critiques have commented, however, that the problem in cases of sexual violence including rape frequently seems to lie in the state connection requirement. Applications involving sexual violence are dealt with in a bewildering way. In the United States, the cases of *Campos-Guardado* and *Lazo-Manjano* have both been widely cited as examples in which rape was interpreted by the judge as not being

---

[13] UNHCR *Handbook* 1979, paragraph 65
[14] Macdonald and Blake *Macdonald's Immigration Law and Practice in the United Kingdom* 1995, 390 paragraph 12.39
[15] Spijkerboer 1991, 29
[16] See this volume at 4.2
[17] See also this volume at 4.2.6

political but 'personal'.[18] In *Campos-Guardado*[19] the court concluded that the persecutor's motives for raping her were different from the political motivation behind the torture and execution of her male family members which she was forced to witness. More recently in the case of *Klawitter*,[20] where the applicant feared the unwanted sexual advances of a colonel in the Polish secret police, the court agreed with the position of the Board that there was no motive behind his behaviour towards her aside from personal ones:

"However distasteful his apparent treatment of the respondent may have been, such harm or threats arising from a personal dispute of this nature, even one taking place with an individual of a high governmental position, is not a ground for asylum...Although the petitioner's testimony recounts an unfortunate situation, harm or threats of harm based solely on sexual attraction do not constitute persecution."[21]

Noting that this line of reasoning seems to be specific to acts of sexual abuse, Spijkerboer criticises the implicit view of sexual violence in asylum-related situations "as derailed sexuality and not as torture,"[22] and suggests that it presupposes a very particular conception of male sexuality; male sexuality is seen as an innate, independent and quasi-biological drive which seeks satisfaction and can suddenly overwhelm a man. As a result it is viewed as 'private' even when it is committed during an interrogation, and dismissed as the aberrant act of an individual which is to be expected, rather than as behaviour condoned or encouraged by the government.[23] In this context it is critical that representatives argue that the failure of state protection of women has occurred in cases of sexual violence including rape which are perpetrated by the state or an agent of the state. This position finds support in both the UNHCR's *Guidelines on the Protection of Refugee Women* and *Macdonald*:

---

[18] See Castel 1992 for further details
[19] *Campos-Guardado v INS* [1987] 809 F.2d 285 (5th Circuit)
[20] *Klawitter v INS* [1992] 970 F.2d 149 (6th Circuit)
[21] ibid.
[22] Spijkerboer 1994
[23] Kelly 1993

> "Sexual violence against women is a form of persecution when it is used with the consent or acquiescence of those acting in an official capacity to intimidate or punish."[24]

> "The security forces of the country do not cease to be agents of official persecution because it is not the policy of central government to persecute the victims in question."[25]

4.1.2 Gender-Based Discrimination Enforced Through Law

Persecution need not take the form of direct attacks on the physical integrity of women. Gender-based discrimination is often enforced through law as well as through social practices. In cases of legislated discrimination, a female applicant will have to prove that the nature of the discrimination was sufficient to rise to the level of persecution.[26] It should also be noted however that a woman's claim to Convention refugee status cannot be based solely on the fact that she is subject to a national law or policy to which she objects.[27] As is suggested in the Canadian *Guidelines*, the claimant will need to establish *one* of the following:

A. The law or policy is inherently persecutory

> "The *Hudood* laws affect all citizens of Pakistan, but are applied to women with particularly disastrous effects. Women are discriminated against by law. They find it extremely difficult to prove rape and may face criminal prosecution if they fail to do so. Women who behave in ways their husbands or fathers dislike, or who seek to divorce and re-marry, or who choose to marry against the will of their parents, or who happen to be related to a man wanted by the authorities and thus get wrongly accused of *Hudood* offences as a means of intimidating their relatives, all risk criminal prosecution under the *Hudood* laws, often with no basis in fact."[28]

---

[24] UNHCR *Guidelines on the Protection of Refugee Women* 1991, 40

[25] Macdonald and Blake *Macdonald's Immigration Law and Practice in the United Kingdom* 1995, 390-391 paragraph 12.40

[26] See this volume at 3.2

[27] CIRB *Guidelines on Women Refugee Claimants Fearing Gender-Related Persecution: UPDATE* November 1996, B (Annex 5, 194)

[28] Human Rights Watch 1992

An example of legislated discrimination which could be construed as persecutory is Pakistan's *Hudood* laws. One component of these laws requires that a woman alleging rape corroborate her complaint with the testimony of four male witnesses. Failure to prove that sexual contact occurred without consent leaves the complainant vulnerable to criminal prosecution for adultery or fornication.

B. The policy or law, although having 'legitimate' goals, is administered through persecutory means

An example of a discriminatory policy with a 'legitimate' end pursued through persecutory means is the one-child policy in the People's Republic of China. While the goal of population control might be defensible, forced sterilisation and abortions are each persecutory means of achieving the objective. Whilst the Chinese government maintains that "forced abortion and sterilisation are strictly prohibited by Chinese law and offenders will be punished according to the law,"[29] the reality is very different:

"The Chinese Government maintains a comprehensive and highly intrusive family planning program. Individual and family decisions about bearing children are controlled by the state, with severe sanctions against those who deviate from official guidelines... Physical compulsion to submit to abortions or sterilisations is not authorised but continues to occur as officials strive to meet population targets."[30]

C. The penalty for non-compliance with the law or policy is disproportionately severe

This approach to the issue of state culpability is particularly relevant in cases from countries such as Iran, where those in contravention to the dress code are subject to punishment which may range from a verbal reprimand, to a fine, to 74 strokes of the lash, to a prison sentence of up to one year. Women are regularly harassed and arrested or detained under legal pretexts for wearing make-up or being improperly veiled. Meanwhile, sexual segregation means that any form of friendship or association between the sexes outside the marriage contract is punishable by flogging, imprisonment, forced marriage or stoning to death. A

---

[29] Fact Sheet 3 'Family Planning in China' issued by the Chinese Embassy in the UK. Online at http:///www.oneworld.org/news/partner_news/china_factsheet3.html

[30] US Department of State, Country Report 1989

similar argument could also be made with regard to Pakistan's *Hudood* laws and has been discussed in a recent UK precedent.[31]

4.2 Unwillingness or Inability of the State to Protect

"A Convention refugee is someone who is at risk because their country of nationality has failed to protect them from persecution. A failure to protect can occur in several ways. It may be that the authorities themselves are the perpetrators of persecution. However, it may be that the perpetrator is another party from whom the authorities do not protect the person either because they are unwilling or unable to do so. Claims of gender-based persecution often involved persecution committed by non-state agents."[32]

Exposing the gendered harms that women endure may not always be sufficient to sustain a finding of persecution. Because violence against women often assumes the form of a social or cultural norm, it is frequently not recognised as a violation of women's human rights for which the state is accountable. Whilst there is no shortage of episodes where women are directly victimised by the state or by agents of the state, much of the violence committed against women is committed by non-state agents. It is perpetrated by husbands, fathers, boyfriends, in-laws, and, in the case of female genital mutilation, women in the local community:

"For most women, indirect subjection to the State will almost always be mediated through direct subjection to individual men or groups of men."[33]

As a result, the problem for many female applicants may lie not in demonstrating that the abuse constitutes 'serious harm', but rather that the state is implicated in, or has failed to protect them from, that harm. In this context, and assuming that except in situations where the state is in a condition of complete breakdown *states must be presumed capable of protecting their citizens*,[34] it is necessary to determine whether the state is

---

[31] See this volume at 4.3

[32] ADIMA *Guidelines on Gender Issues for Decision Makers* July 1996, paragraph 4.11 (Annex 6)

[33] Wright 1992, 249 cited in Macklin 1995, 232

[34] *Canada (Attorney General) v Ward* [1989] 2SCR 689

liable for the acts of private individuals which violate protected human rights and, if so, when.

Although there is no universally accepted definition of persecution in refugee law, the conclusion that state complicity in persecution is not a prerequisite to a valid refugee claim is supported in the drafting history of Article 1(A), the prevailing authorities and academic commentary. According to the UNHCR *Handbook* persecution can take the form of government *inaction* as well as government action:

> **"Where serious discriminatory or other offensive acts are committed by the local populace, they can be considered as persecution if they are knowingly tolerated by the authorities, or if the authorities refuse, or prove unable, to provide effective protection."[35]**

Furthermore, where an applicant's country has denied her protection such denial may confirm or strengthen the applicant's fear of persecution and may indeed be an element of persecution.[36] Commentators have consistently supported this approach to the failure of state protection:

> **"Behaviour tolerated by the government in such a way as to leave the victims virtually unprotected by the agencies of the State constitutes persecution for the purposes of refugee determination."[37]**

> **"Persecution includes failure, voluntary or involuntary, on the part of the state authorities to prevent or suppress violence."[38]**

> **"Persecution [arises] not only from a conscious intent to harm (malfeasance) but also from misfeasance or nonfeasance."[39]**

Under international law therefore, the state has an obligation to exercise due diligence to prevent, investigate, prosecute and punish individuals, including non-state actors, who have committed acts that constitute human rights violations.

---

[35] UNHCR *Handbook* 1979, paragraph 65
[36] UNHCR *Guidelines on the Protection of Refugee Women* 1991, paragraph 98
[37] Grahl-Madsen 1966, 191
[38] Goodwin-Gill 1982, 291
[39] Young 1982

"The state must be held liable for human rights violations by private actors. State liability may be found where the state refuses or is unable to provide protection or redress from such abuses. International law imposes a standard of due diligence or reasonable care on the state to prevent, investigate and punish individuals, even non-state actors, who have committed acts that constitute human rights violations. The failure of the state to do so is a breach of its duties, and as such implicates the state in the commission of these human rights violations."[40]

In cases where the persecutor is not directly related to the government, the representative should consider whether the government was *unwilling* or *unable* or to protect the applicant. It is the responsibility of the representative to establish the following:

- **Whether the applicant sought and was denied protection by the government;**

- **Whether governing institutions and/or government agents were aware of the harm to the applicant and did nothing to protect her;**

- **Whether the applicant has other reasons to believe that it would be futile to seek the protection of the government (for example, if the government has denied protection to similarly situated women, or if the government has systematically failed to apply existing laws).**

The following is a discussion of some of the gender-specific types of 'serious harm' experienced by female asylum-seekers. This list is by no means definitive or exhaustive. It is intended to assist those representing female asylum-seekers to establish that a failure of state protection has occurred.

4.2.1 Sexual Violence Including Rape
In addition to the issues raised in 4.1.1 - where sexual violence is at the hands of the authorities or individuals connected to them - there are a variety of other scenarios where sufficient state connection can be said to exist. This includes cases where sexual violence has been committed by non-state agents and where the authorities are unwilling to give

---

[40] Goldberg 1993, 584-585

protection, either because they support the actions of the individuals concerned, because they tolerate them or because they have other priorities.[41] This position is supported in the UNHCR's *Sexual Violence Against Refugees: Guidelines on Prevention and Response* (1991):

> **"The Government on whose territory the sexual attack has occurred is responsible for taking diligent remedial measures, including conducting a thorough investigation into the crime, identifying and prosecuting those responsible, and protecting the victims from reprisals."[42]**

Representatives and their clients should collate evidence indicating a failure of state protection in that governing institutions and/or their agents in the claimant's country of origin may have condoned the instances of sexual violence if they had been aware of them or did nothing to prevent them.[43]

4.2.2 Social Mores and Discrimination

> **"Fundamental rights of women...have been repeatedly violated by Muslim clerics and Islamist groups in Bangladesh...women who do not fully conform to socially accepted behaviour patterns are most likely to be tried and sentenced by a *salish* [local village arbitration council without legal authority]...the government, by not condemning such acts against women, by not investigating such incidents and by not bringing to justice those who issued death threats or carried out attacks on individual women or women's organisations, appears to have condoned such acts."[44]**

The interpretation of state responsibility advocated in this Handbook extends to those instances where social mores dictate gender-related abuse as an acceptable practice and where there are no viable means of legal recourse to prevent, investigate or punish such acts. In this sense, as

---

[41] Spijkerboer 1994, 24

[42] UNHCR *Sexual Violence Against Refugees; Guidelines on Prevention and Response* 1995, 53

[43] CIRB *Guidelines on Women Refugee Claimants Fearing Gender-Related Persecution* 1993, A. III (Annex 5, 193-194)

[44] Amnesty International, '*Bangladesh: Fundamental Rights of Women Violated With Virtual Impunity*', ASA 13/09/94

long as the state fails adequately to protect the claimant, it does not matter whether inaction derived from collusion, indifference or genuine impotence.

4.2.3 Female Genital Mutilation (FGM)

Formal legislation forbidding FGM, or more specifically infibulation, exists in the Sudan and in Kenya whilst official declarations against FGM have been made in Burkina Faso and Senegal.[45] Moreover FGM is explicitly prohibited in CEDAW, the *UN Declaration on the Elimination of Violence Against Women* and in the *UN Platform for Action* to which many of the countries in which FGM takes place are signatories.[46] The reality of the situation however, is that such laws are rarely applied and that perpetrators act with virtual impunity:

"In some societies, particular types of violence against women may be officially condemned or even illegal but in fact be so endemic that local authorities turn a blind eye to its occurrence. Sometimes these forms of abuse are systemic or culturally acceptable so that the local authorities may effectively participate or be complicit in the harms suffered."[47]

"The toleration of [FGM] by the authorities, or the unwillingness of the authorities to provide protection against them, amounts to official acquiescence."[48]

In this context the general line of argument which was made at 4.2 is relevant. The inefficacy of that state in preventing FGM has been accepted in the Canadian case of *Farah.*[49]

"The panel is satisfied that the authorities in Somalia will not protect the minor female claimant from the physical and emotional ravages of FGM given the evidence of its widespread practice in that country."[50]

---

[45] Minority Rights Group 1993
[46] See this volume at 4.6 and Annex 3
[47] ADIMA *Guidelines on Gender Issues for Decision Makers* July 1996, paragraph 4.12 (Annex 6)
[48] Letter to Refugee Legal Centre from UNHCR, 1994
[49] *Farah v Canada (MEI)* (13 July 1994). See also this volume at 3.2.2
[50] ibid.

4.2.4 Violence Within the Family

It is clearly important that representatives establish that violence within the family constitutes 'serious harm'.[51] However this may not in itself be sufficient to constitute persecution. Acts of serious harm, no matter how severe they may be, cannot be based solely on personal dispute.[52] The failure of the state to protect against the perpetration of such violence must also be shown and this has proved highly problematic; women fleeing violence within the family do not fit the popular conception of a refugee because of the source and location of the persecution.[53] Such violence generally occurs in the home and by definition the assailant has a personal relationship with the potential claimant and is not an anonymous representative of the state. As a result, the state connection required in the definition of a refugee may be difficult to see since the state never actively commits and seldom overtly condones this type of violence against women. This problem is exacerbated by the fact that there is little documentary evidence concerning the particular treatment of women in this area and in many countries, statistics regarding violence within the family are not available.

Just as local police are reluctant to intrude into the 'private' sphere of the home, the international human rights regime is reluctant to intrude into the 'private' sphere of domestic law and its enforcement. Until very recently there has been no discussion about whether women fleeing domestic violence can claim refugee protection, and case law has almost invariably gone against women in these circumstances. In the UK, cases involving violence within the family are routinely dismissed as 'frivolous' and the failure of the state to protect women against violence within the family disputed. For example in *Ranjbar*,[54] the Secretary of State appealed against the decision of an adjudicator to allow the appeal of an Iranian woman who had been beaten by her father. In the grounds of the appeal it was argued that the applicant could look to the Iranian state for protection against maltreatment and that such violence is not condoned by the authorities. The IAT upheld the appeal:

---

[51] See this volume at 3.4
[52] See Goldberg 1993
[53] Stairs and Pope 1990
[54] *SSHD v Fatemah Firouz Ranjbar*, IAT 28th June 1994 (11105) (unreported)

"There is no acceptable evidence in our view that the authorities in Iran would not accord protection to those severely ill-treated within a family. No doubt the standards which would be applied by the authorities in Iran would differ from those in some other countries: no doubt the status of women and children will be differently regarded. The Convention however is not designed to give relief to all those who live under a less liberal social order than that in some Western countries."[55]

The concept of state responsibility must be expanded in practice as well as doctrine, to include not only actions directly committed by states, but also states' systematic failure to prosecute acts committed by private actors. Understanding how the state can be seen to condone activities within the home both justifies and lays the basis for the establishment of state connection to persecution that takes the form of violence within the family. This has been recognised in a recent determination from New Zealand in the case of an Iranian woman who was persecuted by her male family members:

"Because the religious and political imperatives which operate at state level are intended to operate and in fact operate at the domestic or family level as well, we see no distinction on these facts between persecution by the state and persecution by male family members."[56]

In such cases, state inaction may take the form of official legislation (for example, marital rape exemptions in law), lack of police response to pleas for assistance, refusal to investigate or prosecute individual cases and/or a reluctance to convict or punish:

"When a woman has sought, to no avail, police or court protection, or where such efforts would be futile because no protection is available to her, the state may be held responsible for, if not complicitous in, those acts."[57]

---

[55] *SSHD v Fatemah Firouz Ranjbar*, IAT 28th June 1994 (11105) (unreported)
[56] New Zealand Refugee Status Appeals Authority Appeal No. 2039/93, (12th February 1996)
[57] Goldberg 1993, 574

"Where a state facilitates, conditions, accommodates, tolerates, justifies, or excuses private denials of women's rights...the state will bear responsibility. The state will be responsible not directly for the private acts but for its own lack of diligence to prevent, control, correct, or discipline such private acts through its own executive, legislative or judicial organs."[58]

Developments at the international level strengthen the argument of female asylum claimants that the state is sufficiently implicated in the harm done to them to constitute persecution within the parameters of the refugee definition. Most notable among these is the *UN Declaration on the Elimination of Violence Against Women* (1993), which refers explicitly to violence against women occurring in public and private life, and which delineates the obligations of states to develop enforceable laws and appropriate sanctions to prevent violence against women from occurring and to punish those acts to the full extent of the law, whether perpetrated by the state or by private individuals.[59]

4.2.5 Marriage Related Harm
Although the institution of dowry was legislatively abolished in 1961 in India and in 1980 in Bangladesh, the giving and accepting of dowry persists. Many cases are not reported, but it is difficult to prosecute those that are. If brought to court, the cases tend to linger for months or even years and the accused are usually acquitted due to lack of evidence. In this context it can be argued that although state legislation does exist in some cases, in reality the state is unwilling to enforce this so that protection is effectively unavailable. A similar argument can be made in cases of *sati* and in forced marriage including *Mut'a* (temporary pleasure marriage) and child marriage, although the Home Office has typically been unwilling to fulfil its international obligations in these cases:

Ms B is from the Rajput community who originate from Rajasthan, India. The Rajputs are known for their highly restrictive, traditional beliefs on the role of women in society, marriage and divorce, and the practice of *sati* originates in Rajasthan so many accept it as part of their cultural heritage. After Ms B came to the UK, her marriage to a British citizen who mentally abused her broke down, and she was thrown out of the matrimonial home. Her family have said that they

---

[58] Cook 1994, 229
[59] See this volume at 4.6 and Annex 3

would rather she kill herself in the UK than return to India. Ms B is fearful that she will be ostracised and vulnerable to violence, persecution and even death should she be deported. Although Ms B is not a widow, she would be encouraged to kill herself because she is a divorced woman. Suicide in this case would be seen as a substitute for *sati* and regarded as a sacrifice which will help to restore the honour of the family. Her application for asylum has been refused and she is now waiting for the appeal to be heard. Her refusal letter says that the "the Secretary of State...does not consider that the remit of the 1951 Convention extends to people who fear personal difficulties due to their marital status...the expectation is that persecution normally relates to action by the authorities of a country."[60]

However in a recent appeal case where an Algerian woman was told that she must marry the local Emir of the GIA in the form of a *Mut'a* or temporary pleasure marriage, the adjudicator recognised that the Algerian state had failed to protect her against this arrangement, and even though it was not directly implicated, upheld her appeal and granted full status:

"I am satisfied of the authorities' inability to guarantee the safety even of VIPs, not to talk about ordinary citizens. Certainly, as far as women in Algeria are concerned, in my view they are not a top priority as far as the government is concerned and I am not surprised that the appellant did not think it was worth her while to approach the authorities to seek protection. I am satisfied that she was unlikely to receive effective protection from the authorities against the GIA groups who were threatening her safety."[61]

4.2.6 War and Effective State Collapse

"A gender-related claim cannot be rejected simply because the claimant comes from a country where women face generalised oppression and violence."[62]

---

[60] Case study provided by Southall Black Sisters
[61] Appeal No. HX/66670/96 (22nd October 1996) (unreported)
[62] CIRB *Guidelines on Women Refugee Claimants Fearing Gender-Related Persecution* March 1993, C (Annex 5, 193)

Women are frequently subjected to various forms of serious harm during civil wars and other internal or generalised armed conflicts where the state effectively collapses. The problems that were discussed in 4.1.1 regarding the 'privatisation' of sexual violence are particularly apparent in these contexts where it continues to be viewed as a 'normal' by-product of war. This problem is acknowledged by the UNHCR[63] which accepts that women who are attacked by military personnel may find difficulty in showing that they are victims of persecution rather than random violence:

"Even victims of rape by military forces face difficulties in obtaining refugee status when the adjudicators of their claim view such attacks as a *normal* part of warfare."[64]

It should also be noted, however, that even where harm is not inflicted by an agent of the state during war, persecution can exist where the state *is unable* to provide protection.[65] The UNHCR *Handbook* gives specific examples of circumstances in which an applicant may be unable to gain the protection of her state:

"These can include a state of war, civil war or other grave disturbance, which prevents the country of nationality from extending protection or makes such protection ineffective."[66]

The inability of the state to protect women fleeing countries where there is generalised violence or state collapse has been recognised in some jurisdictions:

---

[63] UNHCR *Guidelines on the Protection of Refugee Women* 1991
[64] ibid. 36 (emphasis in original)
[65] UNHCR *Handbook* 1979, paragraph 65. Paragraphs 164 to 166 of the *Handbook* also outline the protection available for victims of war who are not considered refugees under the 1951 Convention or 1967 Protocol. They do have the protection provided for under other international instruments eg. the Geneva Conventions of 1949 on the Protection of War Victims and the 1977 Protocol additional to the Geneva Conventions of 1949 (see Annex 1)
[66] ibid. paragraph 98

"We can find no justification for...restrictive interpretation, leading as it does to the exclusion of asylum seekers from countries affected by civil war such as Angola, Liberia, Somalia and the former Yugoslavia."[67]

However representatives should be aware that some countries are also attempting to negate their international obligations in this respect. For example, in an Act adopted by the member states of the European Union pursuant to Title VI of the Treaty setting out their Joint Position as at 4th March 1996 on the meaning of the term 'refugee', victims of generalised armed conflict are seen to fall outside the meaning of the Convention;[68] Section 6 of the Act deals specifically with civil war and other internal or generalised armed conflicts:

"Reference to a civil war or internal or generalised armed conflict and the dangers which it entails is not in itself sufficient to warrant the grant of refugee status. Fear of persecution must in all cases be based on one of the grounds in Article 1A and be individual in nature...in principle, use of armed forces does not constitute persecution where it is in accordance with international rules of war and internationally recognised practice."[69]

In the UK asylum seekers from countries where there is generalised violence have typically been granted ELR and have not been recognised as Convention refugees:

"There is no government in Somalia, therefore it follows that there is no government persecution...in those circumstances, the appellant's claim must fail."[70]

---

[67] Refugee Status Appeals Authority, New Zealand Appeal No. 2039/93, (12th February 1996)
[68] Council of the European Union *Joint Position Defined by the Council on the Basis of Article K.3 of the Treaty on European Union on the Harmonised Application of the Definition of the Term 'Refugee' in Article 1 of the Geneva Convention of 28th July 1951 Relating to the Status of Refugees.* See also this volume, page 86.
[69] ibid.
[70] Appeal No. TH/5074/92 (1994) (unreported)

However, in this case the appellant, a citizen of Somalia, appealed against the decision to grant her ELR and the IAT, in upholding her appeal, held that the conclusion of the adjudicator was flawed:

"It does *not* follow that because there is no government, or effective government, in a country riven by civil war like Somalia, an individual with identifiable tribal or factional loyalties cannot claim refugee status within the Convention."[71]

More recently in *Lazarevic, Radivojevic, Adan and Nooh*,[72] the Court of Appeal upheld the asylum claims of two Somali applicants fleeing civil war, and agreed with the decisions of the special adjudicator in each case that the state was unable to offer *effective* protection:

"The Convention is, in short, concerned in the last analysis to provide substitute protection (surrogate protection as it is sometimes called) to those who cannot find it from the authorities in their own country."[73]

4.3 Case Law
Canada
In *Fathi-Rad*[74] the Court had to deal with the issue of whether the Islamic dress code is a policy of general application applied to all citizens of Iran. In its decision it is clear that the Court regarded the law as persecutory against women. In the alternative, the court concluded that the punishment for minor infractions of the Islamic dress code was disproportionate to the objective of the law, and therefore constituted persecution:

---

[71] *Hawa Nur Ali v SSTD*, IAT 15th November 1994 (11544) (unreported)

[72] *Lazarevic, Radivojevic, Adan and Nooh v SSTD*, CA 13th February 1997 (unreported). It should be noted that leave to appeal to the House of Lords is being sought by the Home Office at the time of writing.

[73] ibid.

[74] *Fathi-Rad v SSC* (13th April 1994) (unreported). It is worth noting that, since this decision, the Documentation, Information and Research Branch of the CIRB has published a document entitled *Human Rights Brief: Women in the Islamic Republic of Iran* (June 1994), which indicates that the dress code in Iran applies equally to men and women.

"The Islamic dress code is a law applicable only to women in Iran. It dictates the manner in which Iranian women must dress to comply with the beliefs of the theocratic governing regime and prescribes any punishment for any violation of the law. A law which specifically targets the manner in which women dress may not properly be characterised as a law of general application which applies to all citizens."[75]

Canada has also recognised state liability for private actions in its *Guidelines on Women Refugee Claimants Fearing Gender-Related Persecution*:[76]

"A sub-group of women can be identified with reference to the fact of their exposure of vulnerability for physical, cultural or other reasons, to violence, including domestic violence, in an environment that denies them protection. These women face violence amounting to persecution because of their particular vulnerability as women in society *and because they are so unprotected.*"[77]

This position reflects long-standing decisions in both *Rajudeen*[78] and *Surujpal*.[79] Since then both of these cases, as well as paragraph 65 of the UNHCR *Handbook* have been specifically approved by the Supreme Court of Canada in *Ward*[80] which ruled unequivocally that "state complicity in persecution is not a pre-requisite to a valid refugee claim."

United States
The INS *Manual* states that a person is a refugee for purposes of asylum eligibility if "he or she has a well-founded fear of persecution (as a result of one of the five factors in the definition) *because he or she is not adequately protected by his or her government.*"[81] Case law in the US,

---

[75] *Fathi-Rad v SSC* (13th April 1994) (unreported)
[76] See Annex 5
[77] CIRB *Guidelines on Women Refugee Claimants Fearing Gender-Related Persecution* March 1993, 6 (emphasis in original). It should be noted that this provision is no longer explicit in the *UPDATE* to the *Guidelines* which was released in November 1996 (see Annex 5).
[78] *Rajudeen v MEI* [1984] 55 NR 129
[79] *Surujpal v MEI* [1985] 60 NR 73
[80] *Canada (Attorney General) v Ward* [1993] 2 SCR 689
[81] INS *Manual* 1988, paragraph 25 (emphasis added)

most notably *McMullen*[82] and *Matter of Villalta*,[83] establishes that the persecutor can be either the government or a non-government entity that the government is unable or unwilling to control.

United Kingdom

The recent case of *Shah*[84] clearly raises the issue of state responsibility in cases of gender-related persecution. The applicant, a citizen from Pakistan, was a battered wife who had been forced to flee to the UK but who on arrival discovered that she was pregnant. She was afraid to return because she believed that she would be accused of adultery and exposed to the operation of the Sharia law statutes which prescribe stoning to death as punishment. Mr Justice Sedley in quashing the determination of the IAT, by which leave to appeal was refused, implicitly accepted that where gender-based discrimination is enforced through law - either in the form of a law or policy which is inherently discriminatory or as a law or policy for which the penalty for non-compliance is disproportionately severe[85] - then state responsibility and hence persecution can be said to exist. Conclusions may also be drawn from the judgement regarding the responsibility of states to protect women from violence within the family.

The leading case in the UK on the inability of the state to protect against non-state agents of persecution is *Mahmood*.[86] In allowing the appeal, the IAT found that there was a reasonable degree of likelihood that the appellant, if returned to Egypt, would be persecuted for his political opinions and added that:

"We accept that the Egyptian authorities would try to protect him but, in our opinion, there is a serious possibility that they will be unable to do this."[87]

Moreover in *Jeyakumaran*,[88] the argument by the Home Office that the applicant, a Tamil from Sri Lanka, was not sought out or persecuted as

---

[82] *McMullen v INS* [1982] 658 F.2d 1312, 1315 n.2 (9th Circuit)
[83] *Matter of Villalta* [1990] Int. Dec. No. 3126 (BIA)
[84] *R v IAT and SSHD ex parte Syeda Khatoon Shah*, QBD 25th October 1996 (unreported). It should be noted that this decision is being appealed at the time of writing.
[85] See this volume at 4.1.2
[86] *Ibrahim Hussein Mahmood v SSHD*, IAT 10th December 1991 (8405) (unreported)
[87] ibid.
[88] *R v SSHD ex parte Jeyakumaran* [1994] Imm AR 45 (QBD)

an individual and therefore did not qualify for Convention refugee status, was dismissed as a 'startling proposition' and a 'dismal distinction'. Endorsing paragraph 65 of the UNHCR *Handbook*, it was accepted that there is no requirement for an asylum applicant to have been 'singled out' in this context:

> **"It can be little comfort to a Tamil family to know that they are being persecuted simply as Tamils rather than individuals. How can this dismal distinction bear upon whether the applicant has a well-founded fear of persecution?... I ask what solace is it to the victim to know that he is being persecuted by soldiers out of control rather than the Government?"[89]**

Both of these important rulings are reinforced by recent determinations. In addition to the decision of the Court of Appeal in *Lazarevic, Radivojevic, Adan and Nooh*[90] as detailed at 4.2.6, *Yousfi*[91] provides clear guidance on recognising the inability of the state to provide effective protection and endorses paragraph 65 of the UNHCR *Handbook*:

> **"The real question is not whether the State authorities are doing the best they can in all the circumstances, but whether viewed objectively the domestic protection offered by or available from the state to the appellant is or is not reasonably likely to prevent persecution...or as paragraph 65 puts it: are the Algerian authorities *able* to provide *effective* protection against the GIA?...In short it is because the Algerian authorities are *unable* to provide *effective* protection domestically, that the appellant's fear is rendered well-founded and he qualifies for international protection via asylum under the Convention."[92]**

---

[89] *R v SSHD ex parte Jeyakumaran* [1994] Imm AR 45 (QBD)
[90] *Lazarevic, Radivojevic, Adan and Nooh v SSTD*, CA February 1997 (unreported)
[91] *Hocine Yousfi v SSHD*, IAT 1st April 1997 (14779) (unreported)
[92] ibid., (emphasis in original)

4.4 Must State Protection Be Sought?

"When considering whether it is objectively unreasonable for the claimant not to have sought the protection of the state, the decision-maker should consider, among other relevant factors, the social, cultural, religious and economic context in which the claimant finds herself."[93]

"It should also be noted that it is not always reasonable or possible for a woman to alert the authorities to her need for protection. State protection should be effective - with provision of mechanisms for dealing with complaints and also assurance that such avenues for redress are realistic and accessible to a woman of her culture and position."[94]

In the context of gender-related persecution, a further problem is raised by Hathaway: there is no obvious failure of state protection "where a government has not been given an opportunity to respond to a form of harm in circumstances where protection might reasonably have been forthcoming."[95] But when can one reasonably expect a person to turn to the authorities?

"There is a sufficient state connection if violence has been committed by others and theoretically speaking it is conceivable that the authorities could give effective protection, but the woman concerned cannot reasonably be expected to turn to the authorities, because she would run the risk of having to endure further violence or harassment, or because she can have reasonable doubts as to whether she will be given protection."[96]

Both Spijkerboer (cited above) and Castel[97] argue that a woman cannot be expected to alert the authorities if this would put her life in danger.

---

[93] CIRB *Guidelines on Women Refugee Claimants Fearing Gender-Related Persecution: UPDATE* November 1996, C.2 (Annex 5, 194)

[94] ADIMA *Guidelines on Gender Issues for Decision Makers* July 1996, paragraph 4.14 (Annex 6)

[95] Hathaway 1990, 130

[96] Spijkerboer 1994, 24

[97] Castel 1992

This position is supported by Justice la Forest in the much cited Canadian case of *Ward:*[98]

"It would seem to defeat the purpose of international protection if a claimant were required to risk his or her life seeking ineffective protection of a state, merely to demonstrate that ineffectiveness."[99]

In cases such as these, however, where there is not a complete failure of state protection, the burden of proof is on the applicant. Given that refugee law comes into effect only once there has been an exhaustion of other possible remedies, the representative must find whether there were remedies which were meaningful, accessible and effective in the country of origin. In the UK, the problems for women of gaining meaningful state protection have sometimes been acknowledged. For example, a woman from Iran feared that if she were to return to Iran her life and liberty would be in danger, either from the authorities directly, or through her husband who had been violent towards her, and who under Islamic law has permission to kill her for being an unfaithful wife. The Home Office representative argued that if she did suffer at the hands of her husband she would have reported this to the authorities and obtained their protection as well as a divorce, but this was rejected by the adjudicator:

"The appellant did not go to the authorities in Iran for herself or her daughter to complain about her husband's violence because her husband had threatened that he would kill her if she did."[100]

In a similar appeal case, the adjudicator recognised the futility of any approaches that the appellant might make to the Algerian authorities in protecting her from *Mut'a* (temporary pleasure marriage):

"Certainly, as far as women in Algeria are concerned, in my view they are not a top priority as far as the government is concerned and I am not surprised that the appellant did not think it was worth her while to approach the authorities to seek protection."[101]

---

[98] *Canada (Attorney General) v Ward* [1989] 2SCR 689
[99] ibid.
[100] Appeal No. HX/83732/95 (5th December 1996) (unreported)
[101] Appeal No. HX/66670/96 (22nd October 1996) (unreported)

4.5 Is There an Internal Flight Alternative (IFA)?

> "The fear of being persecuted need not always extend to the *whole* of the territory of the refugee's country of nationality. Thus in ethnic clashes or in cases of grave disturbances involving civil war conditions, persecution of a specific ethnic or national group may occur in only one part of the country. In such situations, a person will not be excluded from refugee status merely because [she] could have sought refuge in another part of the same country, if under all the circumstances it would not have been reasonable to expect [her] to do so."[102]

The principle that international protection becomes appropriate where national protection is unavailable also means that in order to be eligible for refugee status an applicant must demonstrate there is no *reasonable* internal flight alternative to leaving the country. In the UK, the leading case regarding the IFA is *Anandanadarajah*[103] which adopts paragraph 91 of the UNHCR *Handbook*:

> "Both the paragraph in the handbook [paragraph 91 of UNHCR *Handbook*] and the paragraph in the rules [paragraph 343 of the Immigration Rules] use the expression 'it would not be reasonable to expect him' to go or to seek refuge."[104]

This principle of *reasonableness* becomes critical when the applicant alleges that the state will not protect against so-called 'private' actions. In such situations the representative must explore the extent to which the government can or does offer protection or redress, and the extent to which the harm extends nationally. Representatives must carefully examine the circumstances giving rise to the harm or risk of harm, as well as the extent to which government protection would have been available in other parts of the country. The implications of gender in determining the reasonableness of an IFA must be recognised:

---

[102] UNHCR *Handbook* 1979, paragraph 91 (emphasis in original)
[103] *R v IAT ex parte Ponnampalam Anandanadarajah*, CA 4th March 1996 (unreported)
[104] ibid.

> "In determining the reasonableness of a woman's recourse to an internal flight alternative (IFA), decision-makers should consider the ability of women, because of their gender, to travel safely to the IFA and to stay there without facing undue hardship."[105]

> "In considering the issue of relocation, the relevant issue is whether the applicant could safely live in another part of the country. Officers must carefully consider gender-related issues when applying this test. Financial, logistical, social, cultural and other barriers to reaching internal safety may significantly affect persons of one gender over another. In addition, gender-based persecution may be systemic and no protection may be available from the authorities in any part of the country."[106]

This has been recognised in the recent determination from the Court of Appeal in the case of *Lazarevic, Radivojevic, Adan and Nooh*[107] which restored the determinations of the special adjudicator in favour of two Somali asylum seekers. Representatives should however be aware that the level of evidence required to prove that an Internal Flight Alternative was unavailable is very high. Because the burden of proof is upon the applicant to demonstrate that they had no alternative but to flee their country and seek asylum in the UK, extensive investigations will be required to substantiate the claim.[108]

4.6 International Instruments for State Protection
4.6.1 The Convention on the Elimination of All Forms of Discrimination Against Women (CEDAW) (1979)[109]

Gender-based harm against women which is enforced through law or unofficially sanctioned by the state, violates the rights guaranteed in CEDAW. While Article 1 is relevant in this respect,[110] it is Article 2 which is particularly useful in the context of establishing state responsibility in these cases:

---

[105] CIRB *Guidelines on Women Refugee Claimants Fearing Gender-Related Persecution: UPDATE* November 1996 C.4 (Annex 5, 194)

[106] ADIMA *Guidelines on Gender Issues for Decision Makers* July 1996, paragraph 4.21 (Annex 6)

[107] *Lazarevic, Radivojevic, Adan and Nooh v SSTD*, CA 13th February 1997 (unreported). This decision is currently being appealed.

[108] See this volume at 2.7

[109] See Annex 3

[110] See this volume at 3.7.1 and Annex 3

Article 2

"States Parties condemn discrimination against women in all its forms and agree to pursue, by all appropriate means and without delay, a policy of eliminating discrimination against women and, to this end, undertake:

- To embody the principle of the equality of men and women in their national constitutions and other appropriate legislation if not already incorporated therein, and to ensure, through law and other appropriate means, the practical realisation of this principle;

- To adopt appropriate legislative and other measures, including sanctions where appropriate, prohibiting all discrimination against women;

- To establish legal protection of the rights of women on an equal basis with men and to ensure through competent national tribunals and other public institutions the effective protection of women against any act of discrimination;

- To refrain from engaging in any act or practice of discrimination against women and to ensure that public authorities and institutions shall act in conformity with this obligation;

- To take all appropriate measures to eliminate discrimination against women by any person, organisation or enterprise;

- To take all appropriate measures, including legislation, to modify or abolish existing laws, regulations, customs and practices which constitute discrimination against women;

- To repeal all national penal codes which constitute discrimination against women."[111]

---

[111] See Annex 3

4.6.2 The UN Declaration on the Elimination of Violence Against Women (1993)[112]

The UN Declaration on the Elimination of Violence Against Women defines violence against women as "any act of gender-based violence that results in, or is likely to result in, physical, sexual or psychological harm or suffering to women...whether occurring in public or private life". Although the Declaration remains unenforceable as international human rights law, it can be used to strengthen the arguments of female asylum claimants that the state is sufficiently implicated in the harm done to them to constitute persecution within the parameters of the refugee definition. Article 4 is of particular relevance in the context of establishing state responsibility:[113]

Article 4

"States should condemn violence against women and should not invoke any custom, tradition or religious consideration to avoid their obligations with respect to its elimination. States should pursue by all appropriate means and without delay a policy of eliminating violence against women and, to this end, should:

- **Refrain from engaging in violence against women;**

- **Exercise due diligence to prevent, investigate and, in accordance with national legislation, punish acts of violence against women, whether those acts are perpetrated by the State or by private persons;**

- **Develop penal, civil, labour and administrative sanctions in domestic legislation to punish and redress the wrongs caused to women who are subjected to violence; women who are subjected to violence should be provided with access to the mechanisms of justice and, as provided for by national legislation, to just and effective remedies for the harm that they have suffered; States should also inform women of their rights in seeking redress through such mechanisms;**

- **Develop, in a comprehensive way, preventive approaches and all those measures of a legal, political, administrative and cultural nature that promote the protection of women against any form of**

---

[112] See also this volume at 3.7.2 and Annex 3

[113] The provisions outlined here are only a selection of those included in Article 4. For further details see Annex 3.

violence, and ensure that the re-victimization of women does not occur because of laws insensitive to gender considerations, enforcement practices or other interventions;

- Adopt all appropriate measures, especially in the field of education, to modify the social and cultural patterns of conduct of men and women and to eliminate prejudices, customary practices and all other practices based on the idea of the inferiority or superiority of either of the sexes and on stereotyped roles for men and women."[114]

4.6.3 The UN Platform for Action (1995)[115]

"Any harmful aspect of certain traditional, customary or modern practices that violates the rights of women should be prohibited and eliminated. Governments should take urgent action to combat and eliminate *all forms of violence against women in private and public life, whether perpetrated or tolerated by the State or private persons.*"[116]

The following Articles are particularly useful in establishing that a failure of state protection has occurred for refugee women seeking asylum in the UK:

Article 117

- "Acts or threats of violence, whether occurring within the home or in the community, or perpetrated or condoned by the State, instil fear and insecurity in women's lives and are obstacles to the achievement of equality and for development and peace;

- In many cases, violence against women and girls occurs in the family or within the home, where violence is often tolerated;

- The neglect, physical and sexual abuse, and rape of girl children and women by family members and other members of the household, as well as incidences of spousal and non-spousal abuse, often go unreported and are thus difficult to detect;

---

[114] See Annex 3 for further details (emphasis added)
[115] ibid.
[116] UN Platform for Action, Article 224 (Annex 3) (emphasis added)

- Even when such violence is reported, there is often a failure to protect victims or punish perpetrators."[117]

Article 118

- "Violence against women is a manifestation of the historically unequal power relations between men and women, which have led to domination over and discrimination against women by men;

- Violence against women throughout the life cycle derives essentially from cultural patterns, in particular the harmful effects of certain traditional or customary practices and all acts of extremism linked to race, sex, language or religion that perpetuate the lower status accorded to women in the family, the workplace, the community and society;

- Violence against women is exacerbated by social pressures, notably the shame of denouncing certain acts that have been perpetrated against women; women's lack of access to legal information, aid or protection; the lack of laws that effectively prohibit violence against women [and] failure to reform existing laws."[118]

Article 124

Clearly sets out the responsibility of states to ensure that sex-based discrimination is not enforced through the law[119] and to protect women where violence is perpetrated by non-state actors.[120] States must:

- "Condemn violence against women and refrain from invoking any custom, tradition or religious consideration to avoid their obligations as set out in the Declaration;

---

[117] These provisions have been extracted from the UN Platform for Action. See Annex 3 for further details.
[118] ibid.
[119] See this volume at 4.1.2
[120] See this volume at 4.2

- **Refrain from engaging in violence against women and exercise due diligence to prevent, investigate and punish acts of violence against women, whether those acts are perpetrated by the State or by private persons;**

- **Render legislation effective in eliminating all violence against women, emphasising the prevention of violence and the prosecution of offenders;**

- **Enact and enforce legislation against the perpetrators of practices and acts of violence against women, such as female genital mutilation, female infanticide, prenatal sex selection and dowry-related violence;**

- **Create or strengthen institutional mechanisms so that women and girls can report acts of violence against them in a safe and confidential environment, free from the fear of penalties or retaliation, and file charges;**

- **Adopt laws, where necessary, and reinforce existing laws that punish police, security forces or any other agents of the State who engage in acts of violence against women in the course of the performance of their duties."[121]**

---

[121] These provisions have been extracted from the UN Platform for Action. See Annex 3 for further details.

Chapter 5 ESTABLISHING THE PERSECUTION GROUND

'Serious harm', even where there is a sufficient link with the state, must also have a persecution ground if it is to form the basis for a successful asylum claim. Some of the most difficult issues in current jurisprudence arise over whether a gender-related asylum claim involves persecution 'on account of' one of the five enumerated grounds which are norms of non-discrimination:

> **"The risk faced by the refugee claimant must have some nexus to her *race, religion, nationality, political opinion or membership of a particular social group*. The critical question is whether but for her civil or political status she could reasonably be said to be at risk of serious intentional harm. If the risk that motivates her flight to safety is not *causally related* to civil or political status, the requirements of the Convention refugee definition are not met."[1]**

With the exception of 'membership of a particular social group', the enumerated persecution grounds within the Convention are relatively clear and claims to refugee status by women can often be framed within them. It has been increasingly recognised however, that in many cases refugee women face barriers to protection which centre around the issue of ground, even though their claims of a well-founded fear of persecution are comparable to those of members of the delineated groups. For example, it is evident from existing determinations both in the UK and elsewhere, that sexual violence frequently obscures the relationship between persecution and Convention grounds. Survivors of sexual violence perpetrated in prison camps by officials, by the military or paramilitary forces often find it difficult to establish that their victimisation was linked to their religion, race, nationality, political opinion or membership of a particular social group, rather than a random expression of individual sexual violence.[2]

In this context feminist scholars and advocates have criticised the Convention, as well as the asylum law of individual countries, for the failure to recognise gender as a category on which a well-founded fear of persecution may be based, and several authors have called for the addition of gender as a prohibited ground of persecution, arguing that

---

[1] Hathaway 1991 (emphasis added)
[2] See also this volume at 3.1, 4.1.1 and 4.2.1

persecution may be inflicted *because* of the applicant's gender.[3] They suggest, for example, that the persecution of women *as women* exists where there is persecution for violation of societal norms requiring them to live with male relatives or persecution for refusal to conform to norms severely restricting their rights and activities.[4] Although this argument is a powerful one, it is not the principal position adopted in this Handbook. Although there are cases where gender is the only reason for the infliction of serious harm (for example, in some cases involving female genital mutilation), there is a tendency to misinterpret the causal relationship between gender and persecution; the idea of women being persecuted *as* women is not the same as women being persecuted *because* they are women.[5] Often women are not persecuted *because* they are women but, as Spijkerboer suggests, because they refuse to be 'proper' women.[6] This is a political issue and is examined at length in this chapter.[7]

There has been increasing criticism of the failure of representatives and decision-makers to incorporate the gender-based persecution claims of women into one of the existing enumerated grounds. Political opinion and social group in particular need to be broadly interpreted to encompass gender-related persecution claims, but in practice these grounds have been construed in a way which frequently serves to exclude the experiences of women as asylum-seekers. In this context, the approach to the issue of persecution ground in this Handbook clearly follows that of the Canadian *Guidelines*:

> **"Although gender is not specifically enumerated as one of the grounds for establishing Convention refugee status, the definition of *Convention refugee* may properly be interpreted as providing protection for women who demonstrate a well-founded fear of gender-related persecution by reason of any, or a combination of, the enumerated grounds."[8]**

---

[3] For example, Indra (1987, 3) cites the omission of gender from the enumerated grounds of persecution as an illustration of "the depth of gender delegitimation in refugee contexts."

[4] See for example Cipriani 1993 and Kelly 1994

[5] See Macklin 1995

[6] Spijkerboer, 1994

[7] Demands for gender to be added as an additional enumerated persecution ground are also unlikely to be successful in the current political climate.

[8] CIRB *Guidelines on Women Refugee Claimants Fearing Gender-Related Persecution: UPDATE* November 1996, A.I (Annex 5, 187)

"The *Guidelines* encourage decision-makers to let gender inform their assessment under race, religion, nationality, or political opinion. As a last resort, 'women' (or some sub-category thereof) might qualify as a 'particular social group'."[9]

This Handbook suggests that grounds of political opinion and religion can, in many cases, better accommodate the experiences of women fleeing gender-based persecution:

"Most of the gender-specific claims involving fear of persecution for transgressing religious or social norms may be determined on *grounds of religion or political opinion.* Such women may be seen by the governing authorities or private citizens as having made a religious or political statement in transgressing those norms of their society, even though UNHCR *Conclusion No. 39...*contemplates the use of 'particular social group' as an appropriate ground."[10]

It is therefore critical to the asylum applications of refugee women that those who are acting as their representatives challenge the normative interpretation of the grounds enumerated within the Convention. This will also require that detailed information about the social, political and legal position of women in their country of origin is available to the representative.[11] Representatives should also be aware of the possible use of the ECHR, and most notably Articles 3 and 13, where establishing the persecution ground is problematic.[12]

5.1 Race

"Race...has to be understood in its widest sense to include all kinds of ethnic groups that are referred to as 'races' in common usage...[R]acial discrimination...represents an important element in determining the existence of persecution."[13]

---

[9] Macklin 1995, 238
[10] CIRB *Guidelines on Women Refugee Claimants Fearing Gender-Related Persecution: UPDATE* November 1996, A.III (emphasis in original) (Annex 5, 190-191)
[11] See this volume at 2.7
[12] See this volume at 1.4.5 and Annex 2
[13] UNHCR *Handbook* 1979, paragraph 68

Whilst race is clearly not specific to women, persecution of women for reasons of race frequently takes a gender-specific form,[14] and both the Canadian and Australian *Guidelines* note that race and gender may operate in tandem to explain why a claimant fears persecution:

"**There may be cases where a woman claims a fear of persecution because of her race and her gender. For example, a woman from a minority race in her country may be persecuted not only for her race, but also for her gender.**"[15]

"**In general racism knows no gender, however persecution may be expressed in different ways against men and women. For example the persecutor may choose to destroy the ethnic identity and/or prosperity of a racial group by killing, maiming or incarcerating the men whilst the women may be viewed as propagating the ethnic identity and persecuted in a different way, such as through sexual violence.**"[16]

The association of sexual violence with persecution for reasons of race has been noted by the adjudicator in a recent UK case:

"**[She] has suffered discrimination and harassment by reason of her Kurdish ethnic origin since her childhood...The rape of the appellant is linked inextricably to her political activities...and also therefore inextricably linked to her Kurdish ethnic origin...[she] had and has a genuine fear of persecution for a Convention reason at the hands of the Turkish authorities...the maltreatment and sexual abuse were acts of persecution by the State.**"[17]

---

[14] See Chapter 3
[15] CIRB *Women Refugee Claimants Fearing Gender-Related Persecution: UPDATE* November 1995, A.II (Annex 5, 188)
[16] ADIMA *Guidelines on Gender Issues for Decision Makers* July 1996, paragraph 4.29 (Annex 6)
[17] Appeal No. HX/73695/95 (17th May 1996) (unreported). See also Women Against Rape Press Release, 7th June 1996

5.2 Nationality

"The term 'nationality' is not to be understood only as 'citizenship'. It also refers to membership of an ethnic or linguistic group and may occasionally overlap with the term 'race'. Persecution for reasons of nationality may consist of adverse attitudes and measures directed against a national (ethnic, linguistic) minority and in certain circumstances the fact of belonging to such a minority may in itself give rise to a well-founded fear of persecution."[18]

The UNHCR *Handbook* also notes that "it may not always be easy to distinguish between persecution for reasons of nationality and persecution for reasons of political opinion when a conflict between national groups is combined with political movements, particularly where a political movement is identified with a specific 'nationality',"[19] and that "although in most cases persecution for reason of nationality is feared by persons belonging to a national minority, there have been many cases in various continents where a person belonging to a majority group may fear persecution by a dominant minority."[20] Although persecution on the grounds of nationality (as with race) is clearly not specific to women, in many instances the nature of the persecution takes a gender-specific form, most commonly that of sexual violence including rape directed particularly, although not exclusively, against women and girls.[21] This has been recognised in a recent appeal case where refugee status was granted to a Bosnian woman seeking asylum in the UK:

"I note and accept that rape and sexual abuse of women has taken place throughout the war in the former Yugoslavia and that as a woman the appellant is at risk of such abuse...I accept that she is at particular risk by reason of her ethnic origin and her political opposition to the authorities, probably from a non-Serb man or men, once a political opposition is apparent."[22]

A gender-related claim of fear of persecution may also be linked to reasons of nationality in situations where a national law causes a woman

---

[18] UNHCR *Handbook* 1979, paragraph 74
[19] ibid., paragraph 75
[20] ibid., paragraph 76
[21] See this volume at 3.1
[22] Appeal No. HX/75012/94 (24th March 1995) (unreported)

to lose her nationality (i.e. citizenship) because of marriage to a foreign national. Whilst some nationality laws are therefore discriminatory, fear of persecution must arise not from the fact of losing nationality itself but rather the consequences which may be suffered as a result.[23]

> "Rather than the loss of citizenship itself, [representatives] should enquire into what harm results from this loss. For example, whether it leads to loss of right of residence or loss of other privileges or benefits."[24]

5.3 Religion
As is acknowledged in the UNHCR *Handbook*, persecution for reasons of religion may assume various forms:

- **prohibition of membership of a religious community;**

- **prohibition of worship in public or private;**

- **prohibition of religious instruction;**

- **serious measures of discrimination imposed on persons because they practice their religion or belong to a particular religious community.[25]**

The asylum claims of refugee women on the grounds of religion are in many cases relatively straightforward. However it should be recognised that in addition to the forms indicated in the UNHCR *Handbook,* the religious practices of many countries have significant implications for gender relations, and in consequence for the persecutory harm suffered or feared by the applicant.[26] Thus the role ascribed to women in certain

---

[23] See Macklin, 1995

[24] ADIMA *Guidelines on Gender Issues for Decision Makers* July 1996, paragraph 4.31(Annex 6)

[25] UNHCR *Handbook* 1979, paragraph 71

[26] It is impossible however to generalise about the implications of any specific religion for women *per se* because much will depend upon the political context in which particular religious tenets are interpreted by the state. For example Islam, as a religious philosophy, is interpreted through laws, regulations and social norms governing behaviour which differ significantly between countries such as Afghanistan, Algeria, Iran, Pakistan, the Sudan and Turkey.

societies may be attributable to the requirements of the state or official religion:

> **"The failure of women to conform to this role or model of behaviour may then be perceived by the authorities or other agents of persecution as the failure to practise or to hold certain religious beliefs and as such an attempt to corrupt the society or even as a threat to the religion's continued power. This may be the case even though the woman actually holds the official religious faith but it is not evidenced by her outward behaviour."[27]**

> **"The *political nature* of oppression of women in the context of religious laws and ritualisation should be recognised. Where tenets of the governing religion in a given country require certain kinds of behaviour exclusively from women, contrary behaviour may be perceived by the authorities as evidence of an unacceptable political opinion that threatens the basic structure from which their political power flows."[28]**

The asylum applications of some refugee women therefore clearly reflect more generalised oppression of women through social mores which have been developed as an interpretation of certain religious principles by both the state and society:

> **"A woman who, in a theocracy for example, chooses not to subscribe to or follow the precepts of a state religion may be at risk of persecution for reasons of religion. In the context of the Convention refugee definition, the notion of religion may encompass, among other freedoms, the freedom to hold a belief system of one's choice or *not to hold* a particular belief system and the freedom to practice a religion of one's choice or *not to practice* a prescribed religion. In certain states, the religion assigns certain roles to women; if a woman does not fulfil her assigned role and is punished for that, she may have a well-founded fear of persecution for reasons of religion."[29]**

---

[27] ADIMA *Guidelines on Gender Issues for Decision Makers* July 1996, paragraph 4.30 (Annex 6)

[28] CIRB *Guidelines on Women Refugee Claimants Fearing Gender-Related Persecution: UPDATE* November 1993, A.II (Annex 5, 189) (emphasis in original)

[29] ibid. (emphasis in original)

A woman may face harm for her particular religious beliefs or practices, including her refusal to hold particular beliefs, to practice a prescribed religion or to conform her behaviour in accordance with the teachings of a prescribed religion:

Mrs S is a 32 year old woman from Pakistan who sought asylum because she no longer believed in Islam. She feared persecution if she were forced to return to Pakistan because she had challenged the fundamentalist laws of Pakistan by trying to divorce her husband who, with his family, had subjected her to a terrifying ordeal of abuse, violence and imprisonment. Having escaped from him and come to the UK she become involved in a relationship with a man who then initiated a campaign of harassment when she ended the relationship. He subsequently contacted her husband and her father informing them of her 'adultery', 'western lifestyle' and 'blasphemous beliefs'. In the eyes of her community, Mrs S is deemed to have blasphemed by rejecting Islam. As a woman she has doubly transgressed by refusing to submit to the will of her husband and family. The case of Mrs S was initially refused by the Home Office but was allowed on appeal on grounds of religious persecution.[30]

In another recent UK appeal case, an Indian woman who had converted to Islam feared retribution from her family and was granted full refugee status on the grounds that her persecution was because of her religious beliefs. Her fear of reprisals were exacerbated because of both her caste and gender, as was suggested by one of the expert reports which her representative used to support her case:[31]

"It is extremely unusual for a woman from such a caste to convert to Islam, and such a conversion, especially by a woman, would almost certainly lead to that person's exclusion from the society of their caste fellows and their own family..."[32]

---

[30] Case study provided by Southall Black Sisters and Women Against Fundamentalism
[31] See this volume at 2.7.1 on the use of expert witnesses and reports
[32] Appeal No. TH/61272/94 (7th February 1996) (unreported)

Clearly there is a considerable degree of overlap between the religion and political opinion grounds in many cases which involve social mores. This reflects, in considerable part, conditions in the country of origin:

"Given the theocratic nature of the current regime in Iran, the appellant's opposition, both to the patriarchal society comprising her extended Arab family and to the male domination of women in Iranian society at large, is conveniently addressed under both the 'religion' and 'political opinion' grounds...We are satisfied on the evidence that a very substantial element of the appellant's case, falls within the 'religion' and 'political opinion' categories of the Convention."[33]

As a result, a substantial component of the analysis relating to religion and gendered social mores is confined to the subsequent section, partly to avoid repetition but also because political opinion is the most accepted - and possibly also the most flexible - ground enumerated within the Convention.[34]

5.4 Actual or Imputed Political Opinion

'Political opinion' - actual or imputed - is probably the least disputed of all the grounds included in the Convention definition, not least because it implies some direct relationship to the state. What constitutes political opinion as a ground for persecution is outlined within the UNHCR *Handbook*:[35]

"Holding political opinions different from those of the Government is not in itself a ground for claiming refugee status, and an applicant must show that [she] has a fear of persecution for holding such opinions. This presupposes that the applicant holds opinions not tolerated by the authorities, which are critical of their policies or methods. It also presupposes that such opinions have come to the notice of the authorities or are attributed by them to the applicant."[36]

---

[33] New Zealand Refugee Status Appeals Authority Appeal No. 2039/93 (12th February 1996)
[34] This is not to imply however that one ground has greater validity than another or that a claim for asylum cannot be based on two grounds simultaneously.
[35] UNHCR *Handbook* 1979, paragraphs 80 to 86 inclusive
[36] ibid., paragraph 80

Persecution for reasons of political opinion implies therefore that an applicant holds an opinion that either has been expressed or has come to the attention of the authorities. However the UNHCR *Handbook* accepts that there may be situations in which the applicant has not given any expression of her opinions:

> **"An applicant claiming fear or persecution because of political opinion need not show that the authorities of [her] country of origin knew of [her] opinions before [she] left the country. [She] may have concealed [her] political opinion and never have suffered any discrimination or persecution. However, the mere fact of refusing to avail [herself] of the protection of [her] Government, or a refusal to return, may disclose the applicant's true state of mind and give rise to a fear of persecution. In such circumstances the test of well-founded fear would be based on an assessment of the consequences that an applicant having certain political dispositions would have to face if [she] returned."[37]**

Such an interpretation is also found in *Macdonald* which accepts that "a person who has not previously expressed [her] political dislike of the regime may be exposed by the very fact of flight and claiming asylum."[38] This aspect of actual or imputed political opinion may be particularly relevant for women fleeing gender-based social mores and discrimination, and also where generalised oppression has rendered the expression of political opinion particularly difficult for women.

Given the overwhelming emphasis and legitimacy placed by the jurisdiction of most states on political opinion as the grounds for persecutory treatment, those representing refugee women clearly need to argue claims on this basis wherever possible. The archetypal image of a political refugee as someone who is fleeing persecution for their direct involvement in political activity does not always correspond with the reality of many women's experiences. The predominant interpretation of persecution on the grounds of political opinion exemplifies the problem of a definition which has typically been seen in terms of male experience and this is reflected, for example, in the nature of the questions asked at

---

[37] UNHCR *Handbook* 1979, paragraph 83
[38] Macdonald and Blake *Macdonald's Immigration Law and Practice in the United Kingdom* 1995, 394 paragraph 12.48. See also *R v IAT ex p d'Joel Aruna Senga*, QBD 9th March 1994 (unreported)

asylum interviews and in Part C of the Self-Completion Questionnaire.[39] Women are less likely than their male counterparts to be involved in high profile political activity and are more often involved in so-called 'low level' political activities which reflect dominant gender roles. They are also frequently attributed with political opinions and subjected to persecution because of the activities of their male relatives. The implications of such an interpretation for female refugees forms the basis of the analysis in this section, not least because women's asylum claims frequently concern declarations of fear on account of a political opinion which relates directly to gender:

"In some societies, overt demonstration of political opinion by women may not be possible as women are not allowed to formally participate in political life...Furthermore, the fact that a woman may challenge particular social conventions about the manner in which women should behave may be considered political by the authorities and may attract persecutory treatment on this basis."[40]

As a strategy for achieving increased recognition of gender-related claims, framing women's asylum claims as related to actual or imputed political opinion avoids the practical and political problems often associated with 'membership of a particular social group',[41] and does not require overly liberal interpretation of the definition. What is required however is a recognition of the conflict over what is 'public' and what is 'private'.

"Whether or not the state may infringe on the religious or political views citizens hold is a deeply political issue. Therefore questions of whether or not a woman is free to choose to wear a veil or not, to be circumcised, to exercise the human right to have an education, to be free from male violence are about the demarcation of the 'public' and 'private' sphere. Conflicts concerning the demarcation of privacy are conflicts of a most essentially political nature, and should be considered as such in evaluating a claim to refugee status."[42]

---

[39] See also this volume at 2.2 and 2.4
[40] ADIMA *Guidelines on Gender Issues for Decision Makers* July 1996, paragraph 4.25 (Annex 6)
[41] See this volume at 5.5 for a detailed analysis of these issues and summaries of case law relating to 'membership of a particular social group'
[42] Spijkerboer 1994, 46

Whilst political opinion therefore appears to suggest traditional 'public' political activity, a broad interpretation of the ground is possible and may include, for example, opposition to social mores and institutionalised discrimination against women.[43]

5.4.1 Women Directly Involved in Political Activity

There are, of course, many cases in which women are actively involved in political activity and where establishing the grounds of the persecutory treatment is relatively unproblematic. These include, *but are not limited to*, the following:

- **women who are members of political parties or organisations;**

- **women who are members of resistance groups;**

- **women who are involved in trade union activities;**

- **women who are members of women's / feminist organisations.[44]**

It should be noted however that in many societies the penalty for this type of political activity may be even more severe for women than for men because of cultural and social norms which have precluded women's involvement. Political women who are imprisoned by the authorities run the risk of 'double punishment'. They are punished not only because they oppose the regime in some way, but because they shirk the traditional role of women by being politically active at all:

"In the case of political activists, women are not only [sexually] assaulted on the basis of their political opinion, but also because, as women, they should not participate in the political arena."[45]

---

[43] See this volume at 5.4.3
[44] The Australian *Guidelines on Gender Issues for Decision Makers* also acknowledge at paragraph 4.25 that "in some societies an organisation of women who are not seeking a public or political profile but who may, for example, possess a feminist ideology, may be viewed as espousing a political opinion hostile to the current administration and be persecuted for that reason" (See Annex 6 for further details)
[45] Spijkerboer 1994, 25

As a result they are often 'put back in their place' by prison guards or military men.[46] Women who are politically active may therefore be dealt with doubly hard by the persecuting authorities and the form of persecution suffered is frequently gender-specific, often involving sexual violence which may include rape.[47] This form of persecution may in itself raise a significant number of procedural difficulties. In cases where the basis of a woman's asylum claim is comparable to that of her male counterpart, credibility problems may arise unless the details of the case are obtained in a gender-sensitive manner from the first interview.[48] It should also be noted that sexual violence including rape has in the past been conceptualised in a way that undermines state responsibility.[49]

5.4.2 Women Indirectly Involved in Political Activity

"In a society where women are 'assigned' a *subordinate status* and the authority exercised by men over women results in a general oppression of women, their political protest and activism do not always manifest themselves in the same way as those of men."[50]

Although many women who claim refugee status are actively engaged in political activity, it remains the case that in general terms, women are less likely than men to be directly involved in political activity. Women are often involved in 'low level' supportive roles:

"The political activities that women are involved in are, in many instances, not as 'public' as making speeches, attending demonstrations and writing publications. Women may provide food, clothing, medical care, hide people, pass messages from one political activist to another and so on. All of these activities may be essential for the ongoing existence of the political organisation, and the knowledge women gain through these activities puts them in danger and at risk. However, these activities are not viewed as having sufficient public profile to attract attention from the authorities to put them at risk"[51]

---

[46] Dutch Refugee Council 1994
[47] See this volume at 3.1
[48] These issues are addressed at length in Chapter 2
[49] See this volume at 4.1.1 and 4.2.1
[50] CIRB *Guidelines on Women Refugee Claimants Fearing Gender-Related Persecution: UPDATE* November 1996, A.II (emphasis in original) (Annex 5, 189)
[51] Legal Aid Commission of NSW, *Submission 588*

> "Women who offer political resistance by carrying out 'odd jobs' often do not label their actions as political resistance, and asylum-granting countries may not judge these activities by their political merits, underestimating the political dimensions of these acts."[52]

The central issue in cases involving this type of political participation is the way in which the concept of 'political' is interpreted. Whilst the UNHCR *Handbook* does not give any clear definition of what is meant by the term, there is considerable evidence that decisions on whether a refugee claimant falls within the political opinion ground have frequently been based, in the past, on the male experience of more overt political activity and that private sphere activities which are most commonly associated with women seeking asylum are viewed as inherently apolitical.[53] However women engaged in 'low level' or indirect political activity may actually be at even greater risk of persecution than their 'high level' or directly involved male counterparts. This was acknowledged by the adjudicator in a recent UK appeal case:

> "The authorities in Uganda would not in any event be so reckless as to persecute ...high profile politicians...who are very much in the eyes of the international community. At the end of the day, it is the "foot soldiers" like the appellant's mother who suffer the brunt of persecution."[54]

In this context Spijkerboer argues that whilst one can say that refugee law is gendered on the basis that the very notion of a refugee is thought of as a 'public' phenomenon, it is not *necessarily* gendered.[55] There are no such things as inherently political or apolitical activities. Rather whether or not activities are political depends on their context; whether or not they can give rise to legitimate claims to refugee status depends on the reaction of the authorities in the country of origin of the claimant. Activities commonly associated with women and occurring in the private sphere are not therefore inherently any less political than those taking place in the public sphere; indeed in some contexts these activities may become inherently political and women may be targeted as a result. It is

---

[52] Dutch Refugee Council 1994
[53] Oosterveld 1996, 12 (footnote 42)
[54] Appeal No. HX/71474/95 (1st February 1996) (unreported)
[55] Spijkerboer 1994

very important that representatives recognise that these activities constitute political opinion and political resistance: they are no less valid than other forms which are dominated by men.

5.4.3 Women to Whom Political Opinion is Imputed

"Where the persecution of women is concerned, it should be recognised that an *imputed* Convention ground is an important aspect to consider."[56]

To make a claim of persecution on the basis of political opinion, the claimant has to demonstrate a relationship between her political opinion and her fear of persecution. In evaluating therefore whether persecution of a female applicant or her fear of persecution is 'on account of political opinion', it will be argued here that where the claimant is not directly involved in political activity in the conventional sense, a claim for refugee status requires that political opinion be broadly defined. Most significantly, the term should be understood to include an opinion regarding the treatment or status of women within her country, culture or social, religious or ethnic group.[57] It should also be recognised that women are often aligned with the views of their male relatives. This interpretation is consistent with the UNHCR *Handbook* which holds that persecution on account of political opinion includes persecution because the authorities attribute an opinion to the applicant and as such does not require prior political activity.[58] It is also compatible with recent case law in the United States, specifically *Hernandez-Ortiz* and *Bolanos-Hernandez* which has concluded that the determination of what is 'political' need not focus solely on the actions of the applicant.[59] This wider interpretation of the definition suggests that political opinion encompasses actions of the government as well, particularly whether the government restricts a person's privilege to hold a certain opinion.

The issues discussed here, as in the preceding section, must therefore be located in the political context in which they occur. Women may not directly claim, in either oral or written statements, that persecution in their home country was due to political opinion although

---

[56] ADIMA *Guidelines on Gender Issues for Decision Makers* July 1996, paragraph 4.23 (emphasis in original) (Annex 6)
[57] Kelly 1994, 524
[58] UNHCR *Handbook* 1979, paragraph 80
[59] See Mulligan 1990, 366

the existing regime may in fact impute them with holding such an opinion.

It is important not to underestimate the political dimension in these cases although women often do not themselves regard themselves as making a political statement, but merely a statement of their discontent.

In cases such as those described below, it is both more accurate and strategically preferable to place the offence in a political context as opposed to arguing that women, or even particular sub-groups of women, constitute a particular social group within the meaning of the Convention.[60]

A. Social Mores and Discrimination

Women face institutionalised discrimination in many countries. For example, women have to keep certain rules for dressing and they are not allowed to receive certain kinds of education, or to practice certain professions,[61] they are forced to marry the man selected for them by their family,[62] or they are denied important civil and political rights. It was argued in Chapter 3 that the nature and extent of such discriminatory measures can be sufficient to rise to the level of persecution, as is the punishment for violation of particular social mores. Yet frequently these challenges to social norms - differing as they do from conventional forms of political contestation - have been considered 'personally motivated' and have not been categorised as political. As a result women persecuted for such transgressions have typically had difficulties bringing themselves within the protection of refugee law.

There is a strong argument that political opinion should include women's opposition to extreme, institutionalised forms of oppression; a woman who opposes institutionalised discrimination against women or expresses views of independence from the social or cultural dominance of men in her society may be found to have been persecuted or to fear persecution because of her actual political opinion or a political opinion that has been or will be imputed to her. She is perceived within the established political/social structure as expressing politically antagonistic

---

[60] See this volume at 5.5
[61] See this volume at 3.2
[62] See this volume at 3.5

views through her actions or failure to act. If a woman resists gendered oppression, her resistance should be regarded as political activity:[63]

"A woman who opposes institutionalised discrimination of women, or expresses views of independence from male social/cultural dominance in her society, may be found to fear persecution by reason of her *actual political opinion or a political opinion imputed to her (i.e. she is perceived by the agent of persecution to be expressing politically antagonistic views).*"[64]

"The fact that a woman may challenge particular social conventions about the manner in which women should behave may be considered political by the authorities and may attract persecutory treatment on this basis."[65]

The strength of this approach is particularly clear in the case of women's refusal to wear the veil. The veil can be a major site of struggle for religious and political freedom and it has been noted with regard to the Iranian *hejab*, that a woman refusing to wear the veil may be looked upon as disloyal to both faith and regime and condemned as "instrumental in the foreign-inspired plot to undermine revolutionary puritanism."[66] Accordingly, religious leaders command the faithful to resist these 'subversives' with the same vigour as they oppose others who have sought to undermine the revolution.

Clearly in this instance women are not being punished solely because they are women - those women who wear the veil are not punished - but because their actions are not accepted. In other words they are punished because they refuse to be 'proper' women.[67]

---

[63] According to Macklin (1995, 260) "identifying women's resistance to gender subordination as political opinion...[is]...profoundly feminist, if indeed one believes that the personal is political and that patriarchy is a system constituted primarily through power relations and not biology."

[64] CIRB *Guidelines on Women Refugee Claimants Fearing Gender-Related Persecution: UPDATE* November 1996, A.II (Annex 5, 189) (emphasis in original)

[65] ADIMA *Guidelines on Gender Issues for Decision Makers* July 1996, paragraph 4.25 (Annex 6)

[66] Afshar 1985, 266 cited in Neal 1988, 219

[67] See Spijkerboer, 1994. The issue of whether women in this context can be seen as a 'particular social group' within the meaning of the Convention is examined further in this volume at 5.5.1

When seen in this context, such an act of defiance is an expression of a political and/or religious opinion.[68]

In addition there are cases where women do not directly or intentionally challenge institutionalised norms of behaviour but are nonetheless imputed with a political opinion as a consequence of their experiences. This may be particularly apparent in contexts where the social implications for a woman who has been divorced from her husband are sufficiently severe to rise to the level of persecution:

Ms A is from Kabul in Afghanistan. She arrived in the UK as a refugee with her husband and three sons and had been subjected to physical and sexual abuse throughout her marriage. In 1994 Ms A finally managed to escape the matrimonial home. Her husband abducted their youngest son and Ms A presently lives in the UK with her two other sons. If her application for asylum is refused she will eventually be sent back to Afghanistan where, in addition to the brutality women have been subjected to throughout the war, the establishment of the Taliban regime in Kabul has led to the drastic reduction of women's rights. As a 'westernised', divorced woman, Ms A would be perceived as being non-Islamic and disobedient. She will be ostracised by the community for having brought dishonour upon her family and will be subject to persecution both from her immediate community and from the Taliban regime. She is already marked as having been politically active in defiance of her husband and this will further mark her out as having transgressed the boundaries women are supposed to operate within. She fears that her husband may arranged to have her killed and will be able to escape criminal prosecution through his considerable wealth, influence and political connections.[69]

In the context of actual or imputed political opinion, the issue then is not one of refugee law *per se*, but of how women's experiences are interpreted by representatives and decision-makers.

---

[68] The distinction between religion and politics is frequently a difficult one to make particularly in the context of Islam. In a case such as this it could equally be argued that the ground for the persecution was religion (see this volume at 5.3). Arguing for either or both grounds are valid approaches in representing such claims.

[69] Case study provided by Southall Black Sisters

"If a woman refuses to oblige with a social practice she finds oppressive, be it a dress code or a denial of education, then that is a political issue. The demarcation of public and private spheres at stake here is a political issue of great importance."[70]

Conceptualising political opinion in a way which goes beyond the public/private dichotomy pervasive in the normative structures of international refugee law reflects the *agency* of those represented. As Indra suggests, refugee images are powerfully imbued with the symbolism of helplessness in the face of forces far larger than themselves.[71] This is exacerbated by the interpretation within customary law of the actions and experiences of refugee women.[72]

B. Guilt by Association

"In many cases there is a societal assumption that women defer to men on all significant issues and that their political views are aligned with those of the dominant members of the family (usually husbands, fathers or brothers). They may thus experience persecution for this reason i.e. imputed political opinion."[73]

The public expression of opinions about politics is to a large extent the preserve of men in many societies whilst women tend to be involved in supportive roles. In addition, many women are persecuted because they have family associations with persons (usually husbands, fathers, brothers or sons) who are politically active in some way. The political opinions or actions of these family members are then imputed to women by the persecuting agent. This was apparent in the case of an Ethiopian woman seeking asylum in the UK:

"The appellant was an Ethiopian citizen. After her brother died [during a demonstration by university students in Addis Ababa] soldiers of the Ethiopian People's Revolutionary Democratic Front (EPRDF) came to her house. They kept on harassing them [the

---

[70] Spijkerboer 1994, 66
[71] Indra 1993
[72] See also Macklin, 1995
[73] ADIMA *Guidelines on Gender Issues for Decision Makers* July 1996, paragraph 4.26 (Annex 6)

appellant and her mother]. They wanted to know which political party they belonged to. They took her and terrorised her by saying that she had to say what they told her to say because she was a woman. They wanted to force themselves on her...They wanted to hear what organisation he [her brother] belonged to and what his role was."[74]

In such cases, it can be argued that the ground for the persecution was a political opinion which was imputed to the applicant because of the actions of her family members. The heightened implications for a female claimant's vulnerability, where both she and male family members have been involved in political opposition, has also been recognised in the case of an Eritrean woman who was the wife of a high profile member of the Eritrean Liberation Front (ELF):

"It appears to me in view of the fact that the appellant's husband had such a high profile in the ELF-RC [Revolutionary Council] and that she also was an active worker in the ELF, that it is possible that she, if anyone, would be vulnerable...she, because of her position and, as I say, the high profile of her husband, would be in a particularly vulnerable position in my view."[75]

It should be noted however, that even though mere association with political activists can render a woman vulnerable to persecution, for many women it may be very difficult to prove the grounds of the persecution, partly because they themselves may not be fully aware of the reasons for their persecution:

"The added difficulty is that, in many societies women have little or no information on the activities of their male relatives and may find it difficult to explain the reasons for their persecution. They may not realise that the authorities, for example, impute a political opinion to them because of their association (by marriage, family links etc.) with others who have attracted the authorities' attention."[76]

---

[74] Appeal No. HX/73267/94 (7th November 1994) (unreported)
[75] Appeal No. HX/76443/95 (4th December 1996) (unreported)
[76] ADIMA *Guidelines on Gender Issues for Decision Makers* July 1996, paragraph 4.24 (Annex 6)

Where it is not possible to 'prove' that a political opinion has been imputed to the applicant, it can instead be argued that the family constitutes a particular social group within the meaning of the Convention; this is an accepted basis in the jurisdiction of several states and, in certain circumstances, in the UK.[77]

C. Forced Sterilisation and Abortion

Forced sterilisation and abortion constitute a fundamental violation of women's human rights as recognised in international law, and in the case of China's one-child policy, the state is directly implicated; the law or policy, although having legitimate goals, is administered through persecutory means.[78] In this context it could be argued that where a woman is subjected to forced abortion or sterilisation or where she is punished through discriminatory measures which rise to the level of 'serious harm', the state is effectively imputing a political opinion to her because it brands her as an opponent of the regime and punishes her on this basis. Arguing imputed political opinion as the grounds for persecution may in some cases therefore be an appropriate strategy and avoids some of the problems associated with the particular social group approach especially given that the social group must exist independently from the persecution itself.[79]

5.4.4 Case Law
Canada

The Canadian *Guidelines* explicitly promote the recognition of resistance to societal mores - such as female genital mutilation and dress codes - as political opinion. This position is reflected in existing jurisprudence. For example, the Canadian Immigration Appeal Board concluded that the unwillingness of an Iranian woman to wear the *chador* and attend Islamic functions constituted political opinion.[80] In a subsequent case it was decided that the claimant's opposition to the government's enforcement of the dress laws, "could possibly result in her being persecuted because of political opinion should she be returned to Iran."[81] The clearest ruling however is in *Namitabar*:[82]

---

[77] See this volume at 5.5.2
[78] See this volume at 4.1.2
[79] See this volume at 5.5
[80] *Shahabaldin, Modjgan v MEI*, IAB 2 March 1987
[81] CRDD T90-01845 (21st Dec 1990)
[82] *Namitabar v MEI* [1994] 2 FC 42

"I consider that in the case at bar the female applicant has demonstrated that her fear of persecution is connected to her political opinion. In a country where the oppression of women is institutionalised any independent point of view or act opposed to the imposition of a clothing code will be seen as a manifestation of opposition to the established theocratic regime."[83]

United States

In the now infamous case of *Campos-Guardado*,[84] the court considered the claim of a woman whose family members had been politically active in El Salvador. Armed attackers came to her home, bound the applicant and other female family members and forced them to watch while the attackers murdered male family members. The attackers then raped the applicant and the other female family members while one attacker chanted political slogans. In what might appear to be an extreme assessment of the evidence, the court affirmed the Board's determination that the applicant had not established that the attackers were motivated by a political opinion they imputed to the victim. This interpretation of the Convention has been explicitly criticised in the INS guidelines.

"Reasonable minds could differ over this record. The court might reasonably have concluded that the chanting of political slogans during the rape indicated not merely that the attackers were politically motivated, but more specifically that they believed the appellant to have contrary political views and that they punished her because of it."[85]

By contrast the Third Circuit in *Fatin*[86] held that there is "little doubt that feminism qualifies as a political opinion within the meaning of the relevant statutes". The political opinion of the applicant in that case did not, however, provide a basis for refugee status; although she had shown that she generally possessed political beliefs about the role of women in society that collided with those prevailing in Iran, the appellant had not shown that she would risk severe enough punishment simply for holding

---

[83] ibid.

[84] *Campos-Guardado v INS* [1987] 809 F.2d 285 (5th Circuit). For further discussion of this case see Castel 1992

[85] INS *Guidelines on Gender Issues for Decision Makers* June 1995, IIIA

[86] *Fatin v INS* [1993] 12 F.3d 1233 (3rd Circuit)

such views.[87] However, the case makes it clear that an applicant who can demonstrate a well-founded fear of persecution on account of her beliefs about the role and status of women in society could be eligible for refugee status on account of actual or imputed political opinion.

United Kingdom

The most significant recent case in which a violation of social mores was interpreted as constituting political opinion is that of *Ahmady*.[88] The Iranian applicant was arrested for wearing make-up and for failing to cover her hair properly. She was detained, taken to court and in place of receiving fifty lashes was fined. She was forced to leave her employment at a primary school due to her incorrect dress and she was unable to find alternative employment. It was argued on appeal that the appellant's behaviour was seen by the regime as opposition to it - a political act - and that the adjudicator was wrong to conclude otherwise. The IAT accepted that in Iran there is no clear and defined boundary to political opinion. In allowing the appeal the Tribunal made a number of comments which are extremely significant in the context of the preceding discussion and which reinforce the argument that refugee women's experiences must be interpreted within the social and political context in which persecution has occurred. It is also strategically an important line of reasoning given the problems associated with the recognition of gender-defined social groups in the UK.

"A woman who is westernised must we think have considerable difficulty in concealing it. If she reveals it in our view it is perceived in Iran to be the expression of a political opinion contrary to the state. It is not merely transgression of Islamic mores, it is transgression of an Islamic mora as interpreted by this particular regime and the two are indistinguishable. We are not going so far as to say that every woman can say that she will not abide by the dress laws and by so doing bring herself within the Convention, it depends on the circumstances, but in this case...the perception will be that she is making a political statement and therefore the persecution will be for a Convention reason on that basis."[89]

---

[87] See this volume at 3.2
[88] *Abdollah Fathi and Mashid Ahmady v SSHD*, IAT 1st December 1996 (14264) (unreported). The IAT also commented with regard to the issue of whether women in Iran could constitute a 'particular social group' that "we cannot see in principle why there should not be one". See this volume at 5.5.1 for further discussion.
[89] ibid.

There has also been some recognition in UK appeals that a political opinion may be imputed to a woman because of her relationship with male family members:

> **"The appellant shares her husband's political opinions and there is a reasonable possibility that if she were returned to Ethiopia she might be persecuted because of her association with her husband's activities. I have therefore concluded that the appellant does have a well-founded fear of persecution for a Convention reason."**[90]

5.5 Membership of a Particular Social Group

The UNHCR *Handbook* includes a definition of social group which is notable for its breadth and simplicity; "a 'particular social group' normally comprises persons of similar background, habits or social status."[91] Whilst noting that mere membership of a particular social group will not normally be enough to substantiate a claim to refugee status, the UNHCR *Handbook* does accept that "there may, however, be special circumstances where mere membership can be a sufficient ground to fear persecution."[92]

Given that the intentions of the drafters of the Convention remain opaque, it is perhaps not suprising that the interpretation of 'membership of a particular social group' should have provided the focus of extensive debate as to its meaning. What is clear however is a general consensus that any attempt at a definition should be open-ended so that it can include different groups suffering persecution:[93]

> **"A broad interpretation of the term social group is...the only reasonable interpretation."**[94]

> **"The intention of the framers of the Convention was...in order to provide a 'safety net' for asylum-seekers who, fleeing persecution, should qualify for refugee status but fail to fall neatly into one of the enumerated categories."**[95]

---

[90] Appeal No. HX/70796/95 (12th February 1996) (unreported)
[91] UNHCR *Handbook* 1979, paragraph 77
[92] ibid., paragraph 79
[93] See for example Grahl-Madsen 1966; Goodwin-Gill 1983; Hathaway 1991
[94] Helton 1983, 59
[95] Neal 1989, 229

Hathaway proposes a taxonomy of three alternative classes for social group membership which is closely reflected in the Supreme Court of Canada decision in *Ward*:[96]

1. Groups defined by an innate or unchangeable characteristic;

2. Groups whose members voluntarily associate for reasons so fundamental to their human dignity that they should not be forced to forsake the association;

3. Groups associated by a former voluntary status, unalterable due to historical permanence.

The most important point to note is that the court named gender, along with linguistic background and sexual orientation, as an example of a particular social group in the first category. Meanwhile as is noted in *Macdonald*[97], the definition of social group in the US case of *Acosta* has been widely cited:

"We interpret the phrase to mean persecution that is directed toward an individual who is a member of a group of persons all of whom share a common immutable characteristic. The shared characteristic might be an innate one such as sex, colour, or kinship ties, or in some circumstances it might be a shared characteristic that defines the group such as former military leadership or land ownership...whatever the common characteristic that defines the group, it must be one that the members of the group cannot change because it is fundamental to their individual identities or conscience. Only when this is the case does the mere fact of group membership become something comparable to the other four grounds for persecution."[98]

In other jurisdictions therefore the concept of social group has been carefully considered, but it has been fully canvassed before the English

---

[96] *Canada (Attorney General) v Ward* [1993] 2SCR 689
[97] Macdonald and Blake *Macdonald's Immigration Law and Practice in the United Kingdom* 1995, 394 paragraph 12.50
[98] *Acosta v INS* [1985] Int. Dec. 2986 (BIA)

courts only very recently in *Savchenkov*.[99] The court was referred to the approach of Hathaway and the decision in *Ward*.[100] The most important aspect of the case is that Treasury counsel advanced the view (not challenged by the court) that social group could be defined as follows:

1. **Membership of a group defined by some innate or unchangeable characteristic of its members analogous to race, religion, nationality or political opinion, for example, *their sex*, linguistic background, tribe, *family* or class;**

2. **Membership of a cohesive, homogenous group whose members are in a close voluntary association for reasons which are fundamental to their rights;**

3. **Former membership of the group covered in 2.[101]**

However, the Court also concluded that a social group for Convention purposes must be identifiable by something other than the risk of persecution and cannot be defined solely by common victimisation:

"The concept of a 'particular social group' must have been intended to apply to social groups which exist independently of the persecution. Otherwise the limited scope of the Convention would be defeated: there would be a social group, and so a right to asylum, whenever a number of persons fear persecution for a reason common to them."[102]

One of the implications of this ruling therefore is that the shared experience of women who have suffered violence is not sufficient to make them a social group unless the fact of their violation will, in the future, make them a target of persecution. In this context, the analysis must inevitably turn to the issue of whether women can be considered as members of a 'particular social group' on the basis of their gender. Family membership and sexuality will also be considered as forming the basis of social group membership especially given that the former is a

---

[99] *SSHD v Sergei Vasilyevich Savchenkov* [1996] Imm AR 28 (CA)
[100] *Canada (Attorney General) v Ward* [1993] 2 SCR 689
[101] *SSHD v Sergei Vasilyevich Savchenkov* [1996] Imm AR 28 (CA) (emphasis added)
[102] ibid.

critical aspect of the claims of many refugee women seeking asylum in the UK.

5.5.1 Gender-Defined Social Group

"While 'gender' is not itself a Convention ground, it may be a significant factor in recognising a particular social group or an identifying characteristic of such a group."[103]

That women constitute a particular social group within the meaning of the Convention definition has been the pervasive position in literature addressing gender-related persecution and the problem of establishing the persecution ground.[104] It is also the position taken by Hathaway:

"Gender is properly within the ambit of the social group category...[g]ender-based groups are clear examples of social subsets defined by an innate and immutable characteristic."[105]

He offers the example of single women living in a Moslem country without the protection of a male relative who suffer persecution as a result, pointing out that in this case group members cannot control gender or the absence of male relatives, and that choice of marital status is a fundamental human right that no one should be required to relinquish. The argument then is that women constitute a social group both because they share certain 'immutable' characteristics and because they are frequently treated differently from men; "[t]o a greater extent than most social groups, women are an easily identifiable 'group'...possessing a combination of biologically and socially attributed characteristics."[106] This position suggests that 'more liberal interpretation', 'innovative use' and 'development' of the concept of social group membership would meet the protection needs of women seeking asylum.

Certainly the use of the particular social group basis of the refugee definition to extend protection to women who face persecution for

---

[103] ADIMA *Guidelines on Gender Issues for Decision Makers* July 1996, paragraph 4.33 (Annex 6)
[104] See for example Neal 1988; Greatbach 1989; Stairs and Pope 1990; Castel 1992; Goldberg 1993; Fullerton 1993; Kelly 1993, 1994; Binion 1995
[105] Hathaway 1991, 591
[106] Stairs and Pope 1990, 167

having transgressed religious or social mores finds strong support in the pronouncements of the UNHCR and governmental bodies and the administrative decisions of several countries. During the 1980s, the UNHCR adopted a series of Executive Committee Conclusions aimed at affording more meaningful protection to women fleeing persecution in their home countries,[107] and its *Guidelines on the Protection of Refugee Women* (1991) encourage states to address the claims of women who face violence as severe as death for violating social mores under the particular social group category. Meanwhile, as early as 1984 the European Parliament adopted a resolution calling upon states to accord refugee status to women within the particular social group category in certain circumstances, a position reflected in the policies of the Dutch Refugee Council.[108] The CIRB has also affirmed gender-related social group classification in cases involving Lebanese, Turkish Moslem and Sri Lankan Tamil women reflecting a recognition of gender-based social groups in its own *Guidelines*:

"Gender is an innate characteristic and, therefore, women may form a particular social group within the Convention refugee definition."[109]

The argument for framing the asylum claims of women with 'particular social group' as their persecution ground is, therefore, a powerful one and has also proved a relatively acceptable approach in some jurisdictions.[110] Yet there are both political and strategic concerns associated with arguing for women as a social group which should be recognised. The first of these relates to the size of the social group itself, although this argument has no basis in fact or reason:

"The fact that the particular social group consists of large numbers of the female population in the country concerned is *irrelevant* - race, religion, nationality and political opinion are also characteristics that are shared by large numbers of people."[111]

---

[107] See Annex 4
[108] See Schilders 1988
[109] CIRB *Guidelines on Women Refugee Claimants Fearing Gender-Related Persecution: UPDATE* November 1996, A.III (Annex 5, 191)
[110] See this volume at 5.5.1.1
[111] CIRB *Guidelines on Women Refugee Claimants Fearing Gender-Related Persecution: UPDATE* November 1996, A.III (Annex 5, 191)

Recognising that some 'women' constitute a 'particular social group' does not lead inexorably to the consequence that all women are automatically entitled to refugee status; the applicant will still be required to establish that the fear of persecution was well-founded, that the nature of the harm inflicted or anticipated rises to the level of serious harm,[112] and that there was a failure of state protection.[113] Nonetheless, the reality is that the perceived size of the prospective social group *is* important in a context where there is an overall trend towards trying to reduce the number of asylum-seekers and limit recognition rates.

Arguing that 'women' *per se* constitute a 'particular social group' is therefore unlikely to be widely accepted not simply because of the issue of numbers but because in reality 'women' are not a cohesive group: even within individual countries, women fall into their own sub-groups - economically, socially and culturally. Whilst there are undoubtedly cases where gender alone is the basis for persecutory treatment, more often the persecution is not applied equally to *all* women. Neal offers the example of a woman who is forced to flee because she has in some way violated oppressive laws and regulations imposed by the government and fears persecution, possibly even in the form of execution, as a result. Whilst these rules are specific to women "not every woman who comes from an oppressive society will qualify [for refugee status],"[114] partly because women have different experiences of these rules but also because the relationship between the persecution and the ground will vary dependent upon the circumstances of the individual woman. Despite the arguments in favour of recognising women as a social group therefore, the very assumption that women have common experiences which can be explained by reference to their gender alone can itself undermine the argument.

Examining more vigorously the relationship between the nature of persecutory measures against women and the potential grounds of the application shows that in many cases such claims can be framed within more conventional and accepted grounds if gender relations, which by implication involve issues of power, are reconceptualised. Going beyond the public/private dichotomy, it could be argued that women who refuse to comply with or transgress social mores, are not being persecuted because they are women but because they are actively

---

[112] See Chapter 3 of this volume
[113] See Chapter 4 of this volume
[114] Neal 1988, 245

opposing a political/religious norm. Returning to the example cited by Hathaway of 'single women living in a Moslem country without the protection of a male relative' as constituting a particular social group within the meaning of the definition, it could be argued that such women are actually being persecuted because they are expressing a political or religious opinion. This case highlights the importance of examining and framing each claim on the basis of the individual woman's experience. If women have chosen to live without a male relative and are then persecuted because of this decision, the ground should be political opinion (or at the very least imputed political opinion). The level of proactivity on the part of the applicant then becomes critical; by subsuming the claims of all women into the social group category proactivity may be lost. In many cases, the asylum claims of women argued on a social group basis are more likely to fail than the claims of men, in part because the relationship between persecution and ground is incorrectly conceptualised.

"The important principle to consider is whether the persecution suffered or feared is *for reasons of* membership of a particular social group."[115]

Framing the appellant's claim with race, nationality, religion or political opinion (actual or imputed) as the grounds for the persecution not only more accurately reflects women's specific experiences in many cases, but also enables the representative to argue that the claim fits comfortably within the Convention and that she should be granted full refugee status. Strategically it is also the favoured approach given the Home Office position on the issue of social group:

"The UK Government interprets paragraph (k) of EXCOM 39 as indicating *no obligation* to grant asylum on the basis of women being a social group...gender is taken into account in the assessment of individual asylum claims where this is relevant. However, casework experience suggests that in practice few, if any, asylum applications made in the UK by women turn solely on the question of gender-based persecution."[116]

---

[115] ADIMA *Guidelines on Gender Issues for Decision Makers* July 1996, paragraph 4.33 (emphasis in original) (Annex 6)

[116] UK Response to a questionnaire to governments participating in the *UNHCR Symposium on Gender-Based Persecution* February 1996, Geneva (unpublished)

Nonetheless, recent case law, most notably *Shah*,[117] has challenged this position. As a result it may be possible to argue that sub-sets of women within a particular context form a social group without defining that group in terms of the persecution itself:

"**These particular social groups can be identified by reference to factors, in addition to gender, which may be innate or unchangeable characteristics. Examples of other such characteristics are age, race, marital status and economic status. In determining whether these factors are unchangeable, consideration should be given to the cultural and social context in which the woman lives, as well as the perception of the agents of persecution and those responsible for providing state protection.**"[118]

"**Gender may be combined with certain other characteristics which could define a particular social group in situations where there is evidence that this group suffers or fears severe discrimination or harsh and inhuman treatment that is distinguished from the situation of others of the same gender.**"[119]

In this context it is important that appropriate case law is developed which responds to the needs of gender-defined social groups:

"**An approach to refugee determination which unjustifiably favours the political opinion ground to the exclusion of the social group ground will tend to reinforce the male gender bias complained of by female asylum seekers, and inhibit the development of refugee jurisprudence which properly recognises and accommodates gender issues within the legitimate bounds of the Refugee Convention.**"[120]

---

[117] *R v IAT and SSHD ex p Syeda Khatoon Shah*, QBD 25th October 1996 (unreported). It should be noted that at the time of writing this decision is in the process of being appealed by the Home Office and the outcome is unknown. The details and reasoning in *Shah* are discussed at 5.5.1.1

[118] CIRB *Guidelines on Women Refugee Claimants Fearing Gender-Related Persecution: UPDATE* November 1996, A.III (Annex 5, 191)

[119] ADIMA *Guidelines on Gender Issues for Decision Makers* July 1996, paragraph 4.33 (Annex 6)

[120] New Zealand Refugee Status Appeals Authority Appeal No. 2039/93 (12th February 1996)

There are clearly cases where gender is the most critical aspect of the applicant's case. For example, when a woman faces the prospect of genital mutilation, dowry burning or being forced to enter an arranged marriage, the grounds of religion or political opinion may prove to be inapposite to her refugee claim. These examples and others are examined below.

"Every day, thousands of women are beaten in their homes by their partners, and thousands more are raped, assaulted and sexually harassed. And, there are the less recognised forms of violence: in Nepal, female babies die from neglect because parents value sons over daughters; in Sudan, girls' genitals are mutilated to ensure virginity until marriage; and in India, young brides are murdered by their husbands when parents fail to provide enough dowry. In all these instances, women are targets of violence because of their sex. This is not random violence; the risk factor is being female."[121]

A. Social Mores and Discrimination

It has been suggested throughout this chapter that religion or political opinion (actual or imputed) may be a more appropriate basis than social group on which to make a claim for asylum for a woman who has been deemed to have violated social mores.[122] This position is reinforced by recent British jurisprudence, most notably in the case of *Ahmady*.[123] However, a woman who is gravely discriminated against without ever offering resistance, for example if she has been divorced by her husband or accused of adultery, may find it difficult to substantiate her plea of being persecuted on one of the other grounds enumerated in the Convention, and the social group strategy may be the preferred, and possibly only, option. **Much will depend upon the details of the particular case and the religious and political context in which the discrimination took place.**

B. Female Genital Mutilation

As with some institutionalised forms of gender-related discrimination, social group may be the only possible ground for claims involving FGM

---

[121] Heise 1989, 12
[122] See this volume at 5.4.3
[123] *Abdollah Fathi and Mashid Ahmady v SSHD*, IAT 1st December 1996 (14264) (unreported). See also this volume at 5.3 and 5.4

because in certain contexts it *is* women *per se* who are targeted for this practice, although the relationship between the harm inflicted or feared and the reason for that harm must, as in all cases, be carefully examined.

It is important that the representative establishes whether it is the practice itself or the consequences of a refusal to submit to female genital mutilation which constitutes the persecution.

If it is the practice itself which is deemed to be inherently persecutory then it may be possible to construct the social group using some other criteria which narrows the grouping further even than nationality, as in 'women from a certain tribe or ethnic affiliation', a construction of social group which was recently accepted in the US case of *Kasinga*.[124]

C. Violence Within the Family

Establishing the failure of state protection in cases involving violence within the family has proved problematic because such violence is conceived of as 'private', a situation which is exacerbated by its occurrence in the geographically and ideologically 'private' sphere of the home[125]. Equally as significant in such cases however has been finding a categorical basis for the persecution. In this context there are two possible ways to characterise the group in claims based upon violence within the family. Firstly, it could be argued that women fleeing violence within the family are members of a social group of 'women':

"This social group must be seen in a social context where women are considered or treated as inferior to men, as property of men and as subject to male domination without regard to their own will. It could be argued that the state is failing to protect [a woman] simply by virtue of the fact of her gender - it is only due to her gender that another individual is allowed to beat her or threaten her on an ongoing basis - and it is only due to her gender that she is denied protection, either through lack of recourse or through failure or refusal to enforce existing laws that could protect her against such conduct."[126]

---

[124] For further details see *The Independent* 06.05.96, *The New York Times* 22.06.96, *The Guardian* 06.07.96 and also this volume at 5.5.1.1
[125] See this volume at 3.4 and 4.2.4
[126] Goldberg 1993, 597

Alternatively the social group could be defined as 'women who are battered and have no recourse to state protection':

"By definition, all victims of crime experience a failure of state protection, yet victims of crime do not qualify as refugees *per se*. What distinguishes women...is that the nature of the abuse and the chronic failure of state protection evince and sustain the unequal status of women in society."[127]

Here the argument is that it is the state's failure to protect the battered woman that makes acts of violence within the family rise to the level of persecution. The woman is not being denied protection because she is a woman *per se* (if that same woman were assaulted on the street by an unknown assailant she would receive police assistance) but because her attacker is her husband, boyfriend, father or other male intimate. The problem with this argument however stems largely from the ruling in *Savchenkov*[128] that the social group must exist independently of the persecution. To describe a social group of 'women who are battered' does not explain *why* such harm occurred; it simply notes that there are characteristics which are common to a number of individuals.[129] This construction also contradicts the concept of social group as constituting those with innate or unchangeable characteristics. Clearly therefore a statistical grouping which is based upon a description of the persecution suffered or feared, even if the victims coincidentally share a particular characteristic, will not be seen to constitute a particular social group within the meaning of the Convention. In the UK this argument can clearly be seen in *Islam*:[130]

---

[127] Macklin 1995, 244
[128] *SSHD v Sergei Vasilyevich Savchenkov* [1996] Imm AR 28 (CA)
[129] There are many examples, even within Canadian jurisprudence, where this line of argument has failed. Fullerton (1993) for example, cites the case of a woman from Trinidad and Tobago who had been abused by her husband for years and whose complaints to the police had been of no avail. After fifteen years of marriage, she fled to Canada and sought asylum based on her persecution due to her membership in 'the social group of Trinidadian women subject to wife beating'. The Federal Court of Appeal upheld the original decision to deny the woman asylum on the basis that her ground was unsatisfactory; in particular the judge questioned whether fear of a particular type of persecution could be the sole distinguishing factor of a 'particular social group'.
[130] *Shahanna Sadiq Islam and others v SSHD*, IAT 2nd October 1996 (13956) (unreported). Representatives should note that this case is being appealed at the time of writing.

"We do not consider that Pakistani women subject to violence within the family are a social group within the Convention. That they are simply women does not make them a social group: the only common characteristic identified is that they are subject to violence within marriage: the only common feature, beyond their sex, is the persecution to which they are alleged to be subject within marriage - that is the persecution itself."[131]

D. Marriage Related Harm[132]

As in cases of social mores and discrimination and FGM, the framing of cases involving marriage related harm within the enumerated ground of social group membership will be dependent upon the particular circumstances of the claim, and in particular whether the persecutory treatment; is the marriage related harm itself (as for example in dowry death and *sati*); the persecutory consequences of refusal to submit to such treatment (as for example in refusing to accept forced marriage or *Mut'a*); or the consequences for a woman of events which may be beyond her control (such as divorce or accusations of adultery).

Potentially there are cases involving marriage related harm which are closely related to social mores and discrimination as a result of which a political opinion has been imputed to the women concerned. In this context it is vital that representatives, through careful consultation with their client and research on conditions for women in the applicant's country of origin, establish at an early stage, the most appropriate basis for the claim.

E. Forced Sterilisation and Abortion

It should be noted that in the context of China's one child policy, there may be cases where the grounds for the persecution are those of actual or imputed political opinion as opposed to social group.[133] For example, if the sterilisation or abortion is seen as effectively constituting punishment for refusal to abide by government policies or if other penalties were imposed which constituted discrimination rising to the level of

---

[131] *Shahanna Sadiq Islam and others v SSHD*, IAT 2nd October 1996 (13956) (unreported)
[132] See also this volume at 3.5, 4.1.2 and 4.2.5
[133] See this volume at 5.4.3

persecution,[134] then the grounds for the claim could be argued as actual or imputed political opinion. The only significant case law on this issue comes from Canada, where following the release of the *Guidelines*, the Federal Court of Appeal held in *Cheung*[135] that Chinese women who bear more than one child, and as a result face forced sterilisation "form a particular social group so as to come within the meaning of a Convention refugee":

> **"These people comprise a group sharing similar social status and hold a similar interest which is not held by their government. They have certain basic characteristics in common. All of the people coming within this group are united or identified by a purpose which is so fundamental to their basic human dignity that they should not be required to alter it on the basis that interference with a woman's reproductive liberty is a basic right ranking high in our scale of values."[136]**

What is of interest in this characterisation is the inclusion of the nature of the persecution feared in defining the particular social group. The Court also found that forced or strongly coerced sterilisation in the context of China's one child policy constitutes persecution because it violates Articles 3 and 5 of the *Universal Declaration of Human Rights*.

5.5.1.1 Case Law
Canada
The Canadian *Guidelines* address the social group category by acknowledging that there is increasing international support for the application of the particular social group ground to the claims of women who allege a fear of persecution by reasons of their gender. The *Guidelines* divide women refugee claimants into four broad categories, although they acknowledge that these categories are not mutually exclusive or exhaustive:[137]

---

[134] See this volume at 3.2, 3.6 and 4.1.2
[135] *Cheung v Canada (MEI)* [1993] F.C.A. no. A-785-91
[136] ibid.
[137] CIRB *Guidelines on Women Refugee Claimants Fearing Gender-Related Persecution: UPDATE* November 1996, A.I (Annex 5, 187-188) (emphasis in original)

- **Women who fear persecution on the *same Convention grounds, and in similar circumstances, as men.*** That is, the risk factor is not their sexual status, *per se*, but rather their particular identity or what they believe in or are perceived to believe in;[138]

- **Women who fear persecution solely for reasons pertaining to kinship i.e. because of the status, activities or views of their spouses, parents and siblings, or other family members;[139]**

- **Women who fear persecution resulting from certain circumstances of *severe discrimination on grounds of gender* or *acts of violence* either by public authorities or at the hands of private citizens from whose actions the state is unwilling or unable to adequately protect the concerned persons;[140]**

- **Women who fear persecution as the consequence of failing to conform to, or for transgressing, certain gender-discriminating religious or customary laws and practices in their country of origin.[141]**

Claims of the fourth category may be determined on grounds of religious or political opinion but also on grounds of membership in 'particular social group' according to the following reasoning:

"Such laws and practices, by singling out women and placing them in a more vulnerable position than men, may create conditions for the existence of a *gender-defined social group*. The religious precepts, social traditions or cultural norms which women may be accused of violating can range from choosing their own spouses instead of accepting an arranged marriage, to matters such as the wearing of make-up, the visibility or length of hair, or the type of clothing a woman chooses to wear." [142]

---

[138] See this volume at 5.1, 5.2, 5.3 and 5.4
[139] See this volume at 5.4.3 and 5.5
[140] See Chapters 3 and 4 of this volume
[141] See this volume at 3.2, 4.1.2, 5.4 and 5.5.1
[142] CIRB *Guidelines on Women Refugee Claimants Fearing Gender-Related Persecution: UPDATE* November 1996, A.I (Annex 5, 188) (emphasis in original)

Even before the *Guidelines* were issued, the CIRB had on several occasions found women refugee claimants to have a well-founded fear of persecution by reason of membership in a particular social group:

A claimant and her two daughters had a well-founded fear of persecution on the basis of their membership of a particular social group, "consisting of women and girls who do not conform to Islamic fundamentalist norms".[143]

A Somali claimant was found to be a refugee on the basis of her membership of a particular social group, "young women without male protection".[144]

A woman who was a divorced woman living under the jurisdiction of Sharia law had a well-founded fear of persecution by reason of her membership in a particular social group of "women".[145]

A woman was found to be a member of a particular social group composed of women who belong to a "women's organisation objecting to the treatment of women in Iran".[146]

Recent Canadian case law supports the argument that claims of women fleeing domestic or intimate violence can be made under the social group category.[147] There have also been successful asylum claims involving FGM:

"The panel finds that the minor female claimant is a member of two particular social groups, namely, women and minors. Her gender is clearly an 'innate or unchangeable characteristic', and the fact that she is below the age of majority is also, for the foreseeable future, something she cannot change."[148]

---

[143] CRDD T-89-06969, T89-06970, T89-06971 (17th July 1990)
[144] CRDD U91-04008 (December 24th 1991)
[145] CRDD T93-05935/36 (31st December 1993)
[146] CRDD T89-02248 (3rd April 1990)
[147] See for example *Narvaex v MCI* [1995] 92 FC 55 and *Diluna v MEI* [1995] 29 2d 156 Imm LR
[148] CRDD Y93-12197,12198,12199 (10th May 1994)

In deciding this case of a Somali woman and her children, the panel explicitly referred to *Ward*,[149] adopting a broad approach to designating the relevant social groups.

United States

The use of 'particular social group' as a grounds for seeking Convention refugee status has evolved in the US through judgements in *Acosta*,[150] *Ananeh-Firempong*[151] and, more recently, *Sanchez-Trijillo*,[152] in which the Court of Appeal used a four point test to evaluate a 'social group' claim. In *Gomez*[153] the Court used the same reasoning as *Sanchez-Trijillo*, adding that it was necessary "that society at large perceive that the women claiming membership to the particular group belong to that group".

It is apparent from both the guidelines released by the INS and the response of the US at the UNHCR *Symposium on Gender-Based Persecution* held in Geneva in February 1996, that the INS can in certain circumstances recognise female asylum seekers as comprising a 'particular social group' within the meaning of domestic and international law:

> **"The concept of 'immutable characteristic' is the most commonly used criterion for determining the existence of a 'particular social group' in the United States. Women asylum seekers appear to satisfy the immutability requirement."**[154]

Although not unchallenged, there is strong authority in US jurisprudence for the proposition that gender, either alone or in combination with other immutable characteristics, can define a 'particular social group'. In *Fatin*[155] for example, the applicant's primary argument was not that she risked harm simply for being female. Rather, she argued that she risked harm as a member of a "very visible and specific subgroup: Iranian women who *refuse to conform* to the government's gender-specific laws and social norms". This group, the court noted, is not made up of all

---

[149] *Canada (Attorney General) v Ward* [1993] 2SCR 689
[150] *Acosta v INS* [1985] Int. Dec. 2986 (BIA)
[151] *Ananeh-Firempong v INS* [1985] 766 F.2d 261 (1st Circuit)
[152] *Sanchez-Trijillo v INS* [1989] 801 F2d 1572 (9th Circuit)
[153] *Gomez v INS* [1991] 947 F2d 660 (2nd Circuit)
[154] US response to a questionnaire to governments participating in the UNHCR *Symposium on Gender-Based Persecution* February 1996, Geneva (unpublished)
[155] *Fatin v INS* [1993]12 F.3d 1233 (3rd Circuit)

Iranian women who hold feminist views, nor even of all those who object to the rules that govern women in that country. It is limited to a smaller group of women who so strongly object that they refuse to conform, despite the risk of severe punishment.[156]

This authority regarding social group has been reinforced by the successful case of *Kasinga*[157] which involved female genital mutilation.[158] In a narrow ruling which "decline[d] to speculate on, or establish rules for, cases that are not before us", an immigration service report was cited which noted that "it remains particularly true that women have little legal recourse and may undergo threats to their freedom, threats or acts of violence, or social ostracisation for refusing to undergo this harmful traditional practice, or attempting to protect their female children."[159] Specific reference was made in the determination to the applicant's tribal grouping.

Australia

The leading cases of the Federal Court in Australia which establish the principles of social group are *Morato*,[160] *Kuldip Ram*[161] and *MIEA v A&B*.[162] It is apparent from these determinations that social group must be recognisable in the sense that a decision-maker has evidence of a common unifying element binding the members of the group. In addition Australian law requires the decision-maker to be satisfied that a particular social group exists because of an individual's inherent characteristics; that is, what a person is, rather than what she has done. In arriving at these conclusions on the proper interpretation of particular social group, it is significant to note that the Federal Court has relied heavily on leading international jurisprudence, especially from Canada and the US. The implication is that women cannot be a social group *per se* because not *all* women are subjected to persecution and that neither can a group of women be defined by the type of harm that they have suffered, for example 'women from Ghana subjected to domestic violence'.

---

[156] INS *Considerations for Asylum Officers Adjudicating Asylum Claims from* Women June 1995, 14
[157] For further details see *The Independent* 06.05.96, *The New York Times* 22.06.96 and *The Guardian* 06.07.96
[158] See this volume at 3.3, 4.2.3 and 5.5.1
[159] See *Feminist News*, 14 June 1996 http://www.feminist.org/news/newsbyte/june96
[160] *Morato v MILGEA* (21st December 1992)
[161] *Kuldip Ram v MIEA* (27th June 1995)
[162] *MIEA v A & B* (16th June 1995)

New Zealand

In a recent case, which was noted at 5.3, an Iranian woman harassed by both the Komiteh and by her male family members to ensure that she acted within the confines of Islamic dress and behavioural codes was found to have been persecuted for reasons of religion and imputed political opinion.[163] In addition the determination considered whether a woman fleeing such treatment could be considered as belonging to a 'particular social group' within the meaning of the Convention. It found that she clearly could:

> "The appellant's case is that the punishment, disproportionately severe penalties and intense discrimination faced by her in Iran are the result of her holding deeply held values, beliefs and convictions fundamentally at odds with the power structure in Iran. But is she a member of a particular social group? On the evidence we have heard and upon an extensive survey of the literature and case law, we are satisfied that there are a number of women in Iran who share the appellant's values, beliefs and convictions. They are characteristics which they ought not to be required to change. We are of the opinion that it would be profoundly abhorrent to require of the appellant that she surrender these values, beliefs and convictions, going as they do to her fundamental civil and political rights, her very identity, her dignity and existence as a human being. Our preliminary view is that the group is clearly cognizable as a social group and is perceived as such by the authorities and Iranian society in general."[164]

France

The Refugee Appeal Commission has accepted that FGM may amount to persecution and that women wishing to avoid FGM can be considered as members of a 'particular social group'. This is reflected in *Aminata Diop*,[165] where the applicant claimed refugee status after she left Mali because of mistreatment by her family for refusing to undergo FGM.

---

[163] New Zealand Refugee Status Appeals Authority Appeal No. 2039/93 (12th February 1996)

[164] ibid.

[165] CCR 164078 (18th August 1991). The Commission did not however grant her refugee status because she could not adequately document her claim.

United Kingdom
There is as yet very limited case law in the UK which recognises gender-defined social groups despite the fact that *Macdonald* refers to the existence of relevant international jurisprudence.[166] In addition decisions at first level appeals are totally contradictory in their approach to this issue.

For many years the only authority on the possibility for claims to be made on the basis of a gender-defined social group was *Gilani*[167] which concerned a woman fleeing discrimination in Iran. Although it was accepted by the IAT that the penalties for transgressing against social mores of dress and behaviour could amount to persecution, it was not accepted that a woman from Iran ran the risk of persecution solely for being a woman. Women were not considered to be a social group because "many women in Iran seem content with their lot", and because the social group did not exist independently of the persecution itself. The Tribunal also considered whether 'Westernised women' constituted a social group in the Iranian context. Whilst the Tribunal agreed that "the transgression of social mores could help to create a social group based on that transgression - just as transgression of a religious belief may create such a group", it did not accept that 'Westernised women' are an identified or identifiable group in Iran:

> "The opposition to the dress and other aspects of the Islamic approach adopted in Iran remains individually based and there is no evidence that there is any recognition that that those opposing look upon themselves as a group distinguished from other women."[168]

This ruling is reflected in *Ranjbar*[169] which involved violence within the family. The IAT overruled the reasoning of the adjudicator that she was a member of a particular social group, "namely those who are subject to physical attack as the result of being female child of a person who expresses his institutionalised attitude to women in the form of physical attacks which fall within the category of inhuman or degrading treatment". The Tribunal accepted the following statements by the Secretary of State in the grounds of the appeal:

---

[166] Macdonald and Blake *Macdonald's Immigration Law and Practice in the United Kingdom* 1995, 396 paragraph 12.54
[167] *Mashid Mahmoudi Gilani v SSHD*, IAT 3rd June 1987 (5216) (unreported)
[168] ibid.
[169] *SSHD v Fatema Fironz Ranjbar*, IAT 28th June 1994 (11105) (unreported)

- "The United Kingdom believes that gender alone is too broad a category to apply; 'persecution' cannot be on the basis of gender alone but must relate to the applicant's race, religion, nationality or political opinion;

- Not all Iranian women will be beaten by their fathers. There is no indication that the applicant was beaten because of her gender or because she had transgressed the social mores of the society in which she lived."[170]

A similar position has also been taken by the IAT in *Islam*.[171]

"We do not consider that Pakistani women subject to violence within the family are a social group within the Convention. That they are simply women does not make them a social group: the only common characteristic identified is that they are subject to violence within marriage: the only common feature, beyond their sex, is the persecution to which they are alleged to be subject within marriage - that is the persecution itself." [172]

The argument by the Home Office that gender cannot form the basis of a claim under social group unless related in some way to the four enumerated grounds is a particularly dangerous one in so far as it totally undermines the independent existence of 'particular social group' as a ground for persecution.[173] It is apparent that these cases have had a significant influence on first level appeal determinations involving violence within the family and/or punishment for transgressing social mores:

"It is submitted that the appellant belongs to a more narrow category of the social group consisting of abused wives...However this would mean that the whole of the female population of such

[170] *SSHD v Fatema Fironz Ranjbar*, IAT 28th June 1994 (11105) (unreported)
[171] *Shahanna Sadiq Islam and others v SSHD*, IAT 2nd October 1996 (13956) (unreported). Currently under appeal.
[172] ibid.
[173] A similar argument has also been made and upheld with regard to family membership as the basis for a claim under the social group ground, and is discussed in detail in this volume at 5.5.2

countries as adopt Islamic law in a fundamentalist or extreme version would automatically acquire the right of asylum or at least those who could show some abuse by their partners would fall into a defined category...an innocent wife who has been abused or may suffer abuse, does not in my view form part of a social group within the meaning of the Convention."[174]

In this case, which concerned a Pakistani woman accused of adultery by her violent husband, the adjudicator dismissed the appeal but strongly recommended that ELR be granted recognising, contradictorily, "that it is clear that the appellant would suffer at least ostracism if not punishment on her return to Pakistan by reason of the vindictive action taken by her husband in the context of society where the appellant would be regarded as having transgressed the norms associated with the wives in particular and women in general in Pakistan".

More recently the case of *Shah*[175] has addressed these issues. The applicant was a battered wife from Pakistan who had finally been forced to flee from her husband and came to the UK with her six children. On arrival however she found that she was pregnant. If she had returned to Pakistan she would have nowhere but her husband's house to go. She has given birth and now credibly fears that if she has to return she will be accused by him of conceiving the child adulterously, exposing her to the operation of the Shiria statute law which prescribes stoning to death as the punishment for adultery. The special adjudicator had initially dismissed her appeal on the grounds that she did not find that the persecution or the fear of persecution fell within the terms of the Convention. The key to the special adjudicator's decision was the meaning of social group. The applicant's case had been that she belonged to a definable group, namely women who had suffered domestic violence in Pakistan, although in the High Court this was recast as women who are perceived to have transgressed Islamic mores. Mr Justice Sedley quashed the determination of the IAT by which leave to appeal from the special adjudicator's decision was refused. He did not however explicitly accept that women could constitute a particular social group in these circumstances, and indeed made comments to the contrary:

---

[174] Appeal No. HX/75169/94 (2nd January 1996) (unreported)
[175] *R v IAT and SSHD ex p Syeda Khatoon Shah*, QBD 25th October 1996 (unreported). *Shah* is currently being appealed and will be heard on 20th May 1997.

159

> **"I am not convinced by the endeavour to fit women in the applicant's prospective situation into the category of a group defined by an innate or unchangeable characteristic."[176]**

Mr Justice Sedley emphasised the dangers of a prescriptive approach to the issue of social group which respects the potential breadth of the category. Nonetheless subsequent determinations have acknowledged the decision to allow the appeal. In the case of an Iranian woman who feared that if she were to return to Iran her life and liberty would be in danger both from the state and/or her husband because of her adultery, the Special Adjudicator, noting *Shah*,[177] concluded that the appellant had established a Convention ground for her persecution on the basis of membership of a particular social group:

> **"She is a woman who forms part of a group of women who face harsh and inhuman treatment due to their having transgressed the social mores of Iran which, to my mind, questionably bring into consideration, a breach of fundamental human rights as it is reasonably likely that she would be killed as a result of her having committed adultery, were she to be returned to that country. For those reasons, I am satisfied that this appellant has established that she has a well-founded fear of persecution for a Convention reason and...I allow this appeal."[178]**

Given that the current jurisprudence on gender-defined social groups is undecided but that *Savchenkov*[179] clearly recognises that gender is an immutable characteristic, the potential for pursuing this line of argument in cases involving women fleeing gender-based persecution is unclear. Following the determination in the case of *Ahmady*,[180] it remains that actual or imputed political opinion is potentially a more useful way of framing cases involving discrimination and the violation of social mores, both strategically insofar as it is a more accepted ground for refugee status, and politically in that it recognises the diversity of women's

---

[176] *R v IAT and SSHD ex p Syeda Khatoon Shah*, QBD 25th October 1996 (unreported). *Shah* is currently being appealed and will be heard on 20th May 1997.
[177] ibid.
[178] Appeal No. HX/83732/95 (30th December 1996) (unreported)
[179] *SSHD v Sergei Vasilyevich Savchenkov* [1996] Imm AR 28 (CA)
[180] *Abdollah Fathi and Mashid Ahmady v SSHD*, IAT 1st December 1996 (14264) (unreported). This case and its implications are considered in this volume at 5.4.4

experiences and locates them in their political and social context.[181] As was suggested earlier however, in cases where gender is the only basis for the persecution, for example in some cases of female genital mutilation, forced sterilisation and abortion, violence within the family and marriage related harm, future developments in *Shah*[182] will clearly be very important.

5.5.2 Family Membership

"Cases of *'persecution of kin'* typically involve violence or other forms of harassment against women, who are not themselves accused of any antagonistic views or political convictions, in order to pressure them into revealing information about the whereabouts or the political activities of their family members."[183]

"There are also cases where persecutors are aware that a woman possesses no political opinion but persecute her as a means of demoralising the rest of her family or community who do hold a political opinion hostile to the current administration."[184]

Many women have been persecuted or face persecution because of the status, activities or views of their spouses, parents, children and siblings or other family members. Such cases often involve violence, arbitrary imprisonment or other forms of abuse of women who are not themselves accused of holding any antagonistic views or political convictions. The harm to these women is often a means of intimidating, coercing or harming the family members who hold dissenting political views or who engage in political activities which are disapproved of by the persecutor. In other cases women are harmed in order to pressure them into revealing information concerning the whereabouts or the political activities of their family members, examples of which have been widely reported by Amnesty International.[185] Recognition of the family as a social group may be crucial therefore in situations where women are threatened, harassed and victimised, either as a means of 'punishing' the man -

---

[181] See this volume at 5.4.3
[182] *R v IAT and SSHD ex p Syeda Khatoon Shah*, QBD 25th October 1996 (unreported)
[183] CIRB *Guidelines on Women Refugee Claimants Fearing Gender Related Persecution: UPDATE* November 1996, A.I (Annex 5, 187)
[184] ADIMA *Guidelines on Gender Issues for Decision Makers* July 1996, paragraph 4.27 (Annex 6)
[185] Amnesty International 1991

whether he be a husband, father, brother, son or uncle - by violating his female kin, or as a means of obtaining information. This view is endorsed by commentators such as Hathaway:

"Wherever there is an indication that the status or the activity of a claimant's relatives is the basis for a risk of persecution, a claim grounded in family background is properly receivable."[186]

Many cases however may be properly argued as having a political ground because the political opinions of their male relatives are imputed to the women.[187] As Macklin notes, women's identities, beliefs and status are frequently subsumed under those of their male kin.[188] Thus it seems reasonable to infer that a woman's kinship association with men could precipitate her persecution on the basis of imputed political opinion regardless of the opinion she actually holds.

Such is the importance of family membership for women seeking asylum that in some cases, her case may be stronger than that of the family member with whom she was associated. It should not be of concern for example, whether that family member was being *prosecuted* as opposed to *persecuted*; the fact remains that the appellant was persecuted on an accepted Convention ground although this has recently been challenged in the UK.[189] It should also be noted that the applicant's gender need not play any role in whether family membership can define a particular social group in the context of a particular case; indeed, some of the most relevant case law may involve male appellants. Nonetheless, claims based on family membership are frequently asserted by female applicants, particularly in countries where men tend to be more politically active than women. ·

5.5.2.1 Case Law
Canada
The Canadian *Guidelines* highlight the family as an example of a particular social group that is more or less uncontroversial in Canadian jurisprudence:

---

[186] Hathaway 1991, 165-166
[187] See this volume at 5.4.3
[188] Macklin 1995
[189] *Fabian Martinez Quijano v SSHD*, CA 18th December 1996 (unreported). See this volume at 5.5.2.1 for further details.

"There is jurisprudential authority for recognising claims grounded in familial association (i.e. where kinship is the risk factor) as coming within the ambit of the 'membership in a particular social group' category."[190]

Several decisions have found women to be members of a particular social group, the family:

- An Iranian woman was recognised as being a member of "a pro-Shah family";[191]

- A Peruvian woman was recognised because of her family membership;[192]

- A Guatemalan woman was found to be a member of the social group, a "targeted family";[193]

- A Salvadoran claimant was found to belong to a particular social group, her husband's family.[194]

United States

"There can, in fact, be no plainer example of a social group based on common, identifiable and immutable characteristics than that of the nuclear family...the link between family membership and persecution is manifest: the Ethiopian security forces applied to the petitioner the time-honoured theory of *cherchez la famille* (look for the family), the terrorisation of one family member to extract information about the location of another family member or to force the family member to come forward."[195]

---

[190] CIRB *Guidelines on Women Refugee Claimants Fearing Gender-Related Persecution: UPDATE* November 1996, A.III (Annex 5, 190)
[191] CRDD M89-00057 (16th February 1989)
[192] CRDD M89-00971 (13th June 1989)
[193] CRDD T89-02313, T89-02314, T89-02315) (17th October 1990)
[194] CRDD C90-00299, C90-00300) (18th December 1990)
[195] *Gebremicheal v INS* [1993] 10 F.3d (1st Circuit). This case concerned an Ethiopian applicant who had been imprisoned and tortured by Dergue government officials seeking information about the applicant's brother.

This decision appears to follow the pronouncement of the BIA in *Acosta*[196] that 'kinship ties' could be the shared characteristic defining a particular social group.

United Kingdom

> **"Clearly, there is no more obvious example of a social group than a family."**[197]

In *Hernandez*,[198] the IAT accepted that a widowed woman from Colombia had been persecuted because of the activities of her husband and that because of his death the appellant and her daughter were unable to leave that particular family. This reasoning has also been accepted in first level appeals. For example, in the case of a woman whose husband was collaborating with the authorities against the drug cartels, the adjudicator referred to Hathaway in making his decision:

> **"It seems to me that it would be a serious anomaly if the appellant formed part of the social group but that his family if they were at risk for precisely the same reasons were held not to be part of a social group but mere victims. In my view the position is accurately set out in Hathaway...and that where there is an indication that the status or activity of a claimant's relative is the basis of the persecution, a claim grounded in family background is properly receivable as falling within the social group category."**[199]

It has also been accepted in *Savchenkov*[200] that the 'family' can constitute a social group; the concept of membership of a particular social group was recognised as including membership of a group defined by some innate or unchangeable characteristic of its members analogous to race, religion, nationality or political opinion, for example, their sex, linguistic background, tribe, *family* or class.

These decisions have however been substantially undermined by the Court of Appeal in *Quijano*,[201] where one of the main questions

---

[196] *Acosta v INS* [1985] Int. Dec. 2986 (BIA). See also this volume at 5.5
[197] *SSHD v Patrice Higuera Hernandez*, IAT 7th December 1995 (12773) (unreported)
[198] ibid.
[199] Appeal No HX/75256/94 (1995) (unreported)
[200] *SSHD v Sergie Vasilyevich Savchenkov* [1996] Imm AR 28 (CA)
[201] *Fabian Martinez Quijano v SSHD*, CA 18th December 1996 (unreported)

addressed was that of whether membership of a particular family is capable of falling within the category of 'a particular social group' if neither the family itself, nor other members of the family on whom the claim is based, are being targeted for one of the four principal enumerated Convention reasons. The IAT had dismissed the appeal and instead accepted the submission of the Secretary of State that it would be anomalous if the applicant's stepfather - the first victim of the persecution - could not claim Convention protection but the appellant - as a later victim - could invoke Convention protection simply by virtue of his relationship to the first victim. This decision was upheld by the Court of Appeal:

> **"It would be absurd that a member of a family of a person threatened would be within the ambit of the Convention when the person threatened would fall outside the Convention. Where a claim is made therefore as a member of the family it is critical to identify the root of a threat and to decide whether that root is the family itself or a particular member of a family. In the latter case any Convention foundation for the claim must be ancillary to and dependent on that of the person threatened. The fact that a member of the family cannot leave that family does not of itself create a social group - the inability to change a characteristic may be an essential element of a social group but it does not of itself create it."** [202]

It is clear from existing case law therefore, that the issue of whether family membership constitutes a 'particular social group' within the meaning of the Convention has yet to be fully resolved in UK jurisprudence. However, this uncertainty coupled with the strength of jurisprudence from elsewhere, most notably Canada and the US, means that this continues to be an appropriate line of reasoning in many cases where women have been targeted directly as a result of their family membership, **where it is clear that a political opinion (or other ground) has not been imputed to the appellant.** [203]

---

[202] *Fabian Martinez Quijano v SSHD*, IAT 16th July 1996 (136930) (unreported)
[203] See this volume at 5.4.3

5.5.3 Sexual Orientation

"If I go back...my father will try to force me to marry. I cannot marry. In this situation I would be forced to flee, and in [my country] no one would protect me. If I told my father that I am a lesbian, my father could subject me to the worst of punishments - perhaps even execution - and no one would protect me."[204]

Violence and discrimination against lesbians pervade the cultural and legal norms of countries around the world.[205] However, despite the advocacy and campaigning work of organisations such as Stonewall,[206] it is apparent from the limited information available in the UK regarding such abuse, that much more research is needed on the ways in which claims for protection based upon sexual orientation can be properly responded to in the process of asylum determination.[207]

"Torture, extrajudicial execution, arbitrary arrest and denial of freedom of expression and of association are examples of violations of fundamental human rights suffered by gay men and lesbians because of their sexual orientation."[208]

---

[204] Testimony of asylum applicant in the US cited in Minter 1996, 3
[205] According to a recent report by Amnesty International (1997), formal laws which criminalise both male and female homosexuality exist in a large number of countries. These include Afghanistan, Algeria, Angola, Bahrain, Bangladesh, Cape Verde, Cuba, Ethiopia, Iran, Kuwait, Morocco, Mozambique, Namibia, Pakistan, Somalia, the Sudan and Zaire. In countries where Sharia laws apply, punishment for lesbianism can include execution by stoning or cleaving in two, amputation of hands or feet and lashing.
[206] See http://www.stonewall.org.uk
[207] Representatives whose clients may have claims for asylum based wholly or in part upon their sexual orientation should ensure that they are aware of the forms of abuse suffered by lesbians in different countries. See for example Rachel Rosenbloom (ed) *Unspoken Rules: Sexual Orientation and Women's Human Rights* (1995) which documents the status of lesbians in 31 countries, Shelley Anderson (ed) *Lesbian Rights are Human Rights* (1995) and Aart Hendricks et al (eds) *The Third Pink Book: A Global View of Lesbian and Gay Oppression* (1993)
[208] Canadian Council for Refugees *Addressing Claims Based on Sexual Orientation*, 26th August 1995. Available on-line at http://www.web.net/~ccr/fronteng.htm

> "In every region of the globe, lesbians experience severe and in some cases life-threatening persecution based on their status as lesbians, including sexual and physical violence, forced psychiatric treatment, and denial of employment, housing, education, health care, and basic social services."[209]

According to Amnesty International's recent publication *Breaking the Silence: Human Rights Violations Based on Sexual Orientation* (1997), human rights violations targeting gay men and lesbians include, *but are not limited to*:

- **extrajudicial executions and disappearances;**

- **arbitrary killings by armed opposition groups;**

- **torture and ill-treatment;**

- **rape and sexual abuse;**

- **forced 'medical treatment' to change sexual orientation;**

- **laws criminalising homosexuality;**

- **detention;**

- **the death penalty;**

- **abuses based on real or perceived HIV status.**[210]

Claims based on sexual orientation raise specific issues for determination and for the process of finding out about women's experiences:[211]

---

[209] Minter 1993, 3. The author also notes that the context and often the form of these abuses vary within and among regions, countries and communities, and are determined not only by a woman's sexual orientation but by race, class, religion, age, ability, and other factors.

[210] Amnesty International 1997

[211] See this volume at 2.2 and Annex 8

> **"Past and continuing homophobia has resulted in a failure to ensure adequate protection of people fleeing persecution on the basis of sexual orientation. The same prejudices that contribute to the persecution play a role in the denial of protection to refugees."[212]**

In addition it has been suggested by the International Gay and Lesbian Human Rights Commission (IGLHRC) that lesbian asylum seekers are at a disadvantage even vis-à-vis gay men: "access to asylum is an all but unreachable goal for the vast majority of lesbians who need protection."[213] Lesbians account for only a fraction of all cases worldwide; for example there are only five known cases in the US in which lesbians have received asylum, and at least two in which claims made on this basis have been denied.[214] As Minter (1996) notes, although rarely acknowledged, lesbians experience different forms of persecution than those characteristically targeted at gay men. Representatives should note for example that social and cultural norms regarding appropriate gender roles and behaviour may mean that even where there are larger groups of persecuted women, lesbians are specifically targeted by the state:

> **"In 1984 in Lima a violent raid was carried out in the capital where about seventy-five lesbian women were beaten up and ill-treated by the police. Prostitutes get a very rough time in jail. But the treatment of lesbians was even worse. Lesbians were beaten up because, however degrading prostitution can be, it is still regarded as normal behaviour, whereas lesbianism is seen as too threatening to the status quo."[215]**

In general terms lesbians are less likely than gay men to be prosecuted under state statutes criminalising same-gender sex; many countries refuse to even acknowledge that lesbianism exists by naming it as a

---

[212] See Canadian Council for Refugees *Addressing Claims Based on Sexual Orientation*, 26th August 1995 (Annex 8).
[213] Minter 1996, 3
[214] International Gay and Lesbian Human Rights Commission (IGLHRC) Asylum Project, *International Asylum Fact Sheet* (10-96)
[215] Testimony of an anonymous Peruvian witness cited in Amnesty International 1997, 23

crime.[216] However the invisibility of lesbianism does not mean that lesbian women will not be persecuted in these contexts:

"The relative invisibility of lesbians in these public places does not mean that lesbians are more insulated from persecution than gay men, but rather that lesbians confront specific forms of persecution that are powerfully affected by gender. Like other women, lesbians are less often persecuted through acts committed by the state than through state failure to address or prevent serious human rights violations by non-state actors."[217]

Many lesbian women have also effectively been denied the right to sexual orientation because they have been forced into a marriage:

"Forced heterosexual marriage is not only a denial of a lesbian's human rights to personal liberty and autonomy. It is also an assault on her *sexual identity as a lesbian* and thus on one of the most deeply felt and central aspects of her personal identity."[218]

In the context of this chapter, the failure to recognise gender-defined social groups and the ways in which refugee women's experiences may differ from those of their male counterparts, can have particular implications in establishing the grounds of the persecution in cases involving sexual orientation. As in claims of persecution based upon race,[219] sexual orientation and gender may interact to explain the *form* that persecution takes in the cases of lesbian applicants:

"Lesbians may face double discrimination, because of their sex as well as their sexual orientation."[220]

---

[216] Amnesty International (1997) have noted that in a significant number of countries formal legislation prohibits male, but not female, homosexuality. These include Armenia, Azerbaijan, Bhutan, Botswana, Chile, Equador, Guyana, India, Jordan, Kenya, Nigeria, Sri Lanka, Tanzania, Uganda and Zambia. Representatives should be aware that the fact that there are no formal laws against lesbianism *does not mean* that lesbians do not suffer persecution, but that this may be more likely to occur indirectly or through non-state agents.
[217] Minter 1996, 5
[218] ibid. (emphasis in original)
[219] See this volume at 5.1
[220] Amnesty International 1997, 9

> "Gender alone...is no more able to account for the specific persecution lesbians confront than is sexual orientation alone. Gender and sexual orientation rarely function as independent bases of persecution. More typically, they intersect in ways that expose lesbians to unique vulnerabilities and unique harms that cannot be accounted for fully on the basis of either status in isolation."[221]

Moreover in some contexts women's fear of persecution for their political activities may be exacerbated because their lesbianism may be used as a pretext to subject them to cruel, inhuman and degrading treatment:

> "The main basis of my claim for asylum was my activities against the prevailing nationalist ideologies in Bosnia. Homosexuality is illegal in Bosnia, but lesbians are not mentioned in the law. However lesbianism is unacceptable. As a lesbian I would have been particularly vulnerable if I had returned to Bosnia as the government would use my sexuality as a pretext to get at me because of my political opinions."[222]

Claims for asylum which are based solely on sexual orientation are not fundamentally different from other claims for asylum and as such should be recognised as being related to the applicant's membership of a 'particular social group'. In addition where sexual orientation is interpreted as a matter of choice (rather than as an innate or unchangeable) characteristic, cases involving persecution because of sexual orientation can equally be argued as suppression of imputed political opinion.[223] For example in Germany it was ruled that gay men in Iran can be perceived as political opponents of the regime because of the peculiarly theological nature of the Iranian state. Asylum was then granted to a gay man from Iran on grounds of the extreme political oppression he would face if he returned to his country of origin.[224]

It is clear from this limited analysis that those representing the asylum claims of refugee women must be sensitive to issues of sexual orientation as well as gender because they often provide the first point of

---

[221] Minter 1996, 6
[222] Testimony of a Bosnian woman recently granted full refugee status in the UK following an appeal, during an interview with the author, April 1997
[223] Haywood and Russell 1996, 11. See also this volume at 5.4
[224] Amnesty International 1997, 31

contact with the legal system for lesbians seeking to determine whether or not they qualify for political asylum. It is particularly critical that representatives make every effort to obtain information relating to their clients case,[225] and that they challenge decision makers to recognise the validity of claims for asylum based upon sexual orientation. In recent years a growing number of countries have granted refugee status to gay and lesbian asylum seekers. These include Australia, Canada, Denmark, Finland, Germany, Ireland, the Netherlands, New Zealand, Norway, the United Kingdom and the United States.

5.5.3.1 Case Law
Canada
In 1992 Jorge Alberto Inaudi, a gay man from Argentina, successfully won his case for asylum before the CIRB on the grounds that, as a member of a particular social group, he would face persecution for his sexual orientation if he were returned to his country of origin. In addition lesbians from both Costa Rica and the Ukraine have been granted asylum on the basis of their sexual orientation.

United States
In the United States, homosexuals from Cuba were recognised as a social group in *Toboso-Alfonso*.[226] When a gay Congressman asked the US Attorney-General if this decision amounted to a precedent in US law, she replied in the affirmative,[227] and Convention refugee status has subsequently been granted to lesbians and gay men from Colombia, Ethiopia, Iran and Guatemala. The IGLHRC has now documented over 40 cases concerning lesbians and gay men who have received asylum in the US.[228]

Australia
In 1992 a gay couple from mainland China were granted refugee status in Australia based upon persecution due to sexual orientation.[229]

---

[225] See this volume at 2.7
[226] Digested in IJLR Vol. 6, 3. See also Hathaway 1991, 163
[227] Amnesty International 1997, 31
[228] The International Gay and Lesbian Human Rights Commission which produces a regular *Asylum Fact Sheet* can be found at http://qrd.tcp.com/qrd/orgs/IGLHRC
[229] Press release from the International Gay and Lesbian Human Rights Commission, March 26th 1992 at http://qrd.tcp.com/qrd/orgs/IGLHRC

The Netherlands
In the Netherlands refugee status was granted to a lesbian from Iran who had been arrested and imprisoned for some time. Lesbians in Iran can be stoned to death.[230]

United Kingdom
As Amnesty International (1997) notes, case law on whether homosexuals can constitute 'a particular social group' within the meaning of the Convention appears to be in some disarray. As is noted in *Macdonald*[231], it was assumed in *Binbasi*[232] that homosexuals could form a social group. However subsequent case law on this issue has been contradictory. For example in *Golchin,*[233] it was not accepted that a gay Iranian asylum seeker belonged to a particular social group, although ELR was granted on the basis that his situation, if he returned to Iran, would be 'intolerable'. However the IAT have recently reviewed their previous decisions and recognised homosexuals as a social group in *Vraciu:*[234]

"It cannot be argued that in Romania homosexuality is not recognised as a characteristic putting that person into a special category."[235]

---

[230] Appeal No. 9007.10.0022 (25th October 1991)
[231] Macdonald and Blake *Macdonald's Immigration Law and Practice in the United Kingdom* 1995, 395 paragraph 12.53
[232] *R v SSHD ex p Zia Mehmet Binbasi* [1989] Imm Ar 595 (QBD)
[233] *Golchin v SSHD*, IAT 1991 (7623) (unreported). See also Amnesty International, 1997.
[234] *Ioan Vraciu v SSHD*, IAT 21st November 1994 (11559) (unreported)
[235] ibid.

ANNEX 1   International Instruments and Where to Obtain Them

- **Universal Declaration of Human Rights** (UDHR) (1948) in *Basic Documents on Human Rights*, Brownlie 3rd Edition 1992, 24*

- **1949 Geneva Conventions on the Laws of War and the two Additional Protocols of 1977**, excerpts in Mulamba Mbuyi (ed) *Refugees and International Law* 1993 , 239 Thompson Canada Ltd

- **European Convention on the Protection of Human Rights** (ECHR) (1950) in UNHCR *Collection of International Instruments Concerning Refugees*, Geneva 1990

- **Convention on Consent to Marriage, Minimum Age for Marriage and Registration of Marriages** (1962)*

- **Convention on the Elimination of All Forms of Racial Discrimination** (1965) *

- **International Covenant on Civil and Political Rights** (ICCPR) (1966) in *Basic Documents on Human Rights*, Brownlie 3rd Edition 1992, 125 *

- **International Covenant on Economic, Social and Cultural Rights** (1966) *

- **Convention on the Elimination of All Forms of Discrimination Against Women** (CEDAW) (1979) *

- **UN Convention Against Torture and Other Cruel, Inhuman or Degrading Treatment or Punishment** (UNCAT) (1984) in *Basic Documents on Human Rights*, Brownlie 3rd Edition 1992, 38 *

- **Convention on the Rights of the Child** (CROC) (1989) in *Basic Documents on Human Rights* Brownlie 3rd Edition 1992, 182 *

- **UN Declaration on the Elimination of Violence Against Women** (1993)*

- **UN Platform for Action** (1995)*

* Full texts can be found in Refworld, UNHCR CD-Rom. Details from:
Case Postale 2500
CH-1211 Geneva Depot 2,
SWITZERLAND Internet: http://www.unicc.org/unhcr

ANNEX 2 European Convention for the Protection of Human Rights (ECHR) (4th November 1950)[1]

Article 3   'No one shall be subjected to torture or to inhuman or degrading treatment or punishment'

Article 4   Prohibition of forced or compulsory labour

Article 5   Deprivation of liberty

Article 6   Right to a fair and impartial hearing 'within a reasonable time'

Article 8   Respect for private and family life

Article 9   Right to freedom of thought, conscience and religion

Article 10   Right to freedom of expression

Article 13   Right to the grant of an effective remedy before a national authority

---

[1] Full text available in UNHCR's *Collection of International Instruments Concerning Refugees*, Geneva 1990 and numerous other sources

ANNEX 3 Relevant Extracts from the Convention on the Elimination of All Forms of Discrimination Against Women (CEDAW), the UN Declaration on the Elimination of Violence Against Women and the UN Platform for Action

I. Convention on the Elimination of All Forms of Discrimination Against Women (CEDAW) (1979)[2]

Article 1

For the purposes of the present Convention, the term 'discrimination against women' shall mean any distinction, exclusion or restriction made on the basis of sex which has the effect or purpose of impairing or nullifying the recognition, enjoyment or exercise by women, irrespective of their marital status, on a basis of equality of men and women, of human rights and fundamental freedoms in the political, economic, social, cultural, civil and any other field

Article 2

States Parties condemn discrimination against women in all its forms, agree to pursue by all appropriate means and without delay a policy of eliminating discrimination against women and, to this end, undertake:

(a) To embody the principle of the equality of men and women in their national constitutions or other appropriate legislation if not yet incorporated therein and to ensure, through law and other appropriate means, the practical realization of this principle;

(b) To adopt appropriate legislative and other measures, including sanctions where appropriate, prohibiting all discrimination against women;

(c) To establish legal protection of the rights of women on an equal basis with men and to ensure through competent national tribunals and other public institutions the effective protection of women against any act of discrimination;

(d) To refrain from engaging in any act or practice of discrimination against women and to ensure that public authorities and institutions shall act in conformity with this obligation;

(e) To take all appropriate measures to eliminate discrimination against women by any person, organization or enterprise;

(f) To take all appropriate measures, including legislation, to modify or abolish existing laws, regulations, customs and practices which constitute discrimination against women;

---

[2] Full text available on the UNHCR's RefWorld on CD-Rom

(g) To repeal all national penal provisions which constitute discrimination against women.

Article 3

States Parties shall take in all fields, in particular in the political, social, economic and cultural fields, all appropriate measures, including legislation, to ensure the full development and advancement of women, for the purpose of guaranteeing them the exercise and enjoyment of human rights and fundamental freedoms on a basis of equality with men.

Other Relevant Articles

Article 4	Equality of Opportunity
Article 6	Traffic in Women and Prostitution
Article 7	Political Participation
Article 9	Nationality
Article 10	Access to Education
Article 11	Employment Rights
Article 12	Health and Family Planning
Article 14	Rural Women
Article 15	Equality in and Before the Law
Article 16	Marriage and Child Custody

II. UN Declaration on the Elimination of Violence Against Women (UN General Assembly Resolution 48/104) (1994)[3]

Article 1

For the purposes of this Declaration, the term 'violence against women' means any act of gender-based violence that results in, or is likely to result in, physical, sexual or psychological harm or suffering to women, including threats of such acts, coercion or arbitrary deprivation of liberty, whether occurring in public or in private life

Article 2

Violence against women shall be understood to encompass, but not be limited to, the following:

(a) Physical, sexual and psychological violence occurring in the family, including battering, sexual abuse of female children in the household, dowry-related violence, marital rape, female genital mutilation and other traditional practices harmful to women, non-spousal violence and violence related to exploitation;

---

[3] Full text available on-line at gopher://gopher.un.org:70/00/ga/recs/48/104

(b) Physical, sexual and psychological violence occurring within the general community, including rape, sexual abuse, sexual harassment and intimidation at work, in educational institutions and elsewhere, trafficking in women and forced prostitution;

(c) Physical, sexual and psychological violence perpetrated or condoned by the State, wherever it occurs.

Article 3
Women are entitled to the equal enjoyment and protection of all human rights and fundamental freedoms in the political, economic, social, cultural, civil or any other field. These rights include, inter alia:

(a) The right to life;

(b) The right to equality;

(c) The right to liberty and security of person;

(d) The right to equal protection under the law;

(e) The right to be free from all forms of discrimination;

(f) The right to the highest standard attainable of physical and mental health;

(g) The right to just and favourable conditions of work;

(h) The right not to be subjected to torture, or other cruel, inhuman or degrading treatment or punishment.

Article 4
States should condemn violence against women and should not invoke any custom, tradition or religious consideration to avoid their obligations with respect to its elimination. States should pursue by all appropriate means and without delay a policy of eliminating violence against women and, to this end, should:

(a) Consider, where they have not yet done so, ratifying or to the Convention on the Elimination of All Forms of Discrimination against Women or withdrawing reservations to that Convention;

(b) Refrain from engaging in violence against women;

(c) Exercise due diligence to prevent, investigate and, in accordance with national legislation, punish acts of violence against women, whether those acts are perpetrated by the State or by private persons;

(d) Develop penal, civil, labour and administrative sanctions in domestic legislation to punish and redress the wrongs caused to women who are subjected to violence; women who are subjected to violence should be provided with ac ess to the mechanisms of justice and, as provided for by national legislation, to just and effective remedies for the harm that they have suffered; States should also inform women of their rights in seeking redress through such mechanisms;

(e) Consider the possibility of developing national plans of action to promote the protection of women against any form of violence, or to include provisions for that purpose in plans already existing, taking into account, as appropriate, such cooperation as can be provided by non-governmental organizations, particularly those concerned with the issue of violence against women;

(f) Develop, in a comprehensive way, preventive approaches and all those measures of a legal, political, administrative and cultural nature that promote the protection of women against any form of violence, and ensure that the re-victimization of women does not occur because of laws insensitive to gender considerations, enforcement practices or other interventions;

(g) Work to ensure, to the maximum extent feasible in the light of their available resources and, where needed, within the framework of international cooperation, that women subjected to violence and, where appropriate, their children have specialized assistance, such as rehabilitation, assistance in child care and maintenance, treatment, counselling, and health and social services, facilities and programmes, as well as support structures, and should take all other appropriate measures to promote their safety and physical and psychological rehabilitation;

(h) Include in government budgets adequate resources for their activities related to the elimination of violence against women;

(i) Take measures to ensure that law enforcement officers and public officials responsible for implementing policies to prevent, investigate and punish violence against women receive training to sensitize them to the needs of women;

(j) Adopt all appropriate measures, especially in the field of education, to modify the social and cultural patterns of conduct of men and women and to eliminate prejudices, customary practices and all other practices based on the idea of the inferiority or superiority of either of the sexes and on stereotyped roles for men and women;

(k) Promote research, collect data and compile statistics, especially concerning domestic violence, relating to the prevalence of different forms of violence against women and encourage research on the causes, nature, seriousness and consequences of violence against women and on the effectiveness of measures implemented to prevent and redress violence against women; those statistics and findings of the research will be made public;

(l) Adopt measures directed towards the elimination of violence against women who are especially vulnerable to violence;

(m) Include, in submitting reports as required under relevant human rights instruments of the United Nations, information pertaining to violence against women and measures taken to implement the present Declaration;

(n) Encourage the development of appropriate guidelines to assist the implementation of the principles set forth in the present Declaration;

(o) Recognize the important role of the women's movement and non-governmental organizations world wide in raising awareness and alleviating the problem of violence against women;

(p) Facilitate and enhance the work of the women's movement and non-governmental organizations and cooperate with them at local, national and regional levels;

(q) Encourage intergovernmental regional organizations of which they are members to include the elimination of violence against women in their programmes, as appropriate.

III. UN Platform for Action (1995)[4]

Article 113

The term "violence against women" means any act of gender-based violence that results in, or is likely to result in, physical, sexual or psychological harm or suffering to women, including threats of such acts, coercion or arbitrary deprivation of liberty, whether occurring in public or private life. Accordingly, violence against women encompasses but is not limited to the following:

(a) Physical, sexual and psychological violence occurring in the family, including battering, sexual abuse of female children in the household, dowry-related violence, marital rape, female genital mutilation and other traditional practices harmful to women, non-spousal violence and violence related to exploitation;

(b) Physical, sexual and psychological violence occurring within the general community, including rape, sexual abuse, sexual harassment and intimidation at work, in educational institutions and elsewhere, trafficking in women and forced prostitution;

(c) Physical, sexual and psychological violence perpetrated or condoned by the State, wherever it occurs.

Article 114

Other acts of violence against women include violation of the human rights of women in situations of armed conflict, in particular murder, systematic rape, sexual slavery and forced pregnancy.

Article 115

Acts of violence against women also include forced sterilisation and forced abortion, coercive/forced use of contraceptives, female infanticide and prenatal sex selection.

---

[4] The full text of the Platform for Action can be found on the UNHCR's RefWorld on CD-Rom

Article 117

Acts or threats of violence, whether occurring within the home or in the community, or perpetrated or condoned by the State, instil fear and insecurity in women's lives and are obstacles to the achievement of equality and for development and peace. The fear of violence, including harassment, is a permanent constraint on the mobility of women and limits their access to resources and basic activities. High social, health and economic costs to the individual and society are associated with violence against women. Violence against women is one of the crucial social mechanisms by which women are forced into a subordinate position compared with men. In many cases, violence against women and girls occurs in the family or within the home, where violence is often tolerated. The neglect, physical and sexual abuse, and rape of girl children and women by family members and other members of the household, as well as incidences of spousal and non-spousal abuse, often go unreported and are thus difficult to detect. Even when such violence is reported, there is often a failure to protect victims or punish perpetrators.

Article 118

Violence against women is a manifestation of the historically unequal power relations between men and women, which have led to domination over and discrimination against women by men and to the prevention of women's full advancement. Violence against women throughout the life cycle derives essentially from cultural patterns, in particular the harmful effects of certain traditional or customary practices and all acts of extremism linked to race, sex, language or religion that perpetuate the lower status accorded to women in the family, the workplace, the community and society. Violence against women is exacerbated by social pressures, notably the shame of denouncing certain acts that have been perpetrated against women; women's lack of access to legal information, aid or protection; the lack of laws that effectively prohibit violence against women; failure to reform existing laws; inadequate efforts on the part of public authorities to promote awareness of and enforce existing laws; and the absence of educational and other means to address the causes and consequences of violence. Images in the media of violence against women, in particular those that depict rape or sexual slavery as well as the use of women and girls as sex objects, including pornography, are factors contributing to the continued prevalence of such violence, adversely influencing the community at large, in particular children and young people.

Strategic objective D.1. Take integrated measures to prevent and eliminate violence against women

Article 124

Action to be taken by Governments:

(a) Condemn violence against women and refrain from invoking any custom, tradition or religious consideration to avoid their obligations with respect to its elimination as set out in the Declaration on the Elimination of Violence against Women;

(b) Refrain from engaging in violence against women and exercise due diligence to prevent, investigate and, in accordance with national legislation, punish acts of violence against women, whether those acts are perpetrated by the State or by private persons;

(c) Enact and/or reinforce penal, civil, labour and administrative sanctions in domestic legislation to punish and redress the wrongs done to women and girls who are subjected to any form of violence, whether in the home, the workplace, the community or society;

(d) Adopt and/or implement and periodically review and analyse legislation to ensure its effectiveness in eliminating violence against women, emphasizing the prevention of violence and the prosecution of offenders; take measures to ensure the protection of women subjected to violence, access to just and effective remedies, including compensation and indemnification and healing of victims, and rehabilitation of perpetrators.

Article 135

While entire communities suffer the consequences of armed conflict and terrorism, women and girls are particularly affected because of their status in society and their sex. Parties to conflict often rape women with impunity, sometimes using systematic rape as a tactic of war and terrorism. The impact of violence against women and violation of the human rights of women in such situations is experienced by women of all ages, who suffer displacement, loss of home and property, loss or involuntary disappearance of close relatives, poverty and family separation and disintegration, and who are victims of acts of murder, terrorism, torture, involuntary disappearance, sexual slavery, rape, sexual abuse and forced pregnancy in situations of armed conflict, especially as a result of policies of ethnic cleansing and other new and emerging forms of violence. This is compounded by the life-long social, economic and psychologically traumatic consequences of armed conflict and foreign occupation and alien domination.

Article 136

Women and children constitute some 80 per cent of the world's millions of refugees and other displaced persons, including internally displaced persons. They are threatened by deprivation of property, goods and services and deprivation of their right to return to their homes of origin as well as by violence and insecurity. Particular attention should be paid to sexual violence against uprooted women and girls employed as a method of persecution in systematic campaigns of terror and intimidation and forcing members of a particular ethnic, cultural or religious group to flee their homes. Women may also be forced to flee as a result of a well-founded fear of persecution for reasons enumerated in the 1951 Convention relating to the Status of Refugees and the 1967 Protocol, including persecution through sexual violence or other gender-related persecution, and they continue to be vulnerable to violence and exploitation while in flight, in countries of asylum and resettlement and during and after repatriation. Women often experience difficulty in some countries of asylum in being recognised as refugees when the claim is based on such persecution.

Strategic objective E.5. Provide protection, assistance and to refugee women, other displaced women in need of protection and displaced women

Article 147
Actions to be taken by Governments, intergovernmental and non-governmental organizations and other institutions involved in providing protection, assistance and training to refugee women, other displaced women in need of international protection and internally displaced women, including the Office of the United Nations High Commissioner for Refugees and the World Food Programme as appropriate:
(a) Take steps to ensure that women are fully involved in the planning, design, implementation, monitoring and evaluation of all short-term and long-term projects and programmes providing assistance to refugee women, other displaced women in need of international protection and internally displaced women, including the management of refugee camps and resources; ensure that refugee and displaced women and girls have direct access to the services provided;
(b) Offer adequate protection and assistance to women and children displaced within their country and find solutions to the root causes of their displacement with a view to preventing it and, when appropriate, facilitate their return or resettlement;
(c) Take steps to protect the safety and physical integrity of refugee women, other displaced women in need of international protection and internally displaced women during their displacement and upon their return to their communities of origin, including programmes of rehabilitation; take effective measures to protect from violence women who are refugees or displaced; hold an impartial and thorough investigation of any such violations and bring those responsible to justice;
(d) While fully respecting and strictly observing the principle of non-refoulement of refugees, take all the necessary steps to ensure the right of refugee and displaced women to return voluntarily to their place of origin in safety and with dignity, and their right to protection after their return;
(e) Take measures, at the national level with international cooperation, as appropriate, in accordance with the Charter of the United Nations, to find

lasting solutions to questions related to internally displaced women, including their right to voluntary and safe return to their home of origin;

(f) Ensure that the international community and its international organizations provide financial and other resources for emergency relief and other longer-term assistance that takes into account the specific needs, resources and potentials of refugee women, other displaced women in need of international protection and internally displaced women; in the provision of protection and assistance, take all appropriate measures to eliminate discrimination against women and girls in order to ensure equal access to appropriate and adequate food, water and shelter, education, and social and health services, including reproductive health care and maternity care and services to combat tropical diseases;

(g) Facilitate the availability of educational materials in the appropriate language - in emergency situations also - in order to minimize disruption of schooling among refugee and displaced children;

(h) Apply international norms to ensure equal access and equal treatment of women and men in refugee determination procedures and the granting of asylum, including full respect and strict observation of the principle of non-refoulement through, inter alia, bringing national immigration regulations into conformity with relevant international instruments, and consider recognizing as refugees those women whose claim to refugee status is based upon the well-founded fear of persecution for reasons enumerated in the 1951 Convention 28/ and the 1967 Protocol 29/ relating to the Status of Refugees, including persecution through sexual violence or other gender- related persecution, and provide access to specially trained officers, including female officers, to interview women regarding sensitive or painful experiences, such as sexual assault;

(i) Support and promote efforts by States towards the development of criteria and guidelines on responses to persecution specifically aimed at women, by sharing information on States' initiatives to develop such criteria and guidelines and by monitoring to ensure their fair and consistent application;

(j) Promote the self-reliant capacities of refugee women, other displaced women in need of international protection and internally displaced women and provide programmes for women, particularly young women, in leadership and decision-making within refugee and returnee communities;

(k) Ensure that the human rights of refugee and displaced women are protected and that refugee and displaced women are made aware of these rights; ensure that the vital importance of family reunification is recognized;

(l) Provide, as appropriate, women who have been determined refugees with access to vocational/professional training programmes, including language training, small-scale enterprise development training and planning and counselling on all forms of violence against women, which should include rehabilitation programmes for victims of torture and trauma; Governments and other donors should contribute adequately to assistance programmes for refugee women, other displaced women in need of international protection and internally displaced women, taking into account in particular the effects on the host countries of the increasing requirements of large refugee populations and the need to widen the donor base and to achieve greater burden-sharing;

(m) Raise public awareness of the contribution made by refugee women to their countries of resettlement, promote understanding of their human rights and of their needs and abilities and encourage mutual understanding and acceptance through educational programmes promoting cross-cultural and interracial harmony;

(n) Provide basic and support services to women who are displaced from their place of origin as a result of terrorism, violence, drug trafficking or other reasons linked to violence situations

Article 148

Actions to be taken by Governments;

(a) Disseminate and implement the UNHCR Guidelines on the Protection of Refugee Women and the UNHCR Guidelines on Evaluation and Care of Victims of Trauma and Violence, or provide similar guidance, in close co-operation with refugee women and in all sectors of refugee programmes;

(b) Protect women and children who migrate as family members from abuse or denial of their human rights by sponsors and consider extending their stay, should the family relationship dissolve, within the limits of national legislation.

Article 224

Violence against women both violates and impairs or nullifies the enjoyment by women of human rights and fundamental freedoms. Taking into account the Declaration on the Elimination of Violence against Women and the work of Special Rapporteurs, gender-based violence, such as battering and other domestic violence, sexual abuse, sexual slavery and exploitation, and international trafficking in women and children, forced prostitution and sexual harassment, as well as violence against women, resulting from cultural prejudice, racism and racial discrimination, xenophobia, pornography, ethnic cleansing, armed conflict, foreign occupation, religious and anti-religious extremism and terrorism are incompatible with the dignity and the worth of the human person and must be combated and eliminated. Any harmful aspect of certain traditional, customary or modern practices that violates the rights of women should be prohibited and eliminated. Governments should take urgent action to combat and eliminate all forms of violence against women in private and public life, whether perpetrated or tolerated by the State or private persons.

ANNEX 4 UNHCR EXCOM Resolutions on Refugee Women[5]

EXCOM Conclusion No.39 (XXXVI) 1985 - Refugee Women and International Protection:
- stresses the need for UNHCR and host governments to give particular attention to the international protection needs of refugee women
- recommends that States, individually, jointly and in co-operation with UNHCR, redefine and reorient existing programmes, and where necessary, establish new programmes to meet the specific needs of refugee women

EXCOM Conclusion No. 46 (XXXVII) 1987 - General Conclusion on International Protection:
- notes that refugee women had special protection and assistance needs
- recognises the need for reliable information and statistics about refugee women in order to increase awareness of their situation

EXCOM Conclusion No. 54 (XXXIX) 1988 - Refugee Women:
- elaborates on the special vulnerability of refugee women and the particular problems they face

EXCOM Conclusion No. 60 (XL) 1989 - General Conclusion on International Protection:
- reiterates concerns about the physical safety and sexual exploitation of refugee women

EXCOM Conclusion No. 64 (XLI) 1990 - Refugee Women and International Protection:
- urges States and others to ensure that the needs and resources of refugee women are fully understood and integrated
- outlines a number of aims in promoting measures for improving the international protection of refugee women

EXCOM Conclusion No. 73 (XLIV) 1993 - Refugee Protection and Sexual Violence:
- examines the implications of sexual violence for protection
- calls upon states and UNHCR to ensure the equal access of women and men to refugee status determination procedures

---

[5] The full texts of the UNHCR's EXCOM Conclusions can be found on the UNHCR's RefWorld on CD-Rom and on-line at
http://www.unhcr.ch/refworld/unhcr/excom/xconc/menu.htm

ANNEX 5   CIRB *Guidelines on Women Refugee Claimants Fearing Gender-Related Persecution: UPDATE* (November 1996)

The definition of a Convention refugee in the *Immigration Act* does not include gender as an independent enumerated ground for a well-founded fear of persecution warranting the recognition of Convention refugee status. As a developing area of the law, it has been more widely recognised that gender-related persecution is a **form** of persecution which can and should be assessed by the Refugee Division panel hearing the claim. Where a woman claims to have a gender-related fear of persecution, the central issue is thus the need to determine the **linkage** between gender, the feared persecution and one or more of the definition grounds.

Most gender-related refugee claims brought forward by women raise four critical issues which these Guidelines seek to address:

1.   To what extent can women making a gender-related claim of fear of persecution successfully rely on any one, or a combination of, the five enumerated grounds of the Convention refugee definition?

2.   Under what circumstances does sexual violence, or a threat thereof, or any other prejudicial treatment of women constitute persecution as that term is jurisprudentially understood?

3.   What are the key evidentiary elements which decision-makers have to look at when considering a gender-related claim?

4.   What special problems to women face when called upon to state their claim at refugee determination hearings particularly when they have had experiences that are difficult and often humiliating to speak about?

A. DETERMINING THE NATURE AND THE GROUNDS OF THE PERSECUTION

Obviously, not all claims brought forward by women are specifically gender-related. Women frequently claim fear of persecution in common with their male fellow citizens, though not necessarily of the same nature or at the same level of vulnerability, for such reasons as belonging to an ethnic or a linguistic minority, or membership in a political movement, a trade union or a religious denomination.

I. GENERAL PROPOSITION

Although gender is not specifically enumerated as one of the grounds for establishing Convention refugee status the definition of *Convention refugee* may properly be interpreted as providing protection for women who demonstrate a well-founded fear of gender-related persecution by reason of any one, or a combination of, the enumerated grounds.

Before determining the appropriate ground(s) applicable to the claim, decision makers must first identify the **nature** of the persecution feared by the claimant.

Generally speaking, women refugee claimants may be put into four broad categories, although these categories are not mutually exclusive or exhaustive:

1. **Women who fear persecution on the <u>same Convention grounds, and in similar circumstances, as men</u>. That is, the risk factor is not their sexual status, <u>per se</u>, but rather their particular identity (i.e. racial, national or social) or what they believe in, or are perceived to believe in (i.e. religion or political opinion).** In such claims, the substantive analysis does not vary as a function of the person's gender, although the nature of the harm feared and procedural issues at the hearing may vary as a function of the claimant's gender.

2. **Women who fear persecution solely for reasons pertaining to kinship, i.e. because of status, activities or views of their spouses, parents and siblings, or other family members.** Such cases of "<u>persecution of kin</u>" typically involve violence or other forms of harassment against women, who are not themselves accused of any antagonistic views or political convictions, in order to pressure them into revealing information about the whereabouts or the political activities of their family members. Women may also have political opinions imputed to them based on the activities of members of their family.

3. **Women who fear persecution resulting from certain circumstances of <u>severe discrimination on grounds of gender</u> or <u>acts of violence</u> either by public authorities or at the hands of private citizens from whose actions the state is unwilling or unable to adequately protect the concerned persons.** In the refugee law context, such discrimination may amount to persecution if it leads to consequences of a substantially prejudicial nature for the claimant and if it is imposed on account of any one, or a combination, of the statutory grounds for persecution. The acts of violence which a woman may fear include violence inflicted in situations of <u>domestic violence</u> and situations of <u>civil war</u>.

4. **Women who fear persecution as the consequence of failing to conform to, or for transgressing, certain gender-discriminating religious or customary laws and practices in their country of origin.** Such laws and practices, by singling out women and placing them in a more vulnerable position than men, may create conditions for the existence of a gender-defined social group. The religious precepts, social traditions or cultural norms which women may be accused of violating can range from choosing their own spouses instead of accepting an arranged marriage, to such matters as the wearing of make-up, the visibility or length of hair, or the type of clothing a woman chooses to wear.

II. GROUNDS OTHER THAN MEMBERSHIP IN A PARTICULAR SOCIAL GROUP

Race:

There may be cases where a woman claims a fear of persecution because of her race and her gender. For example, a woman from a minority race in her country may be persecuted not only for her race, but also for her gender.

Religion:

A woman who, in a theocracy for example, chooses not to subscribe to or follow the precepts of a state religion may be at risk of persecution for reasons of religion. In the context of the Convention refugee definitions, the notion of religion may encompass, among other freedoms, the freedom to hold a belief system of one's choice or not to hold a particular belief system and the freedom to practise a religion of one's choice or not to practise a prescribed religion. In certain states, the religion assigns certain roles to women; if a woman does not fulfil her assigned role and is punished for that, she may have a well-founded fear of persecution for reasons of religion. A woman may also be perceived as expressing a political view (and have a political opinion imputed to her) because of her attitude and/or behaviour towards religion.

Nationality:

A gender-related claim of fear of persecution may be linked to reasons of nationality in situations where a national law causes a woman to lose her nationality (i.e. citizenship) because of marriage to a foreign national. What would constitute good grounds for fearing persecution is not the fact of losing her nationality as such (notwithstanding that such laws are discriminatory to the extent that they do not apply to men married to foreign nationals), but the consequences she may suffer as a result.

Political Opinion:

A woman who opposes institutionalised discrimination against women, or expresses views of independence from male social/cultural dominance in her society, may be found to fear persecution by reason of her **actual political opinion or a political opinion imputed to her (i.e. she is perceived by the agent of persecution to be expressing politically antagonistic views)**. Two considerations are of paramount importance when interpreting the notion of "political opinion":

1. In a society where women are "assigned" a <u>subordinate status</u> and the authority exercised by men over women results in a general oppression of women, their political protest and activism do not always manifest themselves in the same way as those of men.
2. The <u>political nature</u> of oppression of women in the context of religious laws and rituals should be recognised. Where tenets of the governing religion in a given country require certain kinds of behaviour exclusively from women, contrary behaviour may be perceived by the authorities as evidence of an unacceptable political opinion that threatens the basic structure from which their political power flows.

III. MEMBERSHIP IN A PARTICULAR SOCIAL GROUP

In considering the application of the "membership in a particular social group" ground, decision-makers should refer to the Supreme Court of Canada decision in *Ward*. **The *Ward* decision indicated three possible categories of "particular social group":**

1) groups defined by an innate or unchangeable characteristic;
2) groups whose members voluntarily associate for reasons so fundamental to their human dignity that they should not be forced to forsake the association; and
3) groups associated by a former voluntary status, unalterable due to its historical permanence.

The Court gave examples of the three categories as follows:

> The first category would embrace individuals fearing persecution on such bases as **gender**, linguistic background and sexual orientation, while the second would encompass, for example, human rights activists. The third branch is included more because of historical intentions, although it is also relevant to the anti-discrimination influences, in that one's past is an immutable part of the person.

Depending on the basis of the claim, women refugee claimants may belong to a group defined in any of these categories.

A further holding of the *Ward* decision is that a particular social group cannot be based solely on the common victimisation of its members. A group is not defined solely by common victimisation if the claimant's fear of persecution is also based on her gender, or on another innate or unchangeable characteristic of the claimant.

Family as a particular social group
There is jurisprudential authority for recognising claims grounded in familial affiliation (i.e. where kinship is the risk factor) as coming within the ambit of the "membership in a particular social group" category. See, for example, *Al-Busaidy, Talal Ali Said* v. *MEI*,

> ...the [Immigration and Refugee] Board has committed reviewable error in not giving due effect to the applicant's uncontradicted evidence with respect to his membership in a particular social group, namely, his own immediate family.

Gender-defined particular social group
There is increasingly international support for the application of the particular social group ground to the claims of women who allege a fear of persecution solely by reason of their gender. See *Conclusion No. 39 (XXXVI) Refugee Women and International Protection, 1985*, where the Executive Committee of the United Nations High Commissioner for Refugees (UNHCR) ...

> (k) Recognised that States, in the exercise of their sovereignty, are free to adopt the interpretation that women asylum-seekers who face harsh or inhuman treatment due to their having transgressed the social mores of the society in which they live may be considered as a "particular social group" within the meaning of the Article 2 A(2) of the 1951 United Nations Refugee Convention.

Application of the statutory ground

In evaluating the "membership in a particular social group" ground for a fear of gender-related persecution, two considerations are necessary:

1. Most of the gender-specific claims involving fear of persecution for transgressing religious or social norms may be determined on **grounds of religion or political opinion**. Such women may be seen by the governing authorities or private citizens as having made a religious or political statement in transgressing those norms of their society, even though UNHCR *Conclusion*

No. 39, above, contemplates the use of "particular social group" as an appropriate ground.

2. **For a woman to establish a well-founded fear of persecution by reasons of her membership in a gender-defined particular social group under the first category in *Ward* (i.e. groups defined by an innate or unchangeable characteristic):**

- The fact that the particular social group consists of large numbers of the female population in the country concerned is **irrelevant** - race, religion, nationality and political opinion are also characteristics that are shared by large numbers of people.

- **Gender is an innate characteristic and, therefore, women may form a particular social group within the Convention refugee definition.** The relevant assessment is whether the claimant, as a woman has a well-founded fear of persecution in her country of nationality by reason of her membership of this group.

- **Particular social groups comprised of sub-groups of women may also be an appropriate finding in a case involving gender-related persecution.** These particular social groups can be identified by reference to factors, in addition to gender, which may also be innate or unchangeable characteristics. Examples of other such characteristics are age, race, marital status and economic status. Thus, for example, there may be sub-groups of women identified as old women, indigenous women, single women or poor women. In determining whether these factors are unchangeable, consideration should be given to the cultural and social context in which the woman lives, as well as to the perception of the agents of persecution and those responsible for providing state protection.

- **Because refugee status is an *individual remedy*, the fact that a claim is based on social group membership may not be sufficient in and of itself to give rise to refugee status.** The woman will need to show that she has a genuine fear of harm, that one of the grounds of the definition is the reason for the feared harm, that the harm is sufficiently serious to amount to persecution, that there is a reasonable possibility that the feared persecution would occur if she was to return to her country of origin and that she has no reasonable expectation of adequate national protection.

B. ASSESSING THE FEARED HARM

Claims involving gender-related fear of persecution often fall quite comfortably within one of the five grounds of the Convention refugee definition. The difficulty sometimes lies in establishing whether the various forms of prejudicial treatment or sanctions imposed on women making such claims come within the scope of the concept of "persecution".

CONSIDERATIONS

The circumstances which give rise to women's fear of persecution are often unique to women. The existing bank of jurisprudence on the meaning of persecution is based, for the mot part, on the experiences of male claimants. Aside from the few cases of rape, the definition has not been widely applied to female-specific experiences, such as infanticide, genital mutilation, bride-burning, forced marriage, domestic violence, forced abortion or compulsory sterilisation.

The fact that violence, including sexual and domestic violence, against women is universal is **irrelevant** when determining whether rape, and other gender-specific crimes constitute forms of persecution. **The real issues are whether the violence - experienced or feared - is a serious violation of a fundamental human right for a Convention ground and in what circumstances can the risk of that violence be said to result from a failure of state protection.**

The social, cultural, traditional and religious norms and the laws affecting women in the claimant's country of origin ought to be assessed **by reference to human rights instruments which provide a framework of international standards for recognising the protection needs of women.** What constitutes permissible conduct by the agent of persecution towards women may be determined, therefore, by reference to international instruments such as:

> *Universal Declaration of Human Rights*
> *International Covenant on Civil and Political Rights*
> *International Covenant on Economic, Social and Cultural Rights*
> *Convention on the Elimination of All Forms of*
> *   Discrimination Against Women*
> *Convention on the Political Rights of Women*
> *Convention on the Nationality of Married Women*
> *Convention Against Torture and other Cruel, Inhuman or Degrading*
> *   Treatment or Punishment*
> *Declaration on the Elimination of Violence Against Women*

A woman's claim to Convention refugee status **cannot be based solely on the fact that she is subject to a national policy or law to which she objects**. The claimant will need to establish that:

(a) the policy or law is inherently persecutory; or

(b) the policy or law is used as a means of persecution for one of the enumerated reasons; or

(c) the policy or law, although having legitimate goals, is administered through persecutory means; or

(d) the penalty for non-compliance with the policy or law is disproportionately severe.

C. EVIDENTIARY MATTERS

When an assessment of a woman's claim of gender-related fear of persecution is made, the evidence must show that what the claimant genuinely fears is persecution for a Convention reason as distinguished from random violence or random criminal activity perpetrated against her as an individual. The central factor in such an assessment is, of course, the claimant's particular circumstances in relation to both the general human rights record of her country of origin and the experiences of other similarly situated women. Evaluation of the weight and credibility of the claimant's evidence ought to include valuation of the following considerations, among others:

1. **A gender-related claim cannot be rejected simply because the claimant comes from a country where women face generalised oppression and violence and the claimant's fear of persecution is not identifiable to her on the basis of an individualised set of facts.** This so-called "particularised evidence rule" was rejected by the Federal Court of Appeal in *Salibian* v. *MEI*, and other decisions.

2. **Decision-makers should consider evidence indicating a failure of state protection if the sate or its agents in the claimant's country of origin are unwilling or unable to provide adequate protection from gender-related persecution.** If the claimant can demonstrate that it was objectively unreasonable for her to seek the protection of her state, then her failure to approach the state for protection will not defeat her claim. Also, the fact that the claimant did or did not seek protection from non-government groups is irrelevant to the assessment of the availability of state protection.

When considering whether it is objectively unreasonable for the claimant not to have sought the protection of the state, **the decision-maker should consider, among other relevant factors, the social, cultural, religious and economic context in which the claimant finds herself.** If, for example, a woman has suffered gender-related persecution in the form of rape, she may be ostracised from her community for seeking protection from the state. Decision-makers should consider this type of information when determining if the claimant should reasonably have sought state protection.

In determining whether the state is willing or able to provide protection to a woman fearing gender-related persecution, **decision-makers should consider the fact that the forms of evidence which the claimant might normally provide as "clear and convincing proof" of state inability to protect, will not always be either available or useful in cases of gender-related persecution.**

For example, where a gender-related claim involves threats of or actual sexual violence at the hands of government authorities (or at the hands of non-state agents of persecution, whether the state is either unwilling or unable to protect), the claimant may have difficulty in substantiating her claim with any "statistical data" on the incidence of sexual violence in her country.

In cases where the claimant cannot rely on the more standard or typical forms of evidence as "clear and convincing proof" of failure of state protection, **reference may need to be made to alternative forms of evidence to meet the "clear and convincing" test.** Such alternative forms of evidence might include the testimony of women in similar situations where there was a failure of state protection, or the testimony of the claimant herself regarding past personal incidents where state protection did not materialise.

3. **A change in country circumstances, generally viewed as a positive change, may have no impact, or even a negative impact, on a woman's fear of gender-relating persecution.** In situations where a woman's fear is related to personal-status laws or where her human rights are being violated by private citizens, a change in country circumstances may not mean a positive change for the woman, as these areas are often the last to change. An assessment should be made of the claimant's particular fear and of whether the changes are meaningful and effective enough for her fear of gender-related persecution to no longer be well-founded.

4. **In determining the reasonableness of a woman's recourse to an internal flight alternative (IFA), decision-makers should consider the ability of women, because of the gender, to travel safely to the IFA and to stay there without facing undue hardship.** In determining the reasonableness of an IFA, the decision-makers should take into account factors including religious, economic, and cultural factors, and consider whether and how these factors affect women in the IFA.

D. SPECIAL PROBLEMS AT DETERMINATION HEARINGS

Women refugee claimants face special problems in demonstrating that their claims are credible and trustworthy. Some of the difficulties may arise because of cross-cultural misunderstandings. For example:

1. Women from societies where the preservation of one's virginity or marital dignity is the cultural norm may be reluctant to disclose their experiences of sexual violence in order to keep their "shame" to themselves and not dishonour their family or community.

2. Women from certain cultures where men do not share the details of their political, military or even social activities with their spouses, daughters or mothers may find themselves in a difficult situation when questioned about the experiences of their male relatives.

3. Women refugee claimants who have suffered sexual violence may exhibit a pattern of symptoms referred to as Rape Trauma Syndrome, and may require extremely sensitive handling. Similarly, women who have been subjected to domestic violence may exhibit a pattern of symptoms referred to as Battered Woman Syndrome and may also be reluctant to testify. In some cases it will be appropriate to consider whether claimants should be allowed to have the option of providing their testimony outside the hearing room by affidavit or by videotape, or in front of members and refugee claims officers specifically trained in dealing with violence against women. Members should be familiar with the UNHCR Executive Committee *Guidelines on the Protection of Refugee Women.*

FRAMEWORK OF ANALYSIS

1. Assess the harm feared by the claimant. Does the harm feared constitute persecution?

(a) For the treatment to likely amount to persecution, it must be a serious form of harm which detracts from the claimants fundamental human rights

(b) To assist decision-makers in determining what kinds of treatment are considered persecution, an objective standard is provided by international human rights instruments (see appendix 2)

2. Ascertain whether the claimant's fear of persecution is based on any of the grounds, singly or in combination, enumerated in the Convention refugee definition. Considerations:

- It is necessary to ascertain the characteristic of the claimant which places her or members of her group at risk, and to ascertain the linkage of that characteristic to a Convention ground
- Gender is an innate characteristic and it may form a particular social group
- A subgroup of women may also form a particular social group. Women in these particular social groups have characteristics (innate or unchangeable) additional to gender, which make them fear persecution
- The gender-defined group cannot be defined **solely** by the fact that its members share a common persecution

3. Determine whether the claimant's fear of persecution is well-founded. This includes an assessment of the evidence related to the ability or willingness of the state to protect the claimant and, more generally, the objective basis of the claim. Considerations:

- There may be little or no documentary evidence presented with respect to the inadequacy of state protection as it related to gender-related persecution. There may be a need for greater reliance on evidence of similarly situated women and on the claimant's own experience
- The claimant need not have approached non-state organisations for protection
- Factors including the social, cultural, religious, and economic context in which the claimant finds herself should be considered in determining whether it was objectively unreasonable for the claimant not to have sought state protection
- Where a woman's fear related to personal-status laws or where her human rights are being violated by private citizens, an otherwise positive change in country conditions may have no impact, or even a negative impact, on a woman's fear of gender-related persecution

4. If required, determine whether there is a possibility of an internal flight alternative. Considerations:

- Whether there would be undue hardship for the claimant, both in reaching the location of the IFA and in establishing residence there
- Religious, economic, social and cultural factors, among others, may be relevant in determining the reasonableness of an IFA for a woman fearing gender-related persecution

ANNEX 6 ADIMA *Guidelines on Gender Issues for Decision-Makers* (July 1996)

1 INTRODUCTION

1.1 These guidelines have been developed to help officers in assessing gender based claims by applicants for protection visas in Australia or entry to Australia under the offshore Humanitarian Programme. The purpose of these guidelines is to ensure that applications are dealt with effectively and sensitively.

1.2 In recognising that women may experience persecution and discrimination differently from men, the guidelines provide advice on how decision makers can best approach claims of gender-based persecution. It should be noted that claims of gender based persecution can be made by both men and women. However, the feminine pronoun is used in relation to the applicant throughout the guidelines in recognition of the fact that most gender-based claims are made by female applicants.

1.3 The guidelines provide practical guidance on procedural issues which can influence women applicants and which may affect their ability to present their claims, for example, in relation to receiving applications, managing interviews and ensuring confidentiality of information. They also offer assistance with the interpretation of the regulatory requirements of the various protection, refugee and humanitarian visa classes as they relate to claims put forward by applicants with gender-based claims, with the aim of ensuring that the assessment process is sensitive to gender issues

1.4 The information provided in this guide should be read in the context of the Department's broader guidelines on refugee and humanitarian decision-making:

- for applications in Australia for protection visa: *Onshore Refugee Procedures Manual*, relevant chapters of the *Procedures Advice Manual (PAM III)*, including the *Refugee Law Guidelines;*
- for applications under the offshore Humanitarian Programme: relevant chapters of *the Procedures Advice Manual (PAM III)*, including the *Generic Guidelines B Offshore Humanitarian Visas.*

1.5 This document aims to give decision makers an additional level of understanding of the particular needs of women within existing policy frameworks for refugee and humanitarian applications; as such, it does not replace other relevant policy advice, but is intended to complement it.

1.6 These guidelines are designed to apply to officers in Australia and at overseas posts. Accordingly, they acknowledge that often different operational decision making environments exist. The a vice contained in these guidelines should be adopted as far as practicable.

2 BACKGROUND
The international protection framework
2.1   The international community's response to refugees is based on the *1951 Convention and 1967 Protocol relating to the law of Refugees* (Refugee Convention) and the principle of non-refoulement. lie United Nations High Commissioner for Refugees (UNHCR) is the international body that is responsible for providing international protection to refugees and promoting lasting solutions to their plight.

2.2   There are a number of international instruments in which obligations to protect the human rights of women, including refugee women, may be found. They include:

> *Universal Declaration of Human Rights* (UDHR)
> *International Covenant on CIWI and Political Rights (ICCPR)*
> *International Covenant on Economic, Social and Cultural Rights* (ICESCR) *Convention Against Torture and Other Cruel, Inhuman or Degrading Treatment or Punishment (CAT)*
> *Convention on the Elimination of all Forms of racial Discrimination (CERD) Convention on the Elimination of all Forms of Discrimination Against Women* (CEDAW)
> *Convention on the Rights of the Child* (CROC)
> *Convention on Consent to Marriage, Minimum Age for Marriage and Registration of Marriages*
> *Convention on the Nationality of married Women*
> *1.949 Geneva Conventions on the Laws of War and the two Additional Protocols of 1977*
> *Declaration on the Protection of Women and Children in Emergency and Armed Conflict*
> *Declaration on the Elimination of Violence Against Women*

2.3   The international community has devoted a considerable amount of effort and resources to refugees and displaced people. As a result there now exists a complex, if at times fragile, network of institutions, laws and agreements specifically designed to meet the needs of people who have been forced to leave their homeland. Refugee protection has thus taken a number of forms:

• admission to safety in the country of asylum and observance of the fundamental principle of non-refoulement;

- temporary protection until a lasting solution may be found - this may be (in order of preference) voluntary repatriation, local integration or resettlement in a third country; and
- the development of new strategies on prevention which are designed to address the causes as well as the consequences of forced displacement.

There is also an awareness in the international community that lasting solutions to the problem of human displacement will only be found if a concerted effort is made to protect human rights.

2.4   Recently there has been an increasing awareness and focus on the particular vulnerability of refugee and displaced women.

Recognising the needs of refugee and displaced women
2.5   Women compose the majority of people in vulnerable situations because they have been displaced or are refugees. UNHCR indicate that of an estimated 27 million refugees and displaced people in the world, the vast majority are women and children. Women are often particularly vulnerable - after fleeing persecution and violence they may face new threats of violence and abuse in their country of asylum. In addition, due to social and cultural mores they may not necessarily have the same remedies for state protection as men, or the same opportunities for flight.

2.6   The issue of gender persecution and problems facing women asylum seekers have received attention from the Executive Committee of the United Nations High Commissioner for Refugees' Programme (EXCOM), UNHCR and some governments. UNHCR adopted *Guidelines on the Protection of Refugee Women* in 199 1. A number of EXCOM Conclusions have been adopted recommending the development of appropriate guidelines, culminating in 1995 with EXCOM's recommendation that:

"In accordance with the principle that women's rights are human rights, these guidelines should recognise as refugees women whose claim to refugee status is based upon well-founded fear of persecution for reasons enumerated in the 1951 Convention and 1967 Protocol, including persecution through sexual violence or other gender-related persecution".

2.7   International concerns regarding the plight of refugee women have not been confined to the mechanisms surrounding refugee protection. The 1995 World Conference of Women in Beijing drew attention to the violation of women's human rights experienced by refugee women and recommended the development of gender guidelines. The development of this document should be seen in this international context.

Australia's response

2.8   Australia accords a high priority to the promotion and protection of human rights in the international sphere. Australia also has a long-standing commitment to assist international efforts to prevent and alleviate humanitarian crises through diplomatic initiatives, participation in peace-keeping forces, aid, resettlement of refugees and other humanitarian cases through the offshore Humanitarian Programme and the granting of permanent residence to individuals who have been found in need of protection in Australia in accordance with our international obligations under the Refugee Convention.

2.9   Persons requiring resettlement from overseas may apply under the offshore Humanitarian Programme, which is subdivided into the Refugee component, the Special Humanitarian Programme and the Special Assistance Category. Australia has historically recognised some special needs of women via the Woman at Risk visa subclass of the Refugee component, which is specifically targeted at woman refugees or women registered as 'of concern" to the UNHCR who are in danger of victimisation, harassment or serious abuse because of their sex. In addition, overseas staff of the Department who will be assessing applications under the offshore Humanitarian Programme receive cross-cultural and gender sensitivity g prior to taking up their positions overseas. In terms of the processing of applications by women for protection visas in Australia, officers have also received training in cultural and gender sensitisation.

2.10   Whilst women represent the majority of refugees worldwide, they represent a smaller proportion of the refugees who are resettled in Australia under the offshore Humanitarian Programme or granted protection visas in Australia. . This may be a result of many factors, including women's inability or lack of resources to travel unaccompanied or the tendency of applications to be made by the male head of the household. Nonetheless, women's vulnerability remains.

2.11   Guidelines for officers which specifically address women's needs are important if women's claims of persecution, including gender-based persecution, are to be properly heard and assessed. When applying for humanitarian visas, women may face particular problems, such as difficulties in making their case to decision makers, especially when they have had experiences which are difficult and painful to describe. There may also be social and cultural barriers to lodging applications and/or pursuing claims related to their own experiences. For example: in families where the male head of household seeks asylum, claims relating to female members of the family unit may not be mentioned, may be ignored or may not be given any weight by either the male head of household, or the decision maker, or the female applicant herself.

2.12 Barriers to accessing the refugee and humanitarian visa system and the failure to fully explore women's claims can be compounded by difficulties in gaining recognition of the particular forms of persecution or discrimination manifested against women.

2.13 Guidelines for decision makers which focus on these gender-related issues assist in promoting a consistent, sensitive approach to women's claims. They are also consistent with international practice and meet the Government's objectives to provide equitable and accessible services.

2.14 The following chapters focus on two main areas where women may face difficulty in gaining recognition of their claims for protection:

- procedural issues; and
- the assessment of claims.

Focusing attention on gender-related persecution/discrimination will ensure that officers are conscious of forms of harm that may be inflicted on a woman uniquely or more commonly than on a man

2.15 It should be noted that these guidelines do not advocate gender as an additional ground in the Refugee Convention definition. However, it should be accepted that gender can influence or dictate the type of persecution or harm suffered and the reasons for this treatment. Even where gender is not the central issue, giving conscious consideration to gender-related aspects of a case will assist officers to understand the totality of the environment from which an applicant claims a fear of persecution or abuse of their human rights.

3 PROCEDURES

3.1 The following procedures are primarily focused on women applicants for protection visas in Australia and women applicants applying under the offshore Humanitarian Programme. They may also be applied to male applicants who make claims of gender based persecution. While procedures differ between Australia and overseas posts, reflecting the different criteria for each visa class and decision making environments, there are common elements that can be applied by officers required to examine and process visa applications, regardless of the particular visa class applied for.

3.2 The procedures outlined below should, nonetheless, be read in conjunction with the other instructions relating to specific visa classes. For example, applications for entry into Australian under the offshore Humanitarian Programme should be considered with regard to the *Generic Guidelines B2:*

Offshore Humanitarian Visas and guidelines on specific visa classes and subclasses; applications lodged in Australia for protection visas should be considered with regard to the *Onshore Refugee Procedures Manual* and the *Refugee Law Guidelines.*

Preparing the case

Researching Claims

3.3   Adequate research of the claims made in the application and an understanding of the situation in the country of origin of the applicant is important for the full exploration of a person's claims. Where gender related claims are raised, or suspected, an understanding of the role, status and treatment of women in the country of origin is particularly important. Adequate preparation allows a relationship of confidence and trust with the applicant to be developed and allows an interviewer to ask the right questions and deal with any problems that arise during an interview.

Sources of Information

3.4   There are a variety of sources of information available, depending on the location of the decision maker. Officers in Australia have access to the online information databases of the Country Information Service Section of the Department (CISNET). Officers at overseas posts have access to a variety of local sources, including Department of Foreign Affairs and Trade officers, UNHCR and access to CISNET on CD-ROM.

3.5   The types of information which may be relevant in assessing gender-related claims are often similar to that relevant for other types of claims. However, research should also focus on the following areas:

- legal, economic and civil status of women in the country of origin
- the incidence of violence against women in the country of origin, including both sexual and domestic, and the adequacy of state protection afforded to women
- cultural and social mores of the country with respect to such issues as the role and status of women, the family, nature of family relationships, attitudes towards same sex relationships, attitudes to 'foreign' influences, etc
- respect for and adherence to fundamental human rights the differential application of human rights for women issues directly related to claims raised in the application

3.6   It should be noted that violence against women, particularly sexual or domestic violence, tends to be largely under-reported or ignored in many countries.

> The absence of information on the above topics for any particular country should not necessarily be taken as an indicator that abuses of women's human rights do not occur

3.7   Identifying these issues will enable an officer to become aware of the cultural sensitivities and differences in a particular country before considering the applicant's claims.

Using the Information
3.8   When assessing a woman's claims of well-founded fear of persecution (for the protection visa class and refugee visa subclasses), the evidence must show that what the woman applicant genuinely fears is persecution for a Convention reason as distinguished from random violence or criminal activity perpetrated against her as an individual. The general human rights record of the country of origin, and the experiences of other women in a similar situation, may indicate the existence of systematic persecution for a Convention reason.

- A more detailed examination of assessing claims and facts against the refugee definition can be found in Part 4 'The Assessment of the Claims', the *Onshore Re Refugee Procedures Manual, Refugee Law Guidelines and in PAM3 Generic Guidelines B2 - Offshore Humanitarian Visas.*
- Only the refugee subclasses of the offshore Humanitarian Programme (subclasses 200, 201, 203 and 204) require applicants to demonstrate that they are subject to persecution (ie for a Convention reason). The other visa classes and subclasses of the offshore Humanitarian Programme refer to criteria where applicants are subject to 'substantial discrimination' or who are in vulnerable situations. Policy advice for interpreting these criteria may be found in *PAM3 Generic Guidelines B2 - Offshore Humanitarian Visas* and the PAM3 guidelines on specific visa classes.

Interviews
3.9   The objective of an interview is to obtain further information from the applicant on her claims and to clarify any details that are uncertain or ambiguous in the application. Interviewing officers should seek to clarify all matters material to the final outcome of the application.

3.10   It is important to identify the person included in an application who has the strongest claims. An application written by, or an interview with, a male head of household may place little or no emphasis on a female family unit member's experience of persecution or discrimination, even though her experiences may carry the most weight. A woman who is included in the application as a member of a family unit should be given the opportunity of a separate interview so that she is able, with appropriate assurances of confidentiality, to outline her experiences.

3.11 Interviewing a woman who has/or may come forward with gender-related claims must be done in a sensitive and sympathetic way, with respect for confidentiality.

3.12 Many women face particular difficulties when discussing gender-related claims which may include rape, or other forms of sexual violence, domestic violence and discrimination. In particular, women may experience difficulty in recounting sexual torture or rape in front of family members. Some women, because of the shame they may feel over what has happened to them, may understandably be reluctant to identify the true extent of persecution they have suffered because of their continuing fear and distrust of people in authority. They may also be afraid to reveal their experiences because they are so traumatised by them or because they fear reprisals from their family and/or community. Female applicants who are survivors of torture and trauma, in particular, require a supportive environment where they can be reassured of the confidentiality of the gender-sensitive claims they are making.

3.13 Officers should be aware that female victims of violence, discrimination and abuse often do not volunteer information about their experiences and may be reluctant to do so in the presence of family members. In particular, during interviews where an interpreter is used, a woman applicant may be reluctant to divulge information for fear that the interpreter may be an informer for the authorities in the country of origin or that they will divulge their story to others in the community. The applicant should be assured of the confidential nature of the interview process.

In the vast majority of cases women who have experienced torture and/or trauma have suffered these abuses at the hands of men. Coupled with a fear and distrust of authorities, this fact is likely to seriously inhibit the capacity of a female applicant to divulge details of her experiences to a male interviewer

3.14 It will be a matter of the officer having prior appreciation of women's issues in the country of origin, skillful and sensitive interviewing and an understanding of the psychological effects of torture and trauma that will assist these issues to come forward.

Physical environment
3.15 In order to facilitate discussion of gender-related claims it is important that the interview room and surrounding environment be conducive to open discussion. The interview room should be arranged in such a way as to encourage discussion of the claims, promote confidentiality and to lessen any possibility of perceived power imbalances.

Use of Interpreter

3.16   Before scheduling the interview, ensure that appropriate arrangements have been made for interpreters who are sensitive to any special requirements of the applicant regarding language, dialect or ethno-cultural sensitivities. If an applicant has made claims of a sensitive or traumatic nature every effort should be made to ensure an interpreter and interviewing officer of the same sex.

3.17   Where an officer suspects, as a result of researching the country information relating to the case, that gender-related claims may be raised or discussed, every effort should be made to engage an interpreter of the same sex, with regard to any cultural or religious sensitivities, wherever possible.

3.18   During the interview, both the interviewer and interpreter should be aware of the possible difficulties in interpreting particular words, such as 'rape' or 'assault', which may have different meanings or connotations in the applicant's language.

Establishing rapport

3.19   Establishing good rapport with an applicant is very important and begins with the first contact. At the interview, the interviewer should take the time to introduce him/herself and the interpreter, explain clearly what his/her role is and the exact purpose of the interview. The applicant should be assured that her claims will be treated in an absolutely confidential manner.

3.20   Officers should behave in a culturally and gender sensitive manner throughout the interview. It is essential that the interviewer remain neutral, compassionate and objective during the interview.

3.21   However, it should be remembered that no matter how supportive the interviewing officer and the environment may be, the interview process (because of the imbalance of power between participants) will impact on how women may respond.

Culturally sensitive communication

3.22   Officers are required to deal with a wide range of people and as such they should have a well developed understanding of cultural differences, especially in relation to the way they communicate with others.

3.23   Body language can be interpreted in many different ways. It is therefore important that officers ensure they avoid gestures which may be perceived as intimidating or culturally insensitive or inappropriate. Whilst it is important that officers maintain control of the interview, it is also important to ensure that body language does not inhibit the discussion by making the applicant feel uncomfortable.

3.24   Similarly, an approach which is too relaxed may create the impression that the officer is not listening. The officer should allow the applicant to present her claims with minimal interruption.

> Active listening skills play an important part in the flow of the interview and can assist an applicant who may be finding it difficult to recall painful or sensitive events associated with her claims

3.25   Being aware of cultural sensitivities during the interview may provide the applicant with reassurance. As with most interviews this can most appropriately be demonstrated by attentive listening, including the following:

- reflective listening (ie. paraphrasing what has been said by the applicant)
- not talking at the same time as the applicant not making judgemental comments
- maintaining composure if the applicant gets angry or upset
- nodding affirmatively when appropriate
- ensuring minimum interruptions and/or distractions
- ensuring the interpreting is an accurate reflection of the applicant's testimony (eg relative length of translation, reaction from the applicant)

3.26   If an officer feels that a female applicant has further claims of a sensitive nature that have not been discussed during any stage of the interviewing process, the applicant should be encouraged to provide any supplementary information that she feels may support her claims. Alternatively, if an applicant has difficulty in speaking about her persecution, she may be more comfortable putting her claims in writing.

Assessing and handling information
Credibility/Demeanour
3.27   In many societies the stigma attached to victims of sexual assault are such that women cannot bring themselves to discuss such events. In addition, the effects of abuse and trauma may make it difficult for a woman to accurately recall the details and dates of the events when they finally recount their experiences. It may be that a woman is either unable to discuss a particular experience or may not see its relevance to her claims. It is also unlikely that a woman whose written claims are part of an application supplied by other members of her family unit or who is interviewed in the presence of other family members will discuss the circumstances surrounding a sexual assault.

> The fact that a woman failed to raise a gender-related claim of persecution on several occasions should not necessarily cast doubt on her credibility if it is raised at a later date and should not be responded to as if it does. The pertinent issue, of course, is whether or not the claimed event occurred and, in the protection visa class and refugee visa subclasses, whether it was for a Convention reason

3.28   If such claims are revealed separately from the rest of the family, officers must treat the information provided with great care. This is particularly necessary if the woman has indicated that other members of the family are unaware of her experiences. In some cultures rape and other forms of sexual assault are seen as the women's failing to preserve her virginity or marital dignity - disclosure of this information to family members may have adverse consequences to the applicant.

3.29   Similarly, the level of emotional distress exhibited by a female applicant during the recounting of her experiences should not automatically add more credibility to her claims than that of another who may be very calm and quiet when describing a similar event. A lack of emotion displayed at interview does not necessarily mean that the applicant is not distressed or deeply affected by what has happened.   Cultural differences and trauma can often play an important role in determining demeanor.

3.30   In some circumstances, it may be reasonable to seek, and accept, objective psychological evidence.   It is unnecessary to establish the precise details of the sexual assault as opposed to the fact of its occurrence and the motivation of the perpetrator.   In some circumstances it should be noted that a woman may not be aware of the reasons for her abuse.

Confidentiality
3.31   Any applicant who has provided gender-related claims should be reassured that the details will not be provided, in any form, to another member of their family unit.   All information both written and audio taped should be marked *"Not for release to anyone except with the agreement of the applicant"*.

3.32   All confidential information provided by female applicants, particularly that of a gender-sensitive nature, is protected under the *Freedom of Information Act*.   The only circumstances in which another member of a family unit can obtain access to the gender related claims (or indeed any claims) made by a female member of their family is with the written consent of the female applicant concerned.

3.33   If a visa is refused, some applicants who have provided gender-sensitive claims may wish to personally collect their notification letter and copy of the decision record, or nominate a separate address for the letter to be sent. These issues should be discussed with the applicant at the interview stage.

4 THE ASSESSMENT OF CLAIMS

4.1   The following section provides guidance for officers assessing applications for protection visas and applications for entry to Australia, under the offshore Humanitarian Programme, as a refugee (ie under visa class 866 and subclasses 200, 201, 203 and 204). These types of applications centre on the definition of 'refugee' in the *1951 Convention* and *1967 Protocol relating to the Status of Refugees* (Refugee Convention).

*   Women outside Australia who are refugees or who are registered as being of concern to UNHCR may also be eligible for entry to Australia under the Woman at Risk (WR) 204 visa subclass of the offshore Humanitarian Programme. This visa reflects Australia's response to the circumstances of certain women outside their home country who are in danger of victimisation, harassment or serious abuse because of their gender. Further policy advice in deciding applications of this visa subclass can be found in *PAM3 Schedule 2 - Permanent Visa (Migrant) Woman At Risk - Visa 204.*
*   Under the offshore Humanitarian Programme, applicants who meet the Refugee Convention definition of a refugee must also satisfy the other criteria of the visa subclass before they may be granted a visa.
*   Officers should also refer to other sources of guidance for processing these applications, including: *Onshore Refugee Procedures Manual; Refugee Law Guidelines; PAM Generic Guidelines B2: Offshore Humanitarian Visas.*

4.2   The non-refugee components of the offshore Humanitarian Programme (the Special Humanitarian and Special Assistance Categories) are designed for people who do not meet refugee criteria but who, nonetheless:

*   are subject to substantial discrimination amounting to serious human rights violations and for whom resettlement in Australia is the appropriate solution; or
*   are suffering some form of disadvantage or hardship meriting a humanitarian response and who have close links to Australia.

Although discrimination, disadvantage and hardship constitute lesser tests than persecution, assessment of applications for these visas will also involve an examination of the human rights environment in an applicant's country of origin.   Officers should be aware that women may experience not only persecution but also discrimination, disadvantage or hardship in a manner qualitatively different from men as a result of their gender.

The Refugee Convention is intended to provide protection to persons who have a well founded fear of being persecuted on specified grounds. Recognising that treatment or discrimination amounts to persecution is the first step. An officer must also be satisfied that this fear of persecution is 'well-founded' and that is 'for reasons of' a Convention ground.

Persecution and gender-related persecution

4.3   The types of persecution inflicted on individuals may differ because of their gender. It is important to bear in mind that gender-based persecution is only care of many types of persecution a woman may encounter.

- Accordingly, officers must carefully consider all general claims of persecution before turning to consider gender-related claims, otherwise there is the possibility that a woman's claims of persecution unrelated to gender will be ignored.

    - this will also avoid unnecessary retraumitisation of applicants over their experiences related to sexual violence.

4.4   The process of identifying every abuse of human rights against internationally agreed standards of human rights (the human rights protected in the International Bill of Human Rights which includes the UDHR, ICCPR and ICESCR - see 2.2 above) should allow a decision-maker to properly consider all serious forms of harm a person may face, including those harms that are gender-based.

- the further step of focussing on gender-based persecution will ensure that officers are conscious of forms of harm that may be inflicted on a woman uniquely or more commonly than on a man.
- this emphasis on gender-related persecution, combined with the appropriate techniques and awareness, may assist a decision-maker to elicit such claims which would otherwise have remained untouched.

> Increased emphasis on the role of gender in persecution is not intended to alter the ordinary meaning of persecution. Rather it is intended to ensure that all of the applicant's claims of persecution are fully considered

4.5   Australian case law has referred to internationally agreed standards of human rights in recognizing persecution. Whilst there are areas of uncertainty, it can generally be stated that the more fundamental the right threatened, the more likely that the breach of that right amounts to persecution.

Persecution by torture or cruel, inhuman or degrading punishment or treatment

4.6   Rape and other forms of sexual assault are acts which inflict severe pain and suffering (both mental and physical) and which have been used by many persecutors. Such treatment clearly comes within the bounds of torture as defined by the Convention Against Torture (CAT). Furthermore, sexual violence amounts to a violation of the prohibition against cruel, inhuman or degrading treatment, the right to security of person and in some instances the right to life, as contained in a variety of international instruments. There are many other types of treatment that are specific to women, such as female genital mutilation and forced abortion, that also constitute cruel, inhuman or degrading treatment.

4.7   Rape is often used to punish a woman for her actions or to encourage her to put pressure on others whose activities meet with State disapproval. Systematic rape has also been used as part of 'ethnic cleansing'.

4.8   It should also be remembered that in many nations victims of sexual assault become outcasts or are considered to have committed a criminal offence. This fact can be part of the persecutor's motivation in choosing this form of persecution.

Restrictions imposed by legal, social or religious mores
4.9   The status of women in some societies may be restricted and dictated by legal, social or religious mores. The restrictions will vary from mere inconvenience to oppression. In addition a broad range of penalties may be imposed for disobeying restrictions placed on women. Officers should carefully assess the available country of origin information on those issues.

Possible persecution by violation of thought, conscience and religion
4.10   Gender-based persecution is sometimes more subtle than other forms. It can take the form of restrictions on the way a woman behaves or it can involve forcing her to act in a certain way. It may affect a woman's ability to participate in the public life of a society.

Some examples of gender-based treatment against women which may constitute persecution in particular circumstances are:

- social oppression of women - in some communities the status and behavior of women has been dictated by a State sanctioned religious hierarchy
- denial of participation by women in the political, civil or economic life
- forced marriage - many societies practice arranged marriage and this in itself may not be a persecutory practice. However, the consequences of defying the wishes of one's family when viewed against the background of the State's failure to protect a person should be carefully considered
- infanticide, forced abortion, female genital mutilation, which has serious impact on a woman's physical and mental health.

Agents of persecution

4.11 Convention refugee is someone who is at risk because their country of nationality has failed to protect them from persecution. A failure to protect can occur in several ways. It may be that the authorities are themselves the perpetrators of the persecution. However, it may be that the persecutor is another party from whom the authorities do not protect the person either because they are unwilling or unable to do so. Claims of gender-based persecution often involve persecution committed by non-state agents.

> In assessing gender-based persecution it is important to research the accepted norms of the relevant societies to determine how they operate both through legislation and in terms of actual practice in order to determine the degree of protection available to women

4.12 In some societies, particular types of violence against women may be officially condemned or even illegal but in fact be so endemic that local authorities turn a blind eye to its occurrence. Sometimes these forms of abuse are systemic or culturally acceptable so that local authorities may actively participate or be complicit in the harms suffered.

4.13 It is important to remember that the international protection of the Refugee Convention is only available to those who are not able to gain protection from their national authorities. Where a non-state agent of persecution is involved there is a need to establish that the state is "unwilling or unable' to protect the applicant. Clearly, this is established if the authorities were aware of a person's need for protection (either because of her approach or by some other means) and none was forthcoming.

4.14 It should also be noted that it is not always reasonable or possible for a woman to alert the authorities to her need for protection. State protection should be effective - with provision of mechanisms for dealing with complaints and also assurance that such avenues for redress are realistic and accessible to a woman of her culture and position.

- Officers should investigate why a woman did not seek the protection of the state, as her inability to even request protection may in itself be indicative of a failure of state protection.

Cumulative grounds

4.15 An applicant may put forward accounts of different types of harm, none of which, taken individually, will amount to persecution. In these cases it is necessary to consider the cumulative effect of the individual instances of harm.

4.16 This principle is not gender specific. However, the forms of harm directed against women may be more various and more subtle. This may reflect the fact that the woman may not be the primary focus of the persecutory behaviour, which may be directed primarily at male family members.

Well-founded fear
Past Persecution and the "changed circumstances" test

4.17 There are two ways that a well-founded fear of persecution can be established:

- there is a 'real chance" of future persecution; or
- a person has been persecuted in the past and the 'changed circumstances" test (set down by the High Court in Chan has not been satisfied.

4.18 There is a significant difference between the two. A person who has suffered persecution in the past does not have to prove that there is a 'real chance' of future persecution. Rather, a continuing well-founded fear of persecution should be accepted unless the officer can establish that there has been a substantial and material change in circumstances in the country of origin.

4.19 The application of the 'changed circumstances' test must be carefully applied in cases of gender-related persecution. The subjective state of mind of the applicant has obvious implications for gender-related persecution, especially in cases of sexual assault, where the effects on the victim are long lasting. In addition, an overall understanding of the role and perception of women in the applicant's society will demonstrate the extent of the persecution a woman would face if she were to return.

4.20 Officers must also carefully consider what circumstances, if any, would satisfy the "changed circumstances" test in cases of gender-related persecution. Many cases of gender-based persecution occur at the hands of non-state agents of persecution whose actions are ignored or condoned by the authorities. Even where changes in the national legislation or other state of affairs have occurred, such agents of persecution are seldom brought to justice and the is no accountability by the state for the acts of persecution inflicted on the applicant.

Relocation
4.21 An important consideration in gender-related persecution, as with other persecution, is whether the persecution occurs nation-wide or whether it is regionalised. It may be for example that a person is able to access protection in urbanised parts of the country where there is a real chance of persecution in the rural areas. If so, officers should consider whether the applicant could reasonably be expected to relocate within her own country.

In considering the issue of relocation the relevant issue is whether the applicant could safely live in another part of the country. Officers must carefully consider gender-related issues when applying this test. Financial, logistical, social, cultural and other barriers to reaching internal safety may significantly affect persons of one gender over another. In addition, gender bases persecution may be systemic and no protection may be available from the authorities in any part of the country.

Convention grounds

4.22 There are five Convention grounds: race, religion, nationality, membership of a particular social group and political opinion. In addition to actual membership of a Convention ground, a well-founded fear of persecution may be for reasons of an imputed Convention ground. A woman's claims for refugee status may rest on one or more grounds of the Convention even where the persecution is gender-based.

4.23 Where the persecution of women is concerned, it should be recognised that an imputed Convention ground is an important aspect to consider. Women in many societies are forced into a subordinate role in many areas of life. Therefore, the opportunities to assume a publicly recognisable profile do not occur frequently and women are often aligned with the views of their male relatives.

4.24 The added difficulty is that, in many societies women have little or no information on the activities of their male relatives and may find it difficult to explain the reasons for their persecution. They may not realise that the authorities, for example, impute a political opinion to them because of their association (by marriage, family links etc) with others who have attracted the authorities' attention.

Political opinion

4.25 In some societies, overt demonstration of political opinion by women may not be possible as women are not allowed to formally participate in political life. However, there may be country information about the existence of covert political organisations involving women or about the suspicions of authorities that such organisations exist. Furthermore, the fact that a woman may challenge particular social conventions about the manner in which women should behave may be considered political by the authorities and may attract persecutory treatment on this basis.

> In some societies an organisation of women who are not seeking a public or political profile but who may, for example, possess a feminist ideology, may be viewed as espousing a political opinion hostile to the current administration and persecuted for that reason.

4.26   In many cases there is a societal assumption that women defer to men on all significant issues and that their political views are aligned with those of the dominant members of their family (usually husbands, fathers or brothers). They may thus, experience persecution for this reason, ie imputed political opinion.

4.27   There are also cases where persecutors are aware that a woman possesses no political opinion but persecute her as a means of demoralising the rest of her family or community who do hold a political opinion hostile to the current administration.

4.28   The difficulty in assessing claims of imputed political opinion, of course, is that the woman may not be aware of the reasons why she has been persecuted. Officers faced with unexplained instances of persecution should look to whether the explanation may be traced to her family's political opinion or another Convention ground.

Race
4.29   Race is a Convention ground based on readily identifiable characteristics. In general racism knows no gender, however persecution may be expressed in different ways against men and women. For example the persecutor may choose to destroy the ethnic identity and/or prosperity of a racial group by killing, maiming or incarcerating the men whilst the women may be viewed as capable of propagating the ethnic identity and persecuted in a different way, such as through sexual violence.

Religion
4.30   In certain societies, the role ascribed to women may be attributable to the requirements of the state or official religion. The failure of women to conform to this role or model of behaviour may then be perceived by the authorities or other agents of persecution as the failure to practice or to hold certain religious beliefs and as such an attempt to corrupt the society or even as a threat to the religion's continued power. This may be the case even though the woman actually holds the official religious faith but it is not outwardly evidenced by her behaviour.

Nationality

4.31   Gender-based persecution for reasons of nationality may have its genesis in laws which deprive a woman of her citizenship in certain situations (eg marriage to a foreign national). Alternatively, a woman who has married a foreign national may not be able to live with him in her country of nationality. Rather than the loss of citizenship itself, officers should enquire into what harm results from this loss. For example, whether it leads to loss of right of residence or loss of other privileges or benefits.

Membership of a Particular Social Group

4.32   The Australian Federal Court has laid down some essential principles in the interpretation of the particular social group ground. Those principles are summarised as follows:

- the claimed particular social group must be cognisable
    - a group is cognisable if there is a common unifying element binding the members of the group because of shared common social characteristics and/or shared interest or experience in common *(Morato's case);*
    - cognisability does not require a voluntary association amongst the members of the group *(Morato's case);*
    - a group is not cognisable where the sole criterion defining the group is a common act although it is possible that, over a period of time, individuals who engage in similar actions may form a particular social group *(Morato's case);*

    - the group is not defined solely by the persecution feared *(Morato's case).*

- the nexus between the particular social group and the fear of persecution must be established. That is, there is a well-founded fear of persecution *"for reasons of"* membership of that group *(Morato's case);* and
- the individual is (or is perceived to be) a member of that group, i.e. there is a common unifying element binding members together *(A & B's case).*

4.33   While 'gender' of itself is not a Convention ground, it may, be a significant factor in recognising a particular social group or an identifying characteristic of such a group. Officers should bear in mind that there is no Australian jurisprudence on the issue of women as a 'particular social group'. The Refugee Review Tribunal has found that whilst being a broad category, women nonetheless have both immutable characteristics and shared common social characteristics which may make them cognisable as a group and which may attract persecution. In addition, gender may be combined with certain other characteristics which could define a particular social group in situations where there is evidence that this group suffers or fears to suffer severe discrimination or harsh and inhuman treatment that is distinguished from the situation of others of the same gender. The important principle to consider is whether the persecution suffered or feared is far reasons of membership of a particular social group.

Officers should consider this Convention ground on a case by case basis which takes account of the totality of an applicant's claims and the situation in the applicant's country of origin

ANNEX 7 Gender-Sensitive Techniques for Interviewing Women Refugees (UNHCR)[6]

It may be necessary to use a variety of gender-sensitive techniques to obtain information from women during the status-determination process. The recruitment and training of female interpreters is a precondition for the most effective interviewing:

- Be aware of gender differences in communication, particularly non-verbal communications. As an interviewer avoid intimidating gestures that inhibit responses. In assessing the credibility of the female applicant, for example, do not judge it on the basis of such Western cultural values as the ability to maintain eye contact

- Be patient with female applicants to overcome inhibitions, particularly regarding sexual abuse. Questions may need to be asked in a number of different ways before victims of rape and other abuses feel able to tell their stories. Enough time should be allowed during the interviewing process to permit the female applicant to build a rapport with the interviewer so she is able to recount her experiences. Do not ask for details of the sexual abuse; the important thing in establishing a well-founded fear of persecution is to establish that some form has occurred

- Recognise that women who have been sexually assaulted exhibit a pattern of symptoms that are described as Rape Trauma Syndrome. These symptoms include persistent fear, a loss of self-confidence and self-esteem, difficulty in concentration, an attitude of self-blame, a pervasive feeling of loss of control, and memory loss or distortion. These symptoms will influence how a woman applicant responds during the interview. If misunderstood, they may wrongly be seen as discrediting her testimony

- Understand that women in many societies do not have specific information about the activities of men in their families. Gaps in their knowledge should not be construed as lack of credibility unless there is other evidence of such lack of credibility

- Provide women the opportunity to be questioned by themselves, out of the hearing of other members of their family. Victims of sexual abuse may not feel comfortable recounting their experiences in front of their fathers, husbands, brothers or children

---

[6] UNHCR *Guidelines on the Protection of Refugee Women* 1991, 41-42

ANNEX 8   Addressing Claims Based on Sexual Orientation (CCR)[7]

- There may be a delay in making a claim or in referring to sexual orientation because of bad advice or fears resulting from past experiences

- For gay men and lesbians who have come out only since their arrival in Canada, there are often particular difficulties in substantiating the claim, since documentation (often scarce) from the country of origin must be relied upon

- The universality of homophobia is sometimes used as an argument against accepting gay men and lesbians as refugees

- The implication of laws on homosexuality is not necessarily self-evident
  - Laws prohibiting homosexuality are *prima facie* evidence of persecution but are sometimes used as a basis for arguing claimants are being prosecuted rather than persecuted
  - Laws which do not directly refer to homosexual activity may be used against gay men and lesbians (e.g. China's law on hooliganism)
  - Laws which are not being enforced may still have significant impact because their existence gives an air of illegality to the lives of gay men and lesbians, with the consequence that state agencies may refuse protection to gay men and lesbians

- Gay men, lesbians and bisexuals may enter into heterosexual marriages as a cover to hide their sexual orientation. Gay men and lesbians may also have been in genuine marriages before they came to terms with their sexual orientation

- Documentation on human rights violations against members of sexual minorities is inadequate for a number of reasons
  - Many gay men and lesbians do not report human rights violations they have suffered because the authorities condone or participate in the abuses. In fact reporting abuses may lead to further victimisation
  - In some countries some associations of sexual minorities will not speak out on abuses or will even deny that they occur because of fears for the consequences
  - Few human rights organisations have a well-established tradition of

---

[7] Canadian Council for Refugees (CCR) *Addressing Claims Based on Sexual Orientation*, August 1995. Available on-line at http://www.web.net/~ccr/fronteng.htm

reporting on abuses suffered by sexual minorities and some organisations actually refuse to report these abuses or recognise them as significant human rights violations. Amnesty International included sexual orientation in its mandate only recently. Gay men and lesbians may not have sufficient trust of such organisations to report abuses to them

- The experiences of members of sexual minorities may differ significantly between socio-economic classes. In many cases there may be better documentation on the realities of the upper classes, who are likely to be less vulnerable to persecution

- There are significant differences between the ways in which gay men and lesbians are treated. For example, in some countries forced psychiatric 'treatment' is used against lesbians in particular, while in some countries sodomy laws are directed against men rather than women

- Board Members may be uncertain about how to test a person's claim that he or she is a member of a sexual minority

- Board Members' personal values and beliefs or discomfort with the issues discussed may compromise gay and lesbian claimants' right to a fair hearing

ANNEX 9   Sources of Further Information and Support
(Organisations, Internet and Further Reading)

I. Organisations
General
Immigration Law Practitioners' Association (ILPA)
Lindsey House
40-42 Charterhouse Street
London EC1M 6JH Tel: 0171 251 8383

Refugee Action
240a Clapham Road
Stockwell
London SW9 0PZ   Tel: 0171 735 5361

European Legal Network on Asylum (ELENA)
c/o ECRE
Bondway House
3 Bondway
London SW8 1SJ   Tel: 0171 820 1156

Joint Council for the Welfare of Immigrants (JCWI)
115 Old Street
London EC1V 9JR Tel: 0171 251 8706

Refugee Legal Centre
Sussex House
39-45 Bermondsey Street
London SE1 3XF   Tel: 0171 827 9090

Refugee Council
3 Bondway
London SW8 1SJ   Tel: 0171 582 6922

AIRE Centre (Advice on Individual Rights in Europe)
74 Eurolink Business Centre
49 Effra Road
London SW2 1B2   Tel: 0171 924 0297

Medical
Medical Foundation for the Care of Victims of Torture
96 - 98 Grafton Road
London NW5 3EJ   Tel: 0171 813 7777

Refugee Support Centre
47 South Lambeth Road
London SW8 1RH   Tel: 0171 820 3606

Foundation for Women's Health Research
and Development (FORWARD)
The Africa Centre
King Street
London WC2 8JT   Tel: 0171 379 6889

Traumatic Stress Clinic
73 Charlotte Street
London W1P 1LP   Tel: 0171 530 3666

Women Against Rape/ Black Women's Rape Action Project
PO Box 287
London NW6 5QU Tel: 0171 482 2496

Welfare and Housing
Child Poverty Action Group (CPAG)
1-5 Bath Street
London EC1V 9QA Tel: 0171 253 3406

London Advice Services Alliance (LASA)
Universal House
88-94 Wentworth Street
London E1 7SA   Tel: 0171 377 2738

National Association of Citizen Advice Bureaux (NACAB)
Middleton House
115 - 123 Pentonville Road
London N1 9LZ   Tel: 0171 833 2181

Shelter
88 Old Street
London EC1V   Tel: 0171 505 200

Supporting Information
See ILPA (1997) *Directory of Experts on Countries of Origin and Transit of Asylum Seekers*, 2nd edition, and JCWI (1996) *European Directory of Migrant and Ethnic Minority Organisations*, JCWI and European Research Centre for Migration and Ethnic Relations.

Representatives should develop their own expert networks through universities, consultants, specialist journals, newspapers, the Foreign and Commonwealth Office, community associations and the following organisations:

Amnesty International
99 - 109 Rosebery Avenue
London EC1R 4RE Tel: 0171 413 5500

Asylum Aid
244a Upper Street
London N1 1RU   Tel: 0171 359 4026

Human Rights Watch
33 Islington High Street
London N1 9LN   Tel: 0171 713 1995

Migration News Sheet
172 - 174
rue Joseph 11
B-1000 Brussels   Tel: 0032 2 230 3750

Refugee Studies Programme
Queen Elizabeth House
21 St. Giles
Oxford OX1 3LA   Tel: 01865 270722

Refugee Women's Association
The Print House
18 Ashwin Street
London E8 3DL   Tel: 0171 923 2412

Southall Black Sisters (SBS)
52 Norwood Road
Southall
Middlesex
UB2 4DW   Tel: 0181 571 9595

UNHCR
21st Floor, Millbank Tower
21 - 24 Millbank
London SW1P 4QP Tel: 0171 828 9191

II. Sources of Information Available on the Internet

Organisation	Website Address
AAAS Database of Human Rights Resources on the Internet	http://shr.aaas.org/dhr.htm
ADIMA (Australian Department of Immigration and Multi-Cultural Affairs)	http://164.97.143.2/inet-ser.htm
Amnesty International External Country Reports	http://www.amnesty/ailib/index.html
Canadian Council for Refugees (CCR)	http://www.web.net/~ccr/fronteng.htm
Canadian Immigration and Refugee Board (CIRB)	http://www.ncf.carleton.ca/freeport/government/ federal/irb/menu
Electronic Immigration Network (EIN)	http://www.poptel.org.uk/ein/
European Consultation on Refugees and Exiles (ECRE)	http://www.poptel.org.uk/ein/ecre/index.html
European Legal Network on Asylum (ELENA)	http://www.poptel.org.uk/ein/ecre/elena.html
Home Office Immigration and Nationality Directorate	http://www.open.gov.uk/home.off/ind/hpg.htm
Human Rights Internet	http://www.hri.ca/
Immigration Law Practitioners Association (ILPA)	http://www.poptel.org.uk/ein/ilpa/html
International Gay and Lesbian Human Rights Commission (IGLHRC)	http://qrd.tcp.com/qrd/orgs/IGLHRC
Lesbian and Gay Immigration Rights Task Force	http://www.lgirtf.org/
Reform-L (Project for reformulating refugee law)	http://www.yorku.ca/research/crs/law/RP_HP.html
Refugee Council	http://www.gn.apc.org/refugeecounciluk/
Refugee Network	http://www.nmsu.edu/~lshelton/ref.htm
Refugee Studies Programme (RSP) Documentation Centre	http://www.rsl.ox.ac.uk/cgi-bin/rspnew.tcl
Stonewall Immigration Group (Sexual Orientation Based Claims)	http://www.stonewall.org.uk/sig/intro.9611.html
UN Commission on Human Rights - Reports	http://www.unchr.ch/refworld/un/un.htm
UNHCR Website (for country reports and Refworld)	http://www.unhcr.ch
US Committee for Refugees	http://www.irsa-uscr.org/uscr/uscrindx.htm
US Department of State Country Reports	http://www.state.gov/www/issues/human_rights
US Immigration and Naturalisation Service	http://www.usdoj.gov/ins
Women's Commission for Refugee Women and Children	http://www.hypernet.com/wcrwc.html
WWW Virtual Library of Migration and Ethnic Relations Resources (access to hundreds of sites)	http://www.ruu.nl/ercomer/wwwvl/index.utm/

III. Suggestions for Further Reading

There are numerous publications available which are of interest and relevance to those working with refugee women seeking asylum in the UK, a small number of which are detailed below. It is well worth browsing the shelves of good bookshops (especially in the legal, gender and international relations sections) for further sources of information.

Afshar, H (ed) (1996) *Women and Politics in the Third World*, Routledge, London

Ahmed, L (1992) *Women and Gender in Islam*, Yale University Press, London

Amnesty International (1995) *Human Rights are Women's Right*, London

Bhabha, J and Shutter, S. (1994) *Women's Movement; Women Under Immigration, Nationality and Refugee Law*, JCWI, London

Buijs, G (ed). (1993) *Migrant Women; Crossing Boundaries and Changing Identities*, Berg Books, Oxford

Bunyan, T (ed) (1993) *Statewatching the New Europe*, Statewatch

Carillo, R and Bunch, C (1991*) Gender Violence; A Development and Human Rights Issue*, Centre for Women's Global Leadership, New Jersey

Graycar, R and Morgan, J (1990) *The Hidden Gender of Law*, Federation Press, Australia

Kandoyoti, D (ed) (1991) *Women, Islam and the State*, Temple University Press, Pennsylvania

Kerr, J (ed) (1992) *Ours By Right; Women's Rights as Human Rights*, Zed Books, London

MacKinnon, C (1987) *Feminism Unmodified: Discourses on Life and Law*, Harvard University Press, Cambridge Mass.

Mohanty, C et al (eds) (1991) *Third World Women and the Politics of Feminism*, Indian University Press, Bloomington

Moussa, H (1993*) Storm and Sanctuary; The Journey of Ethiopian and Eritrean Women*, Artemis Enterprises, Ontario, Canada

Peterson, V.S and Runyan, A (1993) *Global Gender Issues*, Westview, Boulder

Smart, C (1989) *Feminism and the Power of Law*, Routledge, London

Tomasevski, K (1993) *Women and Human Rights*, Zed Books, London

References

ADIMA (July1996) *Refugee and Humanitarian Visa Applicants; Guidelines on Gender Issues for Decision Makers*, Australian Department of Immigration and Multicultural Affairs

Afkhami, M and Friedl, E (eds) (1994) *In the Eye of the Storm; Women in Post-Revolutionary Iran*, Tarius, London

Amnesty International (1991) *Women on the Front Line; Human Rights Violations Against Women*, London

Amnesty International (1994) *'Bangladesh: Fundamental Rights of Women Violated With Virtual Impunity'*, London

Amnesty International (1997) *Breaking the Silence; Human Rights Violations Based on Sexual Orientation*, London

Asylum Rights Campaign (1996) *The Short Procedures*, London

Bhabha, J (1993) 'Legal problems of women refugees', *Women; A Cultural Review* 4(3), 240-249

Binion, G (1993) 'The nature of feminist jurisprudence', *Judicature* 77(3), 140-143

Binion, G (1995) 'Human rights: a feminist perspective', *Human Rights Quarterly* 17, 509-526

Bunch, C (1990)'Women's rights as human rights; towards a re-vision of human rights', *Humanitarian Rights Quarterly* 12 (4), 486-498

Camus-Jacques, G (1989) 'Refugee women; the forgotten majority' in G.Loescher and L.Monahan (eds) *Refugees and International Relations* 141-157

Castel, J.R (1992) 'Rape, sexual assault and the meaning of persecution' in *International Journal of Refugee Law* 4(1), 39-56

CIRB (March 1993) *Guidelines on Women Refugee Claimants Fearing Gender-Related Persecution*, Immigration and Refugee Board, Ottawa

CIRB (November 1996) *Guidelines on Women Refugee Claimants Fearing Gender-Related Persecution: UPDATE*, Immigration and Refugee Board, Ottawa

Charlesworth, H et al (1991) 'Feminist approaches to international law', *American Journal of International Law* 85, 613-664

Cipriani, L (1993) 'Gender and persecution; protecting women under international law', *Georgetown Immigration Law Journal*, 511-548

Cook, R (1993) 'Women's international human rights law: the way forward', *Human Rights Quarterly* 15, 230-261

Cook, R (1994) 'State accountability under the Convention on the Elimination of All Forms of Discrimination Against Women', in R. Cook (ed) *op.cit.* 228-258

Cook, R (ed) (1994) *Human Rights of Women; National and International Perspectives*, University of Pennsylvania Press, Philadelphia

Copelon, R (1994) 'Surfacing gender; re-engraving crimes against women in humanitarian law', *Hastings Women's Law Journal* 5(2), 243-266

Dutch Refugee Council (1994) *Female Asylum Seekers; A Comparative Study Concerning Policy and Jurisprudence in The Netherlands, Germany, France and the United Kingdom,* Amsterdam

ECRE (1993) *Asylum in Europe: An Introduction,* London

Forbes-Martin, S (1991) *Refugee Women,* Zed Books, London

Friedmann, A.R (1992)'Rape and domestic violence; the experience of refuge women' in *Women and Therapy* 13(1/2), 65-78

Fullerton, M (1993) 'A comparative look at refugee status based on persecution due to membership in a particular social group', *Cornell International Law Journal* 26(3), 505-564

Goldberg, P (1993) 'Anyplace but home; asylum in the United States for women fleeing intimate violence', *Cornell International Law Journal* 26(3), 565-604

Goldberg, P (1995) 'Where in the world is there safety for me: safe haven for women fleeing gender-based persecution' in J.Peters and A.Wolper (eds) *op.cit*

Goldberg, P and Kelly, N (1993) 'International human rights and violence against women; recent developments', *Harvard Humanitarian Rights Journal* 6,195-209

Goodwin-Gill, G (1983) *The Refugee in International Law,* Clarendon Press, Oxford

Grahl-Madsen, A (1966) *The Status of Refugees in International Law,* Sijthoff

Greatbach, J (1989) 'The gender difference; feminist critiques of refugee discourse' *International Journal of Refugee Law* 3(3), 585-605

Guild, E (1996) *The Developing Immigration and Asylum Policies of the European Union,* Kluwer Law International

Hathaway, J (1990) 'Gender-specific claims to refugee status and membership in a specific social group', paper presented at a workshop of the Toronto Convention Refugee Determination Division (CRDD), Working Group on Refugee Women Claimants, December 5th 1990 (unpublished)

Hathaway, J (1991) *The Law of Refugee Status,* Butterworth

Haywood, P and Russell, S (1996) 'Social group and the 1951 Convention' in *Refugee Legal Centre Annual Report 1996,* 10-14

Heise, L (1989) 'The crimes of gender', *WorldWatch* 2(2), 12-21

Helton, A.C (1983) 'Persecution on account of membership in a social group as a basis for refugee status', *Columbia Human Rights Law Review* 15(1), 39-67

Human Rights Watch (1992) *Double Jeopardy: Police Abuse of Women in Pakistan,* London

ILPA (1996) *The Asylum and Immigration Act 1996: A compilation of ministerial statements made on behalf of the government during the Bill's passage through Parliament,* London

ILPA (1997) *Best Practice Guide to Asylum Appeals*, ILPA, The Law Society and Refugee Legal Group, London

ILPA (1997) *Directory of Experts on Conditions in Countries of Origin and Transit* 2nd edition, London

INS (June 1995) *Considerations for Asylum Officers Adjudicating Asylum Claims From Women*, Immigration and Naturalisation Service

Indra, D.M (1987) 'Gender: a key dimension of the refugee experience', *Refuge* 6 (3), 3-4

Indra, D.M (1989) 'Ethnic human rights and gender differences; gender implications for refugee studies and practice', *Journal of Refugee Studies* 2(2), 221-242

Indra, D.M (1993) 'Some feminist contributions to refugee studies', paper presented at a joint plenary session of *Gender Issues and Refugees; Development Implications* and *Exploring Knowledge, Power and Practice in Society* (CASCA Annual Meetings), York University, Toronto, May 9-11 (unpublished)

James, S.A (1994)'Reconciling international human rights and cultural relativism: the case of female circumcision', *Bioethics* 8(1), 1-26

Johnsson, A.B (1989) 'International protection of women refugees: a summary of principle problems and issues', *International Journal of Refugee Law* 1(2), 221-232

Kelly, N (1989) *Working with Refugee Women: A Practical Guide*, NGO Working Group on Refugee Women, Geneva

Kelly, N (1993) 'Gender-related persecution; assessing the asylum claims of women', *Cornell International Law Journal* 26(3), 625-674

Kelly, N (1994) 'Guidelines for women's asylum claims', *International Journal of Refugee Law* 6(4), 517-534

Macdonald, A.I and Blake, N.J (1995) *Macdonald's Immigration Law and Practice in the United Kingdom* 4th edition, Butterworth, London

Macklin, A (1995)'Refugee women and the imperative of categories', *Human Rights Quarterly* 17, 213-277

Mawani, N (1993) 'Introduction to the Immigration and Refugee Board Guidelines on gender-related persecution', *International Journal of Refugee Law* 5(2), 240-247

Minority Rights Group (1992) *Female Genital Mutilation; Proposals for Change*, London

Minter, S (1996) 'Lesbians and asylum: overcoming barriers to access' in S. Levy (ed) *Asylum Based on Sexual Orientation: A Resource Guide*, International Gay and Lesbian Human Rights Commission and London Legal Defence and Education Fund

Mulligan, M (1990) 'Obtaining political asylum; classifying rape as a well-founded fear of persecution on the grounds of political opinion', *Boston College Third World Journal* 10, 355-380

Neal, D.L (1988) 'Women as a social group: recognising sex-based persecution as grounds for asylum', *Columbia Human Rights Law Review* 20(1), 203-257

Oosterveld, V (1996) 'Women seeking refuge: evaluating the Canadian guidelines on gender-related persecution' (unpublished)

Peters, J and Wolper, A (eds) (1995) *Women's Rights, Human Rights; International Feminist Perspectives*, Routledge, London

Refugee Council (April 1996) *The State of Asylum; A Critique of Asylum Policy in the UK*, Refugee Council, London

Romany, C (1994) 'State responsibility goes private: a feminist critique of the public/private distinction in international human rights law', in R. Cook (ed) *op.cit.*, 85-115

Schilders, N et al (1988) *Sexual Violence; 'You Have Hardly Any Future Left'*, Dutch Refugee Council, Amsterdam

Siemens, M (1988) 'Protection of women refugees', *Refugees* 56, 21-22

Southall Black Sisters (1996) *Domestic Violence and Asian Women; A Collection of Reports and Briefings* SBS, Southall, Middlesex

Spijkerboer, T (1994) *Women and Refugee Status; Beyond the Public/Private Distinction*, Study commissioned by the Emancipation Council, The Hague

Stairs, F and Pope, L (1990) 'No place like home; assaulted migrant women's claims to refugee status and landings on humanitarian and compassionate grounds', *Journal of Law and Social Policy* 6, 148-225

Thomas, D.Q and Beasley, M.E (1993) 'Domestic violence as a human rights issue', *Human Rights Quarterly* 15, 36-62

Thompkins, T.L (1995) 'Prosecuting rape as a war crime: speaking the unspeakable', *Notre Dame Law Review* 70 (4), 845-890

Toubia, N (1995) 'Female Genital Mutilation' in J. Peters and A. Wolper (eds) *Women's Rights, Human Rights; International Feminist Perspectives*, Routledge, London, 224-237

UNHCR (1979) *Handbook on Procedures and Criteria for Determining Refugee Status*, Geneva

UNHCR (1991) *Guidelines on the Protection of Refugee Women*, Geneva

UNHCR (1995) *Sexual Violence Against Refugees; Guidelines on Prevention and Response*, Geneva

UNHCR (1995) *An Overview of Protection Issues in Western Europe: Legislative Trends and Positions Taken by UNHCR*, European Series No 3, Geneva

UNICEF (1995) *Children First; Lifting the Veil on Female Genital Mutilation*

Winter, B (1994) 'Women, the law and cultural relativism in France: the case of excision', *Signs* 19 (4), 939-974